1973

This book may be kept

EN DAYS

WORLD THEATER/ The Structure and Meaning of Drama

SEYMOUR REITER

WORLD THEATER

The Structure and Meaning of Drama

HORIZON PRESS   NEW YORK

To Paula, Harry, and Arnold

PREFACE

Who is really the chief character of Jean Anouilh's play *Becket*—Thomas himself, successively Anglo-Saxon collaborator, Archbishop, martyr? Or is it the Norman king Henry II, Becket's friend and destroyer? Is a modern absurdist play like *Waiting for Godot* truly plotless, as nearly all critics believe? What does Thornton Wilder's *Our Town* have in common with the classics of Sanskrit theater? Is there any resemblance between the way the great Japanese Noh dramatist Zeami formed his dance dramas and the ways Calderón or Racine or Brecht constructed their plays?

This book is the record of an intellectual adventure whose ultimate scope has surprised no one more than the author. For the book began rather simply—not as a book at all, in fact, but as a private attempt to see more clearly into certain rather opaque modern plays. I wanted to find their bones. If, like their predecessors in Western drama, they were vertebrate creatures, inside them lay a skeleton which determined their shape and proclaimed their function. Uncovering this arrangement of bones, finding its joints and learning how they articulated—this would be an intriguing pursuit in itself. My purpose was more. Discovering how the play worked could go far toward telling me what the play meant.

The tool I proposed to use was a concept of plot-structure I had grown familiar with as a student of playwriting. So useful was this concept as a device for shaping dramatic material that I hoped it would be equally helpful in analyzing plays already made. And indeed this proved to be the case. Even a play like Euripides' *The Trojan Women*—so far from being conventionally "well made" that it is generally thought to have no plot-structure at all—could be seen to have a firmly purposed logical design. As I gained skill in applying my critical instrument, I became convinced that meaning in a play could be determined objectively and swiftly—whether in the excitement and immediacy of the theater or in the privacy and reflection of reading.

7

The list of plays which invited analysis grew ever longer and ranged ever wider. It became apparent that I had embarked on a kind of scientific investigation. Beneath it lay the assumption—and it is one of the basic premises of this book—that drama is a large, objectively existent material whose nature and laws are subject to intellectual examination. I had set myself the task—unconsciously at the outset—of exploring the extent to which the properties of plot-structure are common to great drama the world over, of scrutinizing the nature of such common properties, and of determining their relation to esthetic meaning.

The critical instrument I used is a method of analyzing a play to discover the *logic of actions*. The "actions" of a play are ordered, not random, events. To determine the relationships among these events is to discover their logic—that is, to discover how and why the playwright has constructed his microcosm. Learning to distinguish a dramatic "action"—a subtler exercise than is commonly supposed—is of course essential.

The concept of plot-structure and dramatic action which constitutes the critical instrument used in this book exhibits a seductive simplicity. That simplicity is deceptive, however. Considerable practice is needed to master its use, and recourse to specific detail in the plays is often necessary. For that reason, detailed plot summaries have been included. The longer summaries have in each case a particular function. The summary of Brecht's *The Caucasian Chalk Circle* is designed to show how the actions of that play are almost wholly physical; of Racine's *Phaedra*, how the actions are almost entirely mental or emotional. Other summaries concern themselves directly with structure, that of Lope de Vega's *Fuenteovejuna* showing how its plot-structure is submerged almost below the level of visibility.

Making the acquaintance of the critical instrument and acquiring skill in its use become, in this book, a single activity—and a pleasurable one, since it involves exploring in intimate detail works that are among the greatest in world literature. The ultimate value to the lover of drama is his growing capacity to hear with more acuity what a play is saying. The meaning implicit in plot-structure is not a play's whole meaning any more than a skeleton is the whole creature. Yet in itself such meaning is complete, crucial, and sure.

That is not to say that the concept of plot-structure and the method of play analysis discussed in this book have absolutely universal application. If I discovered ways in which the greatest dramas of the world are alike, I also discovered ways in which they differ. On even the most exotic works of non-Western cultures, my inquiry provided a fresh perspective, taking me deeper into an understanding not only of Eastern drama but of the nature of all drama.

ACKNOWLEDGMENTS

First I offer my thanks to Bernard Grebanier, Professor Emeritus of Brooklyn College, without whose work on playwriting this study would not have been made; indeed, to whom I am indebted for having turned me long ago from science to literature. Then to Lillian Feder, Professor of English at Queens College, equally distinguished as a classical scholar, whom I thank for early encouragement when we talked drama while practicing tennis (after a fashion), for her careful reading of the sections on Greek drama, and for a valuable addition to my criticism of *The Trojan Women*. On certain matters philosophical and scientific I had the privilege of consulting with James K. Feibleman, W.R. Irby Professor of Philosophy at Tulane University. Three scholars gave me their help although I was personally unknown to them; to them I therefore owe special thanks. Professor Benito Ortolani of the City University of New York has carefully criticized the entire manuscript and has given meticulous attention to the Japanese sections. Professor Rasik Vihari Joshi, Professor and Head of the Department of Sanskrit of the University of Jodhpur, India, devoted detailed care to the Sanskrit chapter. And finally there is Professor Kao Yu-hung of Princeton University on whom I unwittingly descended out of the blue when I telephoned, my letter explaining my needs never having reached him, and who nonetheless agreed to criticize what I had to say on Chinese drama. Needless to say, if errors remain they are mine. The bibliography, I trust, contains every work I have called upon for this study; it is good to enjoy such collaboration.

A word about the references: Generally, sources are named in the body of the book by author when only one work is listed in the bibliography, by author and title when there are more than one work by the same author listed in the bibliography. Details about the translations used are given in the Notes. It also proved well to use Notes in certain instances for other sources.

10

CONTENTS

1/THE PLAY: ABOUT WHOM?
ABOUT WHAT? A MODERN TEST CASE
Anouilh's *Becket*

On October 5, 1960 Jean Anouilh's *Becket* opened at the St. James Theatre in New York, Sir Laurence Olivier in the title role and Anthony Quinn as Henry II. All the leading reviewers, literate and intelligent, saw the play as Thomas Becket's. During the five-week road tour Quinn left for Hollywood and Olivier, reported by *Time* as saying that he "had always been intrigued by the part," switched to Henry II. The play returned to New York on May 8, 1961. Now it was the king who absorbed the reviewers—as though the center of gravity of the play had changed, giving the play new meaning. Was this change in meaning real or apparent?

Does the play—any play—have an independent existence and reality of its own, and therefore determinable meaning apart from performance, even despite performance? That is the esthetic issue at stake. I shall try to show not only that there is such an absolute meaning but that there is an instrument with which one can objectively penetrate to that meaning. By "an absolute meaning" I do not imply that it is ever the whole meaning or that there is only one valid meaning; nor do I imply that all matters of interpretation are objectively verifiable.

Modern criticism of poetry, indeed the whole tradition of poetic criticism, has greater accomplishment to boast than does that of drama, Shakespearean criticism excepted. Criticism is partly science, partly art; and like other sciences and other arts, advances as a great collaboration. There simply has been less collaboration in drama criticism and therefore, perhaps, less working knowledge has been defined for the criticism of drama than of poetry. Yet the contemporary interest in drama (movies and television plays are drama) is to the interest in poetry what an ocean is to a brook; no literary form has more historical importance than drama; and none can claim greater accomplishment.

Few modern critics or reviewers of poetry try to reach meaning in a poem without assessing the formal elements in which the vision of the poet is revealed. They have instruments to assess with, in the workshop of knowledge that their collaboration has built, and they have the skill of practice to use those instruments.

The play reviewer, of course, has a harder task. Not only must he deal with the interpretation of actors and director, which may or may not give existence to the essence of the play, but if he writes for a daily newspaper, he must also cope with a compounded difficulty, formulating thoughts about what he saw and heard on the stage while he goes up the aisle of the theater, rides in the taxi, and works at his typewriter, a copy boy snatching away the review, as it is written, for the compositor. Nonetheless the best of them write with style, judgment, grace, wit, and they deserve tribute. Few scholars would be hardy or foolhardy enough to attempt what they achieve.

But dramatic criticism needs better instruments with which the practiced critic can lay open meaning in a play by analysis of the form. Such a major esthetic instrument, I believe, is at hand. Had the critics of *Becket* known and used that instrument, the history of their criticism would have been different. They would have at the outset seen the play not as Becket's but as Henry's and would not have been misled by a misapprehension of the play's meaning. Before the critics come front and center, here is a preview of the play.

At Becket's tomb Henry II is naked, waiting for the slain Archbishop of Canterbury's Saxon monks to flog him in ritual pun-

ishment. He must make his peace with their Saint because he needs
the Saxons' support against his rebellious son. The ghost of the
Archbishop appears. Henry thinks Becket hated him because as
King he took the courtier Becket's mistress away.

Henry's memory goes to earlier, happier times. The King
makes Becket, his courtier and friend, Chancellor of England, the
secular power second only to the King, and as Chancellor Becket
brings the Church to heel for Henry. The two friends go hunting,
and we see the collaborator Becket saving a Saxon peasant and
his sister from the King; in return for the girl, Becket promises
anything the King will ask—which turns out to be Becket's mistress.

While Henry is campaigning in France, he learns from Becket
that he must crush the bishops in England or lose his kingdom
to them. Providentially, news comes of the Archbishop of Canterbury's death. Henry appoints Becket, who is his man, as the Primate
of England, although Becket warns he cannot serve both God and
Henry. As Archbishop of Canterbury, Becket seems transformed,
winning over the Saxons and finding joy in God's service.

While Henry is with his mother, wife and sons—an unattractive
lot none of whom, it is apparent, means anything to him—he
receives Becket's resignation as Chancellor of England. Pained by
the loss of the one person he loves, he realizes he must learn to
live alone. He goes to the clever and strong Bishop of London,
whom the King, a changing man, controls masterfully and deftly:
he will use the Bishop against Becket. As Becket acts to defend
the freedom and survival of the Church, the breach with the King
widens; finally Becket must escape to France. For a time he lives
in a French monastery, but safety is a temptation he decides he
must put behind him; he will return to England and as Archbishop
do his life's work.

There is a meeting with Henry in France before he returns.
The issue becomes clear: the King must act for the honor of the
realm and the Archbishop for the honor of God. In England Henry
scores against Becket by having another bishop anoint and consecrate his son as King, but the premature consecration gives his son
ground on which to rebel. We see that Henry has no bond with
anyone in his family or with his barons. In a moment of pain
he cries out, "Will no one rid me of him [Becket]?" Four barons,
responding to the cry, go to murder the Archbishop.

The last scene returns to where the play began, at Becket's tomb.
The whipping has been politically successful: Henry has won the
Saxons to his side and so will control his realm.

In *The New York Times* Howard Taubman's theme was the intellectuality of the play: "the appeal of Jean Anouilh's 'Becket' is to the intellect. It also allows for the splendor of pageantry. As it is being presented . . . the eye is diverted and the mind stimulated. But the heart is not often stirred." Whether a playgoer's heart is stirred is not merely a matter of feeling; it depends also on his understanding of what is happening, his understanding of what the play is about. This is what Taubman saw at the center of the play: "M. Anouilh's essential theme—the portrait of a life that ends by championing God, no matter what the cost—has nobility and exaltation. The trouble is with a pivotal character, Becket himself. He is not humanized; he remains a remote figure, whether charming or saintly. . . . But if M. Anouilh's notion is right that Becket could· love nothing except the honor of God, he has committed himself to a grave dramatic weakness. There is no surprise in this Becket. One always knows that this Becket will be faithful to his duty, whatever shape it takes." That indeed would be a grave dramatic weakness if the play were essentially about Becket. This critic perhaps instinctively felt that the center of gravity was elsewhere. "M. Anouilh," he wrote in the same article, "is much more successful with King Henry"; and he saw that "when Becket as Archbishop turns on him to serve God, the king achieves a bitter maturity." Although the reviewer wrote that Anthony Quinn played the "most interesting role in 'Becket'," he did not expatiate on the phrase.

A few days later Taubman turned to the play again in an article on the French spirit of detachment. " 'Becket' is a grave, if not solemn, inquiry into the events and human relationships leading to a martyrdom." Anouilh's detachment, one of the "shining virtues" of the French mind, "will not do for a subject like 'Becket.' " However, "not all of 'Becket' is objective. The role of Henry is realized from inside. It is a full-length portrait of a rough, emotional sovereign. His intellect is limited but his intelligence is sharper than it seems. He is a warm-blooded human being, but he does not suffice to turn 'Becket' into a moving drama of personal destinies."

Brooks Atkinson, writing in his column "Critic at Large" of T.S. Eliot's *Murder in the Cathedral* and *Becket*, let the Becket of Anouilh's play dominate his essay. He judged that in the "realm of the spirit, 'Murder in the Cathedral' is the finer play" but M. Anouilh, who "is a worldly dramatist, . . . makes a useful and clarifying contribution to the legend. He provides worldly perspective. He puts Becket in a political context." Probably Eliot's play, and perhaps Tennyson's *Becket*, predisposed critics to believe that Becket is the main focus of Anouilh's play. No doubt the title of the play also predisposed them. But there are any number of plays that are not built on the characters who give the plays their titles. The plot-structure of Aeschylus' *Agamemnon* is built on Clytemnestra; of Sophocles' *Antigone*, on Creon; of Shakespeare's *Julius Caesar*, on Brutus; of Racine's *Britannicus*, on Nero; of Chekhov's *The Three Sisters*, on Natasha.

In the New York *Herald Tribune* Walter Kerr thought *Becket* an "unfocussed but fascinating play" in which Anouilh "elected to set two of the pressures of power politics into orbit—the spiritual independence of the individual and the legal right of the monarch—and then send crashing across them the comet of friendship." Kerr stated the "essential themes of the play" as "Henry's need of Becket's gayety and Becket's cultivation, Becket's inability to rest in anything other than an ultimate commitment, the savage sorrow these men feel as they head for the sword." Apparently for Kerr the center of gravity of the play lay *between* these two men, not *in one* of them. Were it so, the play would be "unfocussed," or structurally weak; but, as we shall see, it is not so. Although Kerr understood that "Henry II loves Becket" and saw the "rage" and "heartbreak" in Quinn's acting when Becket, resigning the office of Chancellor, returned the Seal of England to Henry, he missed Henry's importance. He wrote that Henry "is described as a 'great adolescent lout' "— believing that would make it easy to write Henry off. Actually the phrase is not a stage direction by Anouilh, although Anouilh does give Henry a "slightly loutish manner." The phrase is spoken by a bishop whom Henry is masterfully controlling and who is surprised by the king's mental deftness: "I had

always taken your Highness for a great adolescent lout."
Perhaps Kerr, like the other critics, looked too much at
Olivier, to whose acting his review paid tribute.

The *Time* reviewer also thought that Anouilh made "hardly
more than a lout of Henry." The burden of this review was
that Becket defeated Anouilh: his play "has the weaknesses
without the high compensatory moments of *Murder in the
Cathedral*." For this reviewer Becket was the crucial character,
and he rapped Anouilh across the knuckles for "scamping
essentials: Becket's great career as Chancellor is passed over;
his clashes with Henry, on becoming Archbishop of Canterbury, go unused." The statement is inaccurate. If it were
accurate it would be beside the point anyway since the play
is not about Becket.

John McCarten, in *The New Yorker*, like Atkinson came to
Becket from *Murder in the Cathedral*; and *Becket*, "as colloquial
as can be," was "something of a shock." For McCarten Becket
was the main focus. In a short review he wrote his objections
to the play, and did not return to it after Olivier changed
roles.

Only Henry Hewes, in the *Saturday Review,* thought that
both Olivier and Quinn were miscast, that both were
inadequate. Unable, therefore, to "make the play work," the
director had to shape it as "a historical pageant," but " 'Becket'
is intended less as a historical chronicle than as a subtle study
of the relationship between two very different men." That
statement, a misapprehension somewhat like Kerr's, placed
the center of gravity in the *relationship between* the two men,
not *in one* of them.

We have seen that none of the critics, the first time around,
understood that the play was more Henry's than Becket's.
The looming title of the play, the overshadowing *Murder
in the Cathedral*, the brilliance of Olivier's acting—all worked
to obscure the king. There is another triptych of reasons
to explain what happened.

Before the play opened there appeared in *The New York
Times* on October 2, 1960 an article by Anouilh (later
reprinted as an Introduction to the Lucienne Hill translation

of the play). In the beginning of the article the playwright wrote that his original attraction to Thomas Becket came by chance. He had purchased from a bookstall on a quay of the Seine an old green volume—he needed a spot of green on his shelves. The book was *The Conquest of England by the Normans* by Augustin Thierry (who believed Becket was a Saxon), "an historian of the Romantic school, forgotten today and scrapped." Skimming through, Anouilh happened on the story of Becket: "I was dazzled. I had expected to find a saint—I am always a trifle distrustful of saints, as I am of great theatre stars—and I found a man." The rest of the lively account mainly tells of his stops and starts. One of the difficulties was facing the "death in the cathedral, a subject already magnificently treated by Eliot." The account, except for a submerged (but crucial) allusion to Henry, which we shall come to after the reviewers complete their say, would seem to place Becket front and center.[1]

Anouilh found a man. A strange man, and fascinating. Better than the king at drinking and whoring, Becket would come to Henry's room the next morning, smiling and fresh, having already taken a gallop in the cold air for the pleasure of it. He served the king wholly in those days—he liked to—without stinting and (perhaps more rare) without diminishing himself. He "adored" hunting, luxury, and honor (although he had no honor himself). His quick sense of laughter matched the king's. Afraid of nothing, not even of the threat of excommunication that made the king shiver and backtrack, Becket's mind and will defeated the Church in a conflict over money, and then Becket was insolent to the old Archbishop. He loved nobody, not the king and not his own mistress, and did not like being loved. Not that he was incapable of feeling, nor was he absolutely detached. In the hunting scene in the forest he was gentle to the old Saxon and acted to save the Saxon's son from death and his daughter from violation.

Perhaps Becket's was a temperament that could love God but not another human being. In our own day we may discover such a temperament in the person who can love an abstraction—the state, or a cause—better than a person. In Becket's day there was no question as to which was the higher love.

Anouilh, however, makes us look at the story with contemporary values. We see such values in the play's colloquial idiom; having appointed Becket his Chancellor, Henry says to the old Archbishop: "Don't rely too much on Becket to play your game. He is my man!"; and again, of a Saxon girl whom he thinks of as merchandise: "Do we take her with us or shall we have her sent?" We see such values in allusions to collaboration with the conquerors, and in the point of view (that came out of the French Resistance) of a young monk who wants to kill one Norman although he knows he's "just a little grain of sand in the machine . . . [but] by putting more and more grains of sand in the machine, one day it will come grinding to a stop." We see modern values again when Becket tells the king in their final confrontation: "We must only do—absurdly—what we have been given to do—right to the end." It's the *absurdly*, of course, that makes the statement modern. To justify Becket by the historical argument that in his time the love of God was higher than the love of people would, therefore, not hold water.

Certainly he did not love his mistress. The scene in which he relinquishes her to the king shows his capacity for detachment. That detachment is made the sharper by the depth of her love for him. For once his intelligence misses an intimation, as he confesses his lack of honor.

> *Gwendolen*. My lord cares for nothing, in the whole world, does he?
> *Becket*. No.
> *Gwendolen*. (*Moves to him and says gently*) You belong to a conquered race too. But through tasting too much of the honey of life, you've forgotten that even those who have been robbed of everything have one thing left to call their own.
> *Becket*. (*Inscrutably*) Yes, I daresay I had forgotten. There's a gap in me where honor ought to be. Go now.

In the king's litter the girl takes her life. Terribly shaken by his closeness to blood and death, Henry cannot spend the night away from Becket, whose service does not waver. Becket soothes the king's troubled rest.

> *Almost tenderly, he draws the coverlet over the king.*
> *Becket.* My prince . . . If you were my true prince, if you were one of my race, how simple everything would be. How tenderly I would love you, my prince . . . You can sleep peacefully though, my prince. So long as Becket is obliged to improvise his honor, he will serve you. And if one day he meets it face to face . . .
> But where is Becket's honor?

That is the curtain line for Act I.

Being a collaborator, having "cheated" his way to a "place among the conquerors," Becket has no honor, and without honor there can be no spiritual independence. The most remarkable of Becket's qualities is that without honor and spiritual independence he cannot love and cannot take pleasure in being loved.

Becket's conversion comes toward the end of the second act. We have understood—as the old Archbishop, a "true father" to Becket, expressed it—that "He is as it were detached. As if seeking his real self." Even the stupid barons are aware that they do not know who Becket is "as a man" and are waiting for him to show himself. These intimations, like Becket's own "where is Becket's honor?" and his seeing "his own ghost, when young" in the boy-monk who wanted to liberate himself from shame by killing Becket, prepare us for the conversion, unless our intention were to explain it away. His conversion is not from unbelief to belief, but from an esthetic center of being to a religious center.

Even if Becket had not experienced his conversion he would have opposed the king. When Becket served, he served wholly, and in his esthetic center he loved doing well what he had to do, that love being the one thing he was sure of. He warned Henry, "If I become Archbishop, I can no longer be your friend," and again, "This is madness, my Lord. Don't do it. I could not serve both God and you." Without his conversion he would have defended the Church against Henry, but would have had to live alone, without God and without love.

In his conversion discovering the honor of God and himself in devotion to that honor, he wins honor for himself and spiritual independence. Having honor, he can love Henry. At the beginning of Act IV, when the King of France says of Henry, "He really hates you, doesn't he?", Becket replies, simply, "Sire, we loved each other and I think he cannot forgive me for preferring God to him." Humanly enough, seeing the past through the glasses of the present in which he has really learned to love, Becket forgets that before the conversion he loved Henry only in so far as he was "capable of love." And when Louis, thinking to persuade Henry to make peace with Becket, asks, "Should he agree, will you be willing to talk with him?", Becket says—and we are certain that he is speaking the truth—"Sire, ever since we stopped seeing each other, I have never ceased to talk to him." And finally, at the confrontation on the plain at La Ferté-Bernard:

> *King.* You know that I am the King, and that I must act like a King! What do you expect of me? Are you hoping I'll weaken?
> *Becket.* No. That would prostrate me.

Only love could have made that reply.

Becket is going back to England to give himself up to the King's power. On the fields of France Becket was a great fighter, and in England the barons in the lists "fell to him like ninepins." But now he must "fight in the place and with the weapons it has pleased You to give me."

That, indeed, was "a man" whom Anouilh found in the old green volume, and his remarkable portrait co-operated in placing Becket front and center.

The final reason for Becket's prominence that first opening night was that he has all the curtain speeches except the last one. I say "all"; actually there was only one intermission. But any critic who had read the play before seeing it would have been impressed by the act-endings. I have already cited the end of the first act: "But where is Becket's honor?" The last scene of the second act, presenting the first effects of Becket's conversion, takes place immediately after the king has ordered him to be Archbishop. The Primate is selling all his goods to give the money to the poor, and invites the poor to dine with him. He is *"happy, lighthearted, and murmurs* . . . 'The joy I feel in shedding all my riches must be part of Your divine intentions!' " In his curtain line before the intermission he speaks to the crucifix, simply, "Lord, are You sure You are not tempting me? It all seems far too easy." Even a critic who had not read the play must have been much impressed—dramatically—by the conversion scene and the curtain speeches before the intermission, in which Becket has the stage to himself. The third act ends with his decision to return to England. He has come to believe that "Saintliness is a temptation too," that the strict monastic rule he has been living within is designed to safeguard the weak, and that it is a temptation he must put behind him. He will return to England and, as Archbishop, will do his "life's work."

Becket's conversion scene before the intermission may have had more dramatic impress at the St. James than the scene before the final curtain, which is Henry's (the acting all to one side for the moment), because the last scene is part of a frame in which the play takes place. The play opens in the cathedral, where the king is to undergo flogging. Henry dreamily remembers the happy times he and Becket had together, *"a memory relived."* The murder of Becket is the penultimate scene of the play. If one then let his responses relax, the end of the play might seem only part of the frame, as though the story proper ended with the murder.

The reader may wonder, after all this, how anybody ever saw the play as Henry's. But so critics saw it the second time around—because Olivier played Henry II—and so it truly is. Here are their reactions.

In *The New York Times* Lewis Funke wrote: "What a change has been made! This Henry by Mr. Olivier is a vibrant, throbbing ruler, gruff and unpolished, a man of primitive temper who manages through his creator's [i.e., Olivier's] sorcery to win our sympathy, to make a solid jab at our emotions.

"No one needs to be told at this date that Mr. Olivier, when he is on stage, generally is the center of focus. Where he goes, there goes the light. In this creation he insists on riveting attention, even at intervals appearing to be turning

the play into a virtuoso performance. It is utterly impossible
to take one's eyes from him as he makes Henry change from
a gay, roistering king during the first half to a bitterly frustrated, temper-ridden man in the second." Most of the review
was given to praise of Olivier's performance.

Judith Crist of the New York *Herald Tribune* was equally
impressed: "Laurence Olivier . . . gives one of the brilliant
performances of his career and in the course of it gives the
play a clarity and vigor that reveal its riches.

"What has the switch of role brought about? Olivier's Becket
was a cultivated man of irony and dedication, Anthony
Quinn's Henry a coarse, crude bellowing lout who hung upon
prerogative. But Olivier's king is never quite the 'great adolescent lout' the script still terms him. He is a young man brought
through the tutelage of friendship to knowledge and bitter
sorrow, an uncomplicated man suddenly involved in a crude
brawl for power, cut to the heart by unrequited love, his
soul in torment by the very vengeance essential to its survival.

"This is a Henry for whom you can weep as he writhes
in almost epileptic spasm and screams and sobs in his
anguished abandonment. And you weep because you have
followed the course of his tragedy, seen the gay insouciance
of his early confidence in Becket, his complete lack of under-
.standing of his friend's character, his blind destruction of
their relationship. Olivier, the master of the inflection, of
the graceful implication, gives this Henry a tragic stature."

She concluded: "It is a particular pleasure for one who
had so many reservations about the original 'Becket' to find
the production now so satisfying. And it is more than
pleasure—it is a high point in theatrical experience—to see
still another great performance by Laurence Olivier."
Perhaps she found it "now so satisfying" because she was
for the first time seeing a production that approximated the
play about Henry that Anouilh wrote.

The *Time* reviewer had this to say: "Though he lost the
title role, Olivier gained by the switch. It is really the title
role in name only: in his drama of the medieval King who
idolized his chief counselor and then suffered him to be
killed, Anouilh ignored too much that was vital in Becket—his

great career as Chancellor, his shift from worldling to ascetic, his clashes, as Archbishop of Canterbury, with Henry. If Anouilh's Henry is not quite a full portrait either, it is for an Olivier a fat part—a touch too fat, for it hides Henry's bone structure. But Olivier catches him in a whole succession of picturesque moments and shifting moods. As against Quinn's clodlike vigor, Olivier's Henry has an easy swagger, a skipping verve; he can be cruel, capricious, ironic, every inch a king less for greatness of will than assertiveness of whim; and one who loved Becket, not just because of lifelong loneliness—domineering mother, dried-up wife, hen-brained children—but because Becket expertly pleased and amused him."

The reviewer ended with the observation that the play "now has a more flaring sense of worldliness and wiles. But its playful side eats into its prayerful side, leaving Becket half snuffed out. . . . With this second try at Henry, it becomes Henry II's show."

Henry Hewes, in the *Saturday Review,* who thought this production "much better . . . than the earlier version," astutely observed, "The strength of this performance tends to transform the play into a saga of King Henry's tortured journey into loneliness and Pyrrhic victory."

How could the reviewers have seen on the first opening night, at the St. James, that the play was Henry's?

Anouilh apparently intended Henry to be at the center of the play. The reviewers possibly did not take up his statement, which appeared in *The New York Times* before opening night, because it was submerged in an explanation for keeping Becket a Saxon although an historian friend let him know that Augustin Thierry had been wrong: "I decided that if history in the next fifty years should go on making progress it will perhaps rediscover that Becket was indubitably of Saxon origin; in any case, for this drama of friendship between two men, between the king and his friend, his companion in pleasure and in work (and this is what had gripped me about the story), this friend whom he could not cease to love though he became his worst enemy the night he was

named archbishop—for this drama it was a thousand times
better that Becket remained a Saxon." Here it is the king
who is the main focus, who could not cease to love even
in the face of extremest alteration.

What an author originally intended may, of course, be
different from the work he has executed. But he largely
knows what meaning the work he wrote contains, whether
the finished work be distant from or close to the original
intention. In any case Anouilh did build his play around
what had gripped him.

More important than the external evidence of Anouilh's
intention is the objective determination that analytical criticism can make of the play's structure. In Joyce's *A Portrait
of the Artist as a Young Man* Stephen Dedalus said of unity
as corresponding to the "first phase of [artistic] apprehension": "An esthetic image is presented to us either in space
or time. What is audible is presented in time, what is visible
is presented in space. But temporal or spatial, the esthetic
image is first luminously apprehended as selfbounded and
selfcontained upon the immeasurable background of space
or time which is not it. You apprehend it as *one* thing. You
see it as one whole. You apprehend its wholeness. That is
integritas.—" *If we do not apprehend a work's unity, we
may see it as it goes by without our having any real apprehension of what it can mean to us.* In a play our "first phase of
apprehension" must correspond to its structural unity of
action.

For the method of structural analysis that I shall use, I
am indebted to Bernard Grebanier, who clarified and refined
William T. Price's discovery of the law of plot-structure and
expanded its consequences so that the formulation can now
be inclusive and precise.[2] Their understanding of the theoret-
ical principles of plot-structure, although evolved for the
practicing playwright, is, I believe, a major new instrument
for both the critic and the audience. It enables us to determine
with clarity and certainty what the plot-structure is, and thus
what the story is about. Structure is the most important element in dramatic form. It is so because the essence of a
play is the visual presentation of an arrangement of happen-

ings. Through that arrangement the burden of the play is communicated to us. The arrangement, when the play is fully satisfying, almost always in Western drama is shaped according to the dramatic law of unity of action.

By "unity of action" is meant that logical unity which binds the beginning of change, the middle of change, the end of change, and its climax. These four elements of the plot-structure are *actions* which must be performed by one and the same character experiencing the change, who is thus the character central to the plot-structure. More than one central character in a plot-structure is a logical contradiction; there could be no unity. If in *Becket* the actions of the plot-structure were divided between the two friends, we would feel that the play was not holding together. Of course there can be several plot-structures in a play, each with its protagonist, as in Shakespeare's plays (see chapter 11) or in O'Casey's *The Plough and the Stars* (in chapter 14). In a play which is "one whole," in Joyce's phrase, these plot-structures are interdependent; that interdependence is generally accomplished by making an action of one plot-structure the cause of an action in another; the interdependence may be intensified by having the plots illuminate the same theme. In a play that is built well the main plot-structure is the one whose central character gives the play its motion, has the crucial climax, and has the final action of the play.

Although *Becket* has pageantry and, in its twenty-two scenes, the scope of a chronicle, the play is literature and not history, drama and not spectacle. As such, the play's business is the illumination of human values in discord with each other that issue in violence and spiritual desolation. That the main business of the play is connected to the discordant relationships between Becket and Henry nobody could miss. But such imprecision as "connected to the discordant relationships" does not take us much into the meaning of the play. Which man is central?

Becket does little to give the play its motion; it is Henry's actions that keep moving the play along the course it takes. What are the actions of the play? We must first ask, What is a dramatic action? A physical occurrence, even an exciting one, is not necessarily a dramatic action. For example, in the hunting scene Becket scuffles with the Saxon's son to disarm him in order to save the boy from death. The occurrence tells us something about Becket, that he does have feeling for the Saxon; but that is characterization, not action. On the other hand, a discovery or realization, which is mental rather than physical, can be a dramatic action. In like manner, an emotional change such as falling in love is an action. What defines a dramatic action is that it have a consequence. Becket's saving the Saxon from death has no consequence.

In the opening scene of the play, in the cathedral, Henry's first speech has assurance and iron; this Henry is the same king who speaks only moments later in the closing scene of the play, self-controlled and in control, whose motive for being in the cathedral is political strategy. He needs those Saxons of Becket's and so goes through the masquerade of the flogging, ashamed of it, to rally the Saxons to his cause against his rebellious son; he makes "peace with their Saint." In the cathedral the ghost of Becket appears in Archbishop's robes. We understand from their conversation that the "honor of the realm" and the "honor of God" divided these two men. Soon Henry's memory flashes back to their earlier "happy times"; those times were gay, affectionate, smiling. The first action of the play—which is not the first action of the plot-structure, that is, not the beginning of change in the central character—takes place in Henry's council chamber: the king revives the office of Chancellor of England, keeper of the Triple Lion Seal, and entrusts it to Becket. As a consequence Becket makes the Church pay the tax that Henry wants. The play has begun to move toward one of its crucial actions, near the end of Act II, which is Henry's ordering Becket to become Archbishop. That action will be the beginning of change. When Becket asks him not to do it, Henry replies, in large measure because of Becket's performance as Chancellor, "You've never disappointed me, Thomas. And you are the only man I trust."

When the king and Becket take shelter from a storm in the hut of a Saxon peasant, Becket acts in relationship to the Saxons; but that is characterization and exposition for what happens later, as I have said, not dramatic action. The scene gives substance to Becket's lines at the end of the act, when he tells the sleeping Henry, "if you were one of my race, how simple everything would be. How tenderly I would love you, my prince, in an ordered world." The only consequence of the scene with the Saxons is that Henry, having given the Saxon girl to Becket as a favor, can more easily demand Becket's mistress, Gwendolen, in the next scene—"favor for favor." That demand advances the play for the rest of the act, and to the end Henry thinks that his taking Gwendolen was perhaps what Becket could never forgive him.

Becket then has two actions. In Henry's tent in France, Becket teaches Henry that "governing can be as amusing as a game of tennis" and that it is important to win. He also makes Henry realize that if the king does not crush the Church "now, in five years' time there will be two Kings in England. . . . And in ten years' time there will be only one," the Archbishop of Canterbury. These are thus far Becket's most crucial actions, although the scene is neither as "dramatic" nor as entertaining as the earlier ones; these actions move the play toward the dislocation in the relationship of the two men.

The next action is Henry's: he learns that the old Archbishop has died. The consequence is momentous. Having absorbed Becket's political lessons, seeing that the tennis ball of power is in his court and that "This is the time to score a point," he conceives an "extraordinary idea"—"what if the Primate is my man? If the Archbishop of Canterbury is for the King, how can his power possibly incommodate me?" And Henry orders Becket, despite his friend's warning, to become Archbishop. The next and last scene of the second act presents the first effects of Becket's conversion.

The third act begins in the king's palace, with exposition that is necessary occurring just before a crucial action. The comic expository scene shows us that nobody in Henry's family can mean anything to him. Then comes the return of the Seal of England.

> *King. (Stunned)* The Seal? Why has he sent me back the Seal?
> *He unrolls the parchment and reads it in silence. His face hardens.*

The silent pause while he reads is to let the return of the
Seal sink in dramatically. The silence heralds the tragic realization that he must "learn to be alone," that he must live
without love.

In the next scene the king deals masterfully with the Bishop
of London, whom he is going to use against Becket; the
king no longer has any fear of the clergy. Indeed, he has
no fear even of God. The terror-struck Bishop is a measure
of the fear the king has lost.

Becket is seen to be living alone; the Bishops are ranged
against him. But it is much easier for Becket to sustain that
condition than it is for the king, who is alone without God.
Becket refuses to retreat from "open opposition" to the king,
for if he does the Church will lose its freedom and not survive.

The crucial decision is still Henry's to make. Folliot, the
Bishop of London, describes the legal machinery which has
been set in motion to crush Becket.

> *King. (Staggering suddenly)* O my Thomas!
> *Folliot. (Impassively)* I can still stop the machine, your Highness.
> *King. (Hesitates a second then says)* No. Go.

Thereafter the hunt must be relentless; the honor of the
realm is at stake. Only Becket's weakening could change
the case, and that is unimaginable. On the plain at La Ferté-
Bernard, Becket understands what course the king, tormented
by love, will take. His last words in the interview are "Farewell, my prince. I know I shall never see you again." Henry
has promised Becket the royal peace in England.

> *King. (His face twisted with hatred)* How dare you say that to
> me after I gave you my royal word? Do you take me for a traitor?
> *Becket looks at him gravely for a second longer, with a sort of pity
> in his eyes. Then he slowly turns his horse and rides away. The wind
> howls.*

That howling wind is an emblem of Henry's desolation and
pain.

We have followed the course of action which Henry's "No" to the Bishop of London determined. Let us return to that crucial moment. The king's "No" is followed by his wife's "He's doomed, isn't he?" The king turns on her angrily, forbidding her to gloat. Neither his wife nor his mother has ever given him love.

> *Queen Mother.* (*Bitterly*) Well, call him back! Absolve him since he loves you! Give him supreme power then! But do something!
> *King.* I am. I'm learning to be alone, Madam. As usual.

Henry's retort reveals that he clearly understands the meaning to his emotional life of his not stopping the machinery that will condemn Becket.

To the king's momentary delight Becket faces down his accusers, as reported by a page, and escapes to France. There are scenes in France, in the Vatican, again in France, presenting Becket's story; but in these scenes Becket's only dramatic action, his only act with a consequence in the drama, is his decision to return to England.

To score against Becket, Henry will have his successor crowned during his lifetime and—with the Pope's authority, for which Henry has paid the price—he will strip from the Primacy its ancient "exclusive right to anoint and consecrate the Kings of this Realm"; the king ignores his mother's warning that if he crowns his son the boy will try to divide the kingdom. Once more we see that Henry has no bond either with his family or with his barons. Hearing that Becket has landed in England and that the Saxons—peasants, artisans, small shopkeepers—have swarmed around Canterbury to protect their Archbishop with "makeshift shields and rusty lances," Henry roars, "A Saxon! A man loved! (*Shouting like a madman*) I loved him! Yes, I loved him! And I believe I still do! Enough, O God! Enough! Stop, stop, O God, I've had enough!" In his misery and hysteria, he makes a sudden cry: "Will no one rid me of him? . . . Are there no men left in England? Oh, my heart! My heart is beating too fast to bear!"

> *He lies, still as death on the torn mattress. The four barons stand*

around speechless. Suddenly, on a percussion instrument, there rises a rhyth-
mic beating, a sort of muffled tom-tom which is at first only the agitated
heartbeats of the King, but which swells and grows more insistent. The
four barons . . . straighten, buckle their sword belts, pick up their helmets
and go slowly out, leaving the King alone with the muffled rhythm of
the heartbeats, which will continue until the murder. The King lies there
prostrate. . . . A torch sputters and goes out. He sits up, looks around,
sees they have gone and suddenly realizes why. A wild, lost look comes
into his eyes. A moment's pause then he collapses on the bed with a long
broken moan.
  King. O my Thomas!
  A second torch goes out. Total darkness. Only the steady throb of
the heartbeats is heard.

The torches going out are symbolic of something in his
emotional life being destroyed. In the murder scene the
"muffled tom-tom is heard distinctly at first, then closer." The
throbbing grows louder and *"mingles with a loud knocking on
the door."* For a moment as the barons and Becket face each
other the tom-tom gives place to a *"heavy silence."* As Becket
begins the service in the cathedral, *"The throbbing starts again,
muffled."* The barons let fall their sword blows like woodcut-
ters. The percussive throbbing, if perceived in performance
as Henry's heartbeats (they can be, coming as they do right
after Henry's "Oh, my heart! My heart is beating too fast
to bear!"), makes Henry present in the murder scene; I should
go so far as to say that the symbolic throbbing makes the
dramatic value of the scene Henry's. When the barons murder
the Archbishop, the throbbing stops: something has died
in Henry's heart. That theme is sustained in the ultimate
scenes of the play. The king is kneeling, naked, where Becket
fell a moment earlier; *"Four monks are whipping him with ropes,
almost duplicating the gestures of the barons as they killed Becket."*
At the last we watch the king. We may feel of him that
without love he is living in spiritual desolation, but he has
recovered his emotional strength and has learned to live
alone. He controls himself and his realm, head and shoulders
over his barons. Because of his political strategy in submitting
to the whipping in penance for the murder of the Saxon
Archbishop and in expressing his wish that his friend "be

honored and prayed to in this Kingdom as a saint," he can look to incontestable future rule with Saxon allegiance. Our admiration for the distance he has come cannot be unmixed, but admiration there is, and also, perhaps, compassion for his present state.

We have seen the course of the change in Henry, a change revealed by the actions of the play. This *change in condition is the essence of narrative; it is that which happens. What happens, of course, happens to a character* and may take any or all of three forms: the character may change (Henry's mind and will strengthen in his "bitter maturity"); personal circumstances may change (the king becomes master of all England); relationships to other people may change (Henry's friendship changes to enmity, and he learns to live utterly alone).

The course of the change in the condition of the central character is described by the beginning, the middle, and the end of the plot-structure; and we must remember that each of these is an action of the central character. *Since there is a change, there must be a beginning of change. That beginning is the first action of the plot-structure.* From the beginning the middle action of the plot-structure emerges; *the middle may be a direct consequence of the beginning, or may bear an adversative relationship to it. In either case the middle will give rise to a question that the play must settle; in terms of plot, this question is what the play is about. The end or final action of the plot answers the question posed by the middle* and in so doing completes what was begun in the beginning.

The middle action of the plot-structure raises the question that the play must settle; how that question is settled is determined by the climax. Like the beginning and the middle, the climax is an action of the central character that moves the play forward. (To say that the end is "determined" by the climax is not strictly accurate. Although the climax is that act of the central character which influences the course of the rest of the action, it does not absolutely determine the end. Only in tragedy is the logical cause-and-effect relationship between climax and catastrophe inviolable. In other kinds of plays, particularly in plays that depend upon a sudden release of tension for an effect, there can occur in the last moments of the play a reversal of the course of action indicated by the climax. In a melodrama, for example, the hero may be heading for catastrophe but at the end will triumph.)

We may now make a logically precise formulation of the plot-structure of *Becket*, which gives the play its unity of action.

The beginning of change: Henry, who loves and greatly depends on Becket, and who has no bond of love with anybody else, makes his friend Primate against Becket's warning that "If I become Archbishop, I can no longer be your friend."

The middle: When Becket returns the Triple Lion Seal, resigning the office of Chancellor, Henry realizes that the love went only in one direction and that he will have to "learn to be alone."

To be settled by the end: Will he be able to?

Climax: He tells the Bishop of London not to stop the machinery that will condemn Becket. That act, dooming Becket, determines the course of the remaining action.

The end, as we have seen, settles affirmatively the question raised by the middle.

Will Henry "learn to be alone"? That is what the story is mainly about. In that story is involved the contrast between Henry's deep human love and, first, Becket's detachment, then Becket's love for the honor of God. It would take a hard heart, I think, not to go out to the king when *"he collapses onto the throne and sobs like a child,"* after the return of the Seal, moaning "O my Thomas!" Then:

You've sent me back the Three Lions of England, like a little boy who doesn't want to play with me any more. You think you have God's honor to defend now! I would have gone to war with all England's might behind me, and against England's interests, to defend you, little Saxon. I would have given the honor of the Kingdom laughingly . . . for you. . . . Only I loved you and you didn't love me . . . that's the difference.

Will Henry learn to live alone? The values of the play are modern; its central issue is intensely so. Never before in history, perhaps, have the human consciousness and sensibility so generally been made to endure a sense of isolation. We may therefore easily feel in sympathy with Henry. True, in the early Henry are a childishness in his fears and pleasures and a crudeness in his actions; a "sly, brutish way," a "slightly loutish manner" never leave him. But these dissolve in his warmth and brightness on seeing Becket in the early days, in his great love and later his torment, in his noble gratitude always. Only Becket's death can free the king from torment, but that is not why the king dooms the priest. We may take the king at his word when he turns on his wife, forbidding her to gloat: "Becket is attacking me and he has betrayed me. I am forced to fight him and crush him, but at least he gave me, with open hands, everything that is at all good in me. . . . That is why I forbid you to smile as he lies dying." We find here a man.

The logical formulation of plot-structure, after considerable practice, may be quickly made. In making that formulation it is often well to decide first what the beginning of change and the climax are. The climax, as defined here technically, often is *not* the most exciting moment of the play. *It is essential to remember that there can be only one central character and that the four actions of the plot-structure—the beginning, the middle, and the end of change, and the climax—are his.*

This method of structural analysis cannot reveal the total meaning of a play because the total meaning is a product of *all* the elements that go into making the play. But by providing an instrument with which an objective determination may be made of the most important formal elements in a play, this method of analysis makes accessible an absolute meaning in a play. We may validly maintain that a play has an absolute meaning because the vital principle of a play, giving life to the rest, is (I repeat) the visual presentation of happenings which constitute the course of the change we apprehend; and these happenings have not only an independent existence and reality of their own but a determinable logic that binds them together.

2/ THE PLAY: ABOUT WHOM? ABOUT WHAT? A CLASSICAL TEST CASE

Sophocles' *Philoctetes*

If reviewers thinking on the run may miss important meaning in a play, so may unhurried scholars in the privacy of the study. Let us turn from contemporary drama to the classical Greek. In 409 B.C. Sophocles presented *Philoctetes* and won the first prize at the dramatic festival. What the Athenians, perhaps fifteen thousand strong in the Theater of Dionysus, saw in the play with Sophocles there to direct, we do not know. Perhaps they quarreled over the play's meaning. Most scholars today believe, like Gilbert Norwood, that "for the dramatist Philoctetes, and not Neoptolemus, is the central figure: this is proved by the work as a whole and the title." But a "work as a whole," unanalyzed, can prove nothing; nor, as we have already seen, can the title. More than a century ago the German archeologist and writer on ancient art and history Karl O. Mueller, in his *History of the Literature of Ancient Greece* (commissioned in England and translated by George Cornwall Lewe; the German text was never published), made this claim for Neoptolemus: "the intrinsic revolution, the real *peripeteia** in the drama of Sophocles, lies in the . . . return of Neoptolemus to his genuine and natural disposition, and this *peripeteia* is . . . brought about by means of the characters and the progress of the action itself," in contrast to the

* That is, "reversal," which is change.

36

peripeteia brought about by the appearance of Heracles to Philoctetes at the play's end. Mueller has stood almost alone.

Now, the structure of any narrative, whether in poetry or prose, whether a drama or narration, depends on how what happens (the change that takes place) is arranged, and to that arrangement corresponds our first phase of apprehension of meaning. As Thornton Wilder puts it, "The dramatist . . . learns, above all to organize the play in such a way that its strength lies not in appearances beyond his control [e.g., in what the actors do] , but in the succession of events and in the unfolding of an idea, in narration."[1] Let us see whether we can determine *Philoctetes'* narrative meaning, objectively verifying Mueller's claim that the intrinsic *peripeteia* is that of Neoptolemus.

The play opens with Odysseus speaking to Neoptolemus, the son of Achilles: this desolate island is Lemnos, where Odysseus isolated Philoctetes, whose screams and groans of pain stopped the Greek army's sacrifices on the way to Troy. Then Odysseus, seeming only to justify himself but subtly beginning his control of the young Neoptolemus' mind by implanting the rightness of loyalty, says,

I tell you I had orders for what I did:
my masters, the princes, bade me do it.[2]

Now Neoptolemus is to help with the capture of the diseased outcast. The young man climbs to a cave, where there are only leaves for a mattress, a rude wooden cup, some kindling, and stained rags drying in the sun. Odysseus has Neoptolemus set a guard, for with a maimed foot Philoctetes cannot go far, and he is dangerous to Odysseus. Odysseus goes on with the purpose of their coming to Lemnos, to which, he says, Neoptolemus must be loyal with more than his body, no matter what he now hears. What he hears is that he must practice this deceit: he is to say to Philoctetes that although the prayers of the Greeks had moved him, Neoptolemus, to go to Troy (for only with his help could Troy be taken), they thought him not worthy of his father's armor, which they gave to Odysseus, and so with bitter hatred he is sailing

home. (Although the armor had originally been awarded
to Odysseus, the Greeks gave it to Neoptolemus as his due
heritage, for otherwise Troy could never fall.) If Neoptolemus will not do this, he will bring sorrow to the Greeks,
for without Philoctetes' bow Neoptolemus will never sack
Troy. Philoctetes will trust Achilles' son.

I know, young man, it is not your natural bent
to say such things nor to contrive such mischief.
But the prize of victory is pleasant to win.
Bear up: another time we shall prove honest.
For one brief shameless portion of a day
give me yourself, and then for all the rest
you may be called most scrupulous.

Later Odysseus is explicit about the motive of his life:

As the occasion
demands, such a one am I.
When there is a competition of men just and good,
you will find none more scrupulous than myself.
What I seek in everything is to win.

The prize of victory is what Odysseus holds out to Neoptolemus in order to lure him from his natural bent. That
temptation is open enough, but what follows it is subtly cor-
ruptive: "one brief shameless portion of a day" would deci-
sively change the young man's bent for honesty, at least in
the world this play envisions, as again made explicit later.

Men whose wit has been mother of villainy once
have learned from it to be evil in all things.

When Neoptolemus replies to Odysseus,

what I dislike to hear
I hate to put in execution.
I have a natural antipathy
to get my ends by tricks and stratagems,

we may wonder whether the lines are plainly noble or tinged
with the pomposity of the young. He has not yet been tested.
We may judge what the man says by what he does, and what
he does is to agree to the deception. Only craft will take

Philoctetes, Odysseus argues, for he will never listen to persuasion, and his arrows, which carry inevitable death, make
him invulnerable to force. Nor is lying shameful when it
brings gain. "What gain is it for me that he should come
to Troy?" Neoptolemus cannot take Troy without Philoctetes'
weapons. If he wins the weapons, two prizes will be his.
"What? If I know, I will do what you say." He shall be called
wise and valiant. "Well, then I will do it, casting aside all
shame." *That decision is the beginning of change, the beginning
of the logic in the plot.* We must remember that the three actions
of the plot-structure define only the change experienced by
the central character and not the total action of the play,
and that the character whose choices and other actions give
the play its motion and direction is central. Odysseus then
returns to his ship, not to be seen by Philoctetes, saying that
if Neoptolemus is beyond due time, he, Odysseus, will send
a man with a crafty story for Neoptolemus to use.

The chorus, ordinary men aware of their limitations, do
not know what to say or what to hide from Philoctetes and
appeal to their young lord who, they think, as a deputy of
Zeus has pre-eminent judgment. They are to take their cues
from him and help when they can. They pity Philoctetes
his suffering and loneliness, wondering at his endurance and
lamenting the dark dealings of the Gods; and because their
pity is mixed with fear, it has depth and no sentimentality.
Neoptolemus knows that the wound was the work of a deity,
Chryse. (Philoctetes alone knew where the altar of this deity
was to whom the Greek chiefs had to sacrifice. Guiding the
Greeks to the precinct on the island, he was bitten by a snake.
His cries of pain, bad omens, prevented the performance
of the rites, and the stink from his festering foot disgusted
the camp.) And Neoptolemus believes that Philoctetes' long
suffering has been owing to some God, so that he could
not bend his bow against Troy before the destined time for
that city to fall to the divine, invincible arrows. The chorus
hear a bitter cry and caution their lord not to speak of the
plot. When Philoctetes comes to them and speaks, there is
nothing in his speech of the savage killer the chorus feared,

although they are afraid of what he looks like. He asks them
not to shrink in fear because of his wild appearance; asks,
too, for their pity for his suffering, or at least for speech.
In the exchange of speech Philoctetes recounts the nine years
he has "spent dying," evoking tragic pity, and Neoptolemus
tells his prepared lies, beginning a moral descent. Indeed,
his skill in elaborating the story of the Greek refusal to give
him his father's armor, the way he puts partial truth to the
service of a lie, shows him as cunning potentially as Odysseus.
The chorus confirm his story. During the account Philoctetes,
on learning of Apollo's slaying of Achilles, whom he loved
dearly, speaks this epitaph: "Noble was he that killed and
he that died." The epitaph has this importance to the audience, that it clearly portrays Philoctetes' acceptance of the
God's act. Philoctetes learns also of the other dead heroes,
only the good dying, the evil continuing to live (like the villainous Thersites and Odysseus, who is here said to be the son
of the fraudulent and deceitful Sisyphus). Philoctetes wonders what he is to think, how praise the Gods when their
ways are evil. Nevertheless, his acceptance of the Gods is
deep. Whether or not good will survive is crucial to the meaning of the play and to the tragic terror that will be evoked.
Neoptolemus cunningly pretends to end the meeting:

Now I will be going to my ship. Philoctetes, on you God's blessing
and goodbye. May the Gods recover you of sickness, as you would
have it. Let us go, men, that when God grants us sailing we may
be ready to sail.

On his knees Philoctetes begs the young man to take him
from the island, appealing to his nobleness of mind not to
sully his fair name with meanness. Others who put in at
this island never even took a message to his father—such
is the way of the world. The chorus play the ill game, advising
their young prince to take pity, both to baffle the hateful
Greeks and not to offend God. Neoptolemus yields, saying
an ambiguous prayer:

May God give us a safe clearance from this land
and a safe journey where we choose to go.

Before they leave, Philoctetes wants to show the young man how he has lived, how tough his spirit was that did not break—the endurance that he has had in the balance against the terrible years on Lemnos, whose prospect alone would have broken any other man.

At that moment a stranger comes, the sailor disguised as a merchant sent by Odysseus. It is understandable that Philoctetes in his joyous fortune should not suspect the coincidence of the double arrival of the ships. The trader (expecting a reward) informs Neoptolemus that the Greeks are pursuing him with a squadron. The young man says, "Do they intend to bring me back with violence or persuade me?" It is a mirror image of a line Odysseus spoke earlier of Philoctetes, "He will not be persuaded; force will fail," and is echoed by the trader some lines later, after clever preparation, saying that Odysseus and Diomedes (whom Philoctetes thinks one of the evil men who live on while the good die) have sworn to take Philoctetes to Troy "either by persuasion or brute force." But neither persuasion nor force nor craft wins out in this play, only inner necessity. We learn also from the trader the prophecy, accepted as truth, that Troy will never fall unless Philoctetes yields to Greek persuasion. Philoctetes expresses anxiety to sail, apparently not believing, although he does later, that his bow can withstand the Greeks. He will gather the things he needs, an herb to soothe his wounds, and any arrows lying around, for none must fall into anyone else's hand. Is this, then, the famous bow which Philoctetes is holding? Neoptolemus longs to touch it, if such is lawful. His deceit is cunning; he knows that Philoctetes is deeply religious. Philoctetes replies, "Your words are reverent, boy. Your wish is lawful." Neoptolemus alone of the living will be able to boast that he handled the bow, for Philoctetes himself by friendly help had first won the bow. (The young Philoctetes had lighted the funeral pyre for Heracles, who then gave him his bow and arrows, which Heracles had got from Apollo.)

The two men are about to enter the cave, when the chorus speak. They have known of none, of all mankind,

whose destiny was more his enemy when he met it
than Philoctetes', who wronged no one, by force
or fraud, but lived just among the just,
and fell in trouble past his deserts.

Their account of his sufferings is true and has the ring of
sincerity; in some measure their sympathy is real. But they
are practicing deception when they say,

But now he will end fortunate. He has fallen in
with the son of good men . . .
Our prince in his seaworthy craft will carry him
after the fulness of many months to his father's home.

Because they know what they have said about his terrible
sufferings is true, their corruption, which is service to their
prince, strikes us the worse. They will be good or evil as
Neoptolemus is. What follows accounts for the silence and
motionlessness of the two men during the ode. Philoctetes
was transfixed in fear of an attack of his sickness coming
on, the younger man watching him. He is afraid that Neoptolemus, seeing the terrible nature of his sickness, will leave;
but Neoptolemus asks to lend a helping hand. Philoctetes
tells Neoptolemus not to touch him, but to take and guard
the bow during the attack and the sleep that will come upon
him:

by the Gods I beg you do not give up my bow
willingly or unwillingly to anyone.

And when the young man takes the bow, the religious Philoctetes says,

          Bow in prayer to the Gods' envy
that the bow may not be to you a sorrow.

His pain becomes intense, and out of his pain comes the
curse, an expression of his hate, that Agamemnon and
Menelaus should suffer so. Philoctetes calls on Death, as he
does day in and day out, but Death cannot come, and so
Philoctetes pleads that Neoptolemus burn his body.

I had the resolution once to do this for another,

the son of Zeus, and so obtained the arms
that now you hold. What do you say?
What do you say? Nothing? Where are you, boy?

Neoptolemus replies, truly we may believe,

I have been in pain for you; I have been
in sorrow for your pain.

When he ambiguously assures Philoctetes he will not
leave, that "I *may* not go without you," that it would
be unlawful, Philoctetes does not understand his other
meaning, which Neoptolemus makes explicit to his men:

we have hunted in vain,
vainly have captured our quarry the bow, if we sail
without him.
His is the crown of victory, him the God said we must bring.
Shame shall be ours if we boast and our lies still leave
victory unwon.

The chorus urge their prince to take up Philoctetes now,
while he is eyeless and helpless. But Philoctetes awakens,
full of gratitude to Neoptolemus, wanting the young man
to set him on his feet. Neoptolemus at first refuses; let Philoctetes lift himself, or let these men carry him. He refuses
because he does not want to face the consequence of having
Philoctetes in his hands, the literal image betokening the
capture. When Philoctetes persists, not wanting the men to
be disquieted by his stink, Neoptolemus takes hold of the
weakened man. *That action is the middle action of the plot-
structure, for it crucially forces a choice upon Neoptolemus, who
must either yield to his pity for Philoctetes or be loyal to the Greeks.*
He says,

Now is the moment. What shall I do from now on?

The question the play must answer, then, is this: How will he act?
Will he reconcile justice to Philoctetes with loyalty to the
Greeks? Will he be good or evil? With the knowledge of
experience he can now say,

All is disgust when one leaves his own nature
and does things that misfit it.

Philoctetes quickly begins to suspect him:

Unless I am wrong, here is a man who will
betray me, leave me—so it seems—and sail away.

To which, Neoptolemus:

Not I; I will not leave you. To your bitterness,
I shall send you on a journey—and I dread this.
         . . . You must sail to Troy.

To waste Troy, Neoptolemus still believes, is a necessity that
he cannot gainsay; but he is no longer practicing deception,
and so a moral ascent may begin, although he refuses to
give back the bow, for duty and self-interest, he says, both
make him obedient to the Greek generals. Philoctetes speaks
movingly, in anger and despair. The chorus respond:

What shall we do? Shall we sail? Shall we do as he asks?
Prince, it is you must decide.

These lines expose us to tragic terror. For if Neoptolemus
decides against Philoctetes, he will violate himself and the
evil in the world will have its way. Although compassion for
Philoctetes is strong in Neoptolemus, he is filled with indeci-
sion and turns the question back, "What shall we do, friends?"
At that moment Odysseus appears, demanding the bow, and
Philoctetes knows at once where the foul craft of Neoptolemus
came from. His despair makes him lose judgment, and he
fights with words, threatening to throw himself off the precipice and by his death frustrate their design; Odysseus commands the men to seize Philoctetes who, although defeated,
speaks with remarkable self-esteem and, as the chorus say,
with "no yielding to suffering."

You who have never had a healthy thought
nor noble, you Odysseus, how you have hunted me,
how you have stolen upon me with this boy
as your shield, because I did not know him, one
that is no mate for you but worthy of me,
who knows nothing but to do what he was bidden,
and now, you see, is suffering bitterly
for his own faults and what he brought on me.

And he curses Odysseus, thinking still that the Gods care
for justice. The cunning Odysseus changes his tactic against
the hard Philoctetes who will not yield to his suffering.

Let him go, men . . .
Let him stay here. We have these arms of yours
and do not need you, Philoctetes.
Teucer is with us and has the skill and I,
who, I think, am no mean master of them
and have as straight an aim. Why do we need you?
　　　　. . . Perhaps
your prize will bring me the honor you should have had.

As we know, the arms will do the Greeks no good without
Philoctetes, who must go willingly to Troy. Odysseus is counting on Philoctetes not being able to stand his, Odysseus',
using the bow; and indeed, after Odysseus leaves with Neoptolemus, Philoctetes laments,

By the shore of the gray sea he sits and laughs at me.
He brandishes in his hand the weapon which kept me alive,
which no one else had handled. Bow that I loved . . .

You have found a new master, a man of craft.

That feeling explains Philoctetes' immediate response to
Odysseus' speech:

What shall I do? Will you appear
before the Argives in the glory of my arms?

Philoctetes then asks Neoptolemus if he will go away in silence.
Odysseus warns Neoptolemus not to let his generosity spoil
their future. Philoctetes then turns to the chorus, "Do you,
too, have no pity?" Let them not desert him. And they reply,
"This young man is our captain. What he says to you we
say as well." Again we hear that they will be good or not
depending on Neoptolemus. He has them stay with Philoctetes until the ship is ready, hoping that Philoctetes will have
better thoughts of him and Odysseus.

　Philoctetes can say only that he must die. The chorus believe
that he has doomed himself, not choosing the wisdom of
going to Troy; and when Philoctetes would condemn the

doer of treachery, they say that not any craft of theirs but the Gods' will has done what has been done. They keep responding to him, he not listening until they speak of his pain. To them he appeals for a weapon to destroy himself. The chorus, giving up trying to persuade him to go to Troy, say they would have left long ago had they not seen Odysseus and Neoptolemus coming.

The next scene contains the climax of the play. Neoptolemus now thinks that he did wrong to obey Odysseus and the Greeks. Odysseus, using threats, tries to persuade him not to return the bow.

> How can it be just to give to him again
> What you have won by my plans?

The younger man's reply measures their difference in values. "My fault has been shameful, and I must try to retrieve it." *That is his climactic decision.* Persuasion failing, Odysseus threatens force, placing his hand on his sword. When Neoptolemus at once takes his sword hilt in hand, Odysseus runs no unnecessary risk (we have learned that his victories at Troy were by stratagems).

> I will let you alone;
> I shall go and tell this to the assembled Greeks,
> and they will punish.

The irony of Neoptolemus shows the maturing of his mind.

> That is very prudent.
> If you are always as prudent as this,
> perhaps you will keep out of trouble.

Odysseus silently leaves.

Neoptolemus calls on Philoctetes to come speak with him, still wanting Philoctetes to go to Troy. Philoctetes has only a curse for the treachery of Neoptolemus. Neoptolemus then hands over the bow, and as he does Odysseus returns threatening to bring Philoctetes to Troy by force. Philoctetes strings an arrow, but Neoptolemus grips his arms. Odysseus makes his escape; nobody can face that bow. Neoptolemus' values are different not only from Odysseus' but from Philoctetes' as well.

Philoc. Why did you prevent me killing my enemy, with my bow, a man that hates me?

Neopt. This is not to our glory, neither yours nor mine.

Philoctetes grants, having his bow, that there is no cause for anger or complaint against Neoptolemus and praises him. Now Neoptolemus advises Philoctetes, putting what he has to say as a request for favor. Men need to bear the fortunes the Gods give, but clinging to self-imposed misery cannot be justly excused or pitied. Philoctetes will hate the man who advises with good will, thinking him an enemy. But Neoptolemus will go on speaking, calling Zeus to witness. It is heaven's doing, the sickness of Philoctetes, who was bitten by the snake guarding the roofless sanctuary of the Goddess Chryse; and Philoctetes will never know relief until he goes freely to the plains of Troy, where the sons of Asclepius will ease him of the sickness, and where, with his bow and with Neoptolemus, he will take Troy. Let him yield with a good grace.

It is a glorious heightening of gain.
First, to come into hands that can heal you,
and then to be judged pre-eminent among the Greeks,
winning the highest renown among them, taking
Troy that has cost infinity of tears.

We may note that Neoptolemus, like Odysseus, still accepts the desirability of gain and glory, as he did when the crafty man persuaded him to lie; but with this change, he will do nothing dishonorable for gain or glory. He still believes in the rightness of Philoctetes going to Troy, but no longer believes in a loyalty to the Greeks on his own part if that loyalty involves bad acts. Philoctetes is torn, thinking his life hateful that he must either be deaf to his friend's words or expose himself to living with those who ruined him and from whom he will again suffer evil, for such are they. Nor should Neoptolemus go to Troy; "let those bad men die in their own bad fashion." Neoptolemus replies,

What you say
is reasonable; yet I wish that you would trust
the Gods, my words, and, with me as friend, fare forth.

Heracles, who is beyond the reason in what Philoctetes has said, will soon manifest himself. Although Neoptolemus knows that it would be best for them both if Philoctetes went to Troy, he leaves his pleading, ready to fulfil his promise to take Philoctetes home. But how will he escape blame from the Greeks? What if they come to ravage his country? Philoctetes replies that he will be there and drive them away with the bow of Heracles. Even as they are ready to go Heracles, now a God, appears.

What shall we make of Heracles? There is nothing in the play to make us doubt the literal existence of the Gods. Even when Philoctetes hears of the good dying and the evil living, and in his anger finds that the Gods are evil, even then his acceptance of them is deep. And we know that his state of mind then, because of his suffering, because those he loved are dead and those he hates are alive, lets him speak bitterly, without clear judgment, for he could say in that speech, "No evil thing has been known to perish." When Neoptolemus says, after returning the bow, "I wish that you would trust the Gods" and go to Troy, Philoctetes wonders why the younger man saying that has no shame that the Gods should hear those words. No God has spoken; each man's judgment is his own. We know that Philoctetes can think the Gods noble, for he said that of Apollo on hearing that the God had killed the noble Achilles. No wonder then that Heracles—who is closest in meaning of the Gods to Philoctetes—when he announces that it is his face and his voice (which Philoctetes knows well) and that he has come from the heavenly seats to tell the purposes of Zeus, can turn Philoctetes to Troy. Nor is there any possibility that the epiphany is a vision coming from within Philoctetes, unless it is argued that Philoctetes not only saw a vision that came from elements or impulses not in his conscious mind but that he was able to make the vision seen and heard by Neoptolemus, who also accepts injunctions of Heracles. It is possible, of course, to interpret Heracles symbolically, just as it may be valid to give a symbolic or a psychological interpretation to any religious experience. I maintain only that it is not possible to consider Heracles as other than the epiphany of a God *in the play* that Sophocles wrote; that is, whatever other meaning he may have, his real existence is a premise of the play. The play, indeed, makes perfectly clear that before the epiphany of Heracles nothing can make Philoctetes go to Troy, although he was torn in making up his mind. It is also true, I think, that were it not for his experience with Neoptolemus, with goodness in a man, Philoctetes' mind would have hardened against Heracles and disobeyed the God. Earlier, when Neoptolemus left with Odysseus apparently to take the bow to Troy, Philoctetes declared that even if Zeus burned him in the blaze of lightning he would not change his fixed purpose never to go to Troy. The change in Neoptolemus, then, is crucial to the outcome of Philoctetes' life, that through his sufferings he will win glory, even as Heracles did.[3]

3/ THE NATURE OF ACTION IN A PLAY

Brecht's *The Caucasian Chalk Circle*

Racine's *Phaedra*

"All concrete things and events," whether fictive or actual, says the contemporary philosopher James K. Feibleman in *Aesthetics,* "possess formal structures. This formal structure consists in a set of postulates, a chain of deductions which necessarily follow, and rigorous conclusions." As this study of formal structure has to do mainly with those postulates which are actions, let us again consider the nature of dramatic action, which formally means "that which has a consequence" and which may be either physical or mental (by "mental" I mean not only such actions as discoveries, realizations, decisions, but also such as falling in love or becoming afraid). It may seem that physical actions are likely to create the more dramatic interest—certainly they are the stuff of ordinary melodrama and farce—but empirically such a conclusion is not warranted. For example, in Calderón's *The Surgeon of His Honour,* the protagonist, fearing that his wife has dishonored him, enraged and sorrowing, in a monologue of nearly a hundred lines tries to excuse her actions as possibly innocent and to think the circumstantial evidence he discovered is accidental. Torn, he resolves to take remedies against the sickness endangering his honor. He will dissimulate his anguish, returning to his house to make further diagnosis. In the end he exacts a terrible vengeance. The monologue is tensely dramatic: our emotions are engaged with his and we watch in fearful suspense in order to know which way his mind will turn.

The plot-structures of some plays are dominantly physical; of others, mental. Neither kind is intrinsically better or more dramatic. Which kind of action a playwright will use depends on his bent or purposes. Brecht for *The Caucasian Chalk Circle* used the physical; Racine for his *Phaedra,* the mental.

The prologue of *The Caucasian Chalk Circle* (1948)[1], although important thematically, is not to our purpose in observing the nature of dramatic action. We shall consider the play proper as having two parts. The first three sections comprise Part One; as Eric Bentley in his introduction says of Part One, it is "a complete Brecht play in itself."[2] Part Two, the fourth and fifth sections, is a sequel. Grusha, a kitchen maid, is central to the plot-structure of Part One; Azdak, a village scribe who becomes a judge, to that of Part Two.

In section 1, "The Noble Child," revolutionaries decapitate the Governor of Grusinia (Georgia), and the governor's wife in escaping forgets her son. When Grusha, who has accepted the marriage proposal of the soldier Simon and said that she will wait for him, her mouth unkissed, catches sight of the governor's head on the end of a lance, she is horrified; and she hears, or thinks she hears, the governor's child calling for help. Seduced by goodness, she lifts up the deserted child (in acting out a pantomime of a passage sung by the narrator) and creeps away like a thief. That physical act will lead to the beginning of the plot-structure.

Section 2, "The Flight into the Northern Mountains," shows Grusha pursued by the Ironshirts. Grusha, although she already feels affection for the child, leaves him at the threshold of a farmhouse, for as she says to the child, "My sweetheart the soldier might be back soon, and suppose he didn't find me? You can't ask that, can you?" But the Ironshirts catch up, the peasant woman in fear betrays the child, and Grusha in despair hits an Ironshirt, who is about to take the child, over the head with a log and runs away. *This physical act, committing her to the child and making her an enemy of the Ironshirts, is the beginning of change.* She escapes by crossing a deep glacial precipice on a dangerous broken rope-bridge that her pursuers are afraid to cross.

In section 3, "In the Northern Mountains," she makes her way across the glacier and down the slopes to the farm of her prosperous brother; she is ill from the hard journey. The winter passes swiftly and her brother, afraid to have her stay on, suggests her marriage to a peasant who is about to die; marriage would stop talk about the child and, as she realizes, a stamped document for the child would attest that the child is hers. She agrees, and a comic wedding ceremony and party take place. During the party guests say the war is over and nobody can be drafted anymore. So the "dying" peasant gets up from the bed and throws out the guests who have been eating up his money. *The middle of change, then, is the ceremonial action of her marrying,* in order to protect the child she loves, believing that there will be no risk to her betrothal to the soldier. *The question thereby raised, which the end will answer, is, Will she be able to have her soldier?* She works hard for the peasant but never allows him intercourse. The soldier Simon returns, still in love with her. So that he will not leave her, she tells him that the child is not hers. But Ironshirts come for the child, and when an Ironshirt says, "Is this your child?" Grusha asserts "Yes." Simon goes and the Ironshirts take her to trial. That "Yes," unlike her earlier actions in the plot-structure, is mental rather than physical; *that decision is the climax of Part One,* determining the unhappy loss of her lover. The climax works well although unusually late because of the melodramatic elements in Part One, for which a late climax can be formally fitting, and because the end points to the sequel. The comic sequel, "The Story of the Judge" and "The Chalk Circle," reverses the end of Part One, giving Grusha both the child and the soldier in marriage.

Phaedra (1677),[2] generally regarded as the greatest of French tragedies, on the other hand presents only one physical action and that action is not part of the plot-structure (other physical actions in the play, the suicide of Oenone and the violent death of Hippolytus, are narrated, not presented; we do not *see* her suicide or his death. The power of drama is in the direct immediacy of what is presented, of what we see happening). Nonetheless, on the stage the play's dramatic interest never flags.

Act I. Hippolytus confesses to Theramenes that he is leaving Troezen to search for Theseus, his long-missing father (although Theramenes has already searched) because he dare not stay in Troezen—not because of the hatred of Phaedra, who is dying, but because of his love for Aricia (a descendant of rival claimants to the throne of Athens) who, Theseus has ruled, cannot marry.

Phaedra, who has neither slept nor taken food for three days, berated by Oenone for her inhuman silence, confesses to this woman who is devoted to her that she loves her husband's son, Hippolytus—then learns that her husband has died. With Theseus reported dead, Athens is divided into factions over whether its ruler shall be Phaedra's son, or Hippolytus, or Aricia. Oenone, who was going to die with Phaedra, argues that Phaedra must live for her son, and that her husband's death no longer makes her passion a crime and a horror. Let Phaedra unite with Hippolytus against Aricia; Troezen is his, and he knows that the laws give Athens to her son. Phaedra agrees.

Act II. Hippolytus comes to Aricia—he does not yet know that she loves him—to say that he will revoke the laws against her, that she is free, and that he is going to Athens to settle the succession of its throne on her as the last descendant of its former rulers; and because she alludes to his hating her, he says, too, that he loves her. She responds that Athens is not the richest of his gifts to her.

Phaedra, who comes to Hippolytus to beg help for her son, despite herself makes clear her love for Hippolytus, a love that she does not condone. To expiate the sin of her self-betrayal, she asks him to strike his sword into her heart and, if he will not, to let her have the sword. She takes the sword from the amazed Hippolytus. (This is the only physical action presented in the play; the sword is later used as evidence against Hippolytus.) Oenone stops her from using the sword on herself and takes her away from shame as Theramenes approaches.

Athens has voted to give its rule to Phaedra's son. But there is a rumor that Theseus is alive. Hippolytus orders the rumor looked into; if it is unfounded, he will go to Athens to put the scepter into Arcia's hands, at whatever cost.

Act III. Now that Hippolytus knows of her passion, she having crossed "the bounds of modesty," Phaedra cannot leave him, nor can she rule the state, having no rule over herself. Thinking that his heart is not open to love, she instructs Oenone to tempt him with the crown. But Oenone returns quickly: Theseus is alive and near. Phaedra laments that she will die dishonored; she cannot live with her shame. Oenone argues that Phaedra should not by her death, which is a confession, expose her children to insult or corroborate Hippolytus' accusation. Let Phaedra, rather, accuse Hippolytus; the sword that Phaedra has will speak against him. Or let Oenone speak, for whom Phaedra's life is "of such value that all else must yield to it." Theseus and Hippolytus approach. Phaedra thinks she sees her ruin in Hippolytus' eyes, and to Oenone says,

> Do what you will,
> I resign myself to you. In my disorder,
> I can do nothing for myself.

Phaedra leaves Theseus' presence as made unworthy of him by Fortune, and Hippolytus asks his father for permission to leave Troezen. Theseus replies,

> What horror makes my frightened family
> Flee from my sight? . . .
> > Phaedra complains
> That I am wronged. Who has betrayed me?

When his son is silent, Theseus suspects the young man of betrayal and goes off to Phaedra. Hippolytus thinks that Phaedra will accuse herself.

Act IV. Theseus is enraged against his traitorous son, accepting, as evidence of the violence Hippolytus tried to use to execute his passion, the sword he had given to his son. He banishes Hippolytus and prays to Neptune to kill his son. Hippolytus, not wishing to grieve his father, does not tell the truth about Phaedra, pleading only that he has never done anything unlawful, that he hates vice, and that the only woman he burns for is Aricia whom he loves with a virtuous love; but his father believes that he is lying about Aricia. After Hippolytus leaves, Theseus feels his unhappiness for the destruction he is bringing on his son warring with his sense of justice.

Phaedra comes to plead that Theseus spare Hippolytus, but he will not, accusing his son of other crimes, including the lie that he loves Aricia. Theseus goes to the altar of Neptune to pray that the vengeance be executed swiftly.

Knowing that Hippolytus loves Aricia, Phaedra, maddened with jealousy, suffers more than ever. But she takes hold of herself. To her father Minos she says,

A cruel god has doomed thy family.
Behold her vengeance in thy daughter's lust.

Oenone tries to persuade her that her love is a venial fault. Phaedra condemns her for her pernicious, servile arts and orders her to go.

Act V. Aricia tries to persuade Hippolytus to defend himself, but he will not tell the truth to his father. She agrees to escape with him, and he leaves.

Theseus comes looking for truth. Aricia tries to make him repent his murderous prayer. She then leaves. He is troubled by what she has not said and, affected with pity, will interrogate Oenone again. He learns that Oenone has committed suicide and that Phaedra wants to die. He sends for his son to defend himself and asks Neptune to withhold disaster. But it is too late. Theramenes gives the account of Hippolytus' brave death.

To Phaedra, Theseus says,

Joy in his death, whether unjust or lawful
I'll let my eyes forever be abused,
Believe him criminal, since you accuse him.
His death alone gives matter for my tears
Without my seeking harsh enlightenment,
Which would not bring him back, and might increase
The sum of my misfortunes.

He would banish himself from this coast and the bloody image of his son, but his fame will not let him hide. Phaedra has taken a deadly poison to leave her only enough life to exonerate Hippolytus. When she dies, Theseus turns from her. He will mix tears with his son's blood and render him honor; and to appease his son's ghost, will make Aricia his daughter.

Although some may feel the tragic experience of Theseus more deeply than Phaedra's, his plot-structure is subordinate to hers; Phaedra, of course, is the central character. Here is her plot-structure.

The beginning of change: Phaedra, an honorable woman struggling against her passion for her husband's son and dying of that sickness, persuaded on hearing Theseus has died that her passion is no longer a crime and a horror and that she must live for her son's sake, decides to ask Hippolytus to help her young son secure the throne of Athens, which is due her son by the laws of Athens.

The middle: When she speaks to Hippolytus, overcome by her passion she confesses her love, only to find that Hippolytus is monstrously offended by her, and then to learn that her husband is alive.

To be settled by the end: Will she be able to extricate herself?

Climax: In her state of disorder, unable to act for herself, she lets Oenone accuse Hippolytus of attempting outrage, using the sword as evidence (end of Act III, Scene iii; in five-act plays the climax usually occurs in the third act, a practice Shakespeare followed also).

There are subordinate plot-structures for Theseus and for Hippolytus. The climax of the plot-structure for Theseus is his praying to Neptune for swift vengeance against his son (end of Act IV, Scene iv). Hippolytus' climax is his refusal to tell the truth about Phaedra to his father (Act V, Scene i). His refusal to act is itself an action, for it has a consequence, his death: right after he leaves Aricia, Theseus comes with a troubled heart wanting to know the truth. We see that Phaedra's climax gives rise to the actions that are the other climaxes; thus subordinate plot-structures depend on hers.

4/STRUCTURE AND TEXTURE

Although *Phaedra* is well known, I gave the epitome of the play at some length, in order to focus on the mental nature of the actions; but even so, the psychological nature of the play cannot be much experienced in an account of the narrative as its psychological elements are in the language. The influential Antonin Artaud attacked Racinian drama for being psychological and gave only a minor place to language in the theater. "The misdeeds of the psychological theater descended from Racine have unaccustomed us to that immediate and violent action which the theater should possess. . . . Dialogue—a thing written and spoken—does not belong specifically to the stage, it belongs to books . . . ." In another context Artaud said that it is "not a question of suppressing the spoken language, but of giving words approximately the same importance they have in dreams . . . . The stage is a concrete physical space which asks to be filled, and to be given its own concrete language to speak . . . intended for the senses and independent of speech"—a language of "music, dance, plastic art, pantomine, mimicry, gesticulation, intonation, architecture, lighting, and scenery," for by means of these a "sense of old ceremonial magic can find a new reality in the theater"; our theater must evoke "that great metaphysical fear which is at the root of all ancient theater . . . the underlying menace of a chaos as decisive as it is dangerous . . . the terrible and necessary cruelty which things can exercise against us. . . . And the theater has been created to teach us that first of all."[1]

For Racine the resource for theater that counted most was language. He had no use for music or dance or scenery in making his tragedies. Nonetheless, he presented "the underlying menace of a chaos as decisive as it is dangerous" in the human mind. When language is the main resource for theater, the play is also a literary work and (at least in Western drama) will almost always have a plot-structure which is the armature, as in clay modelling, of the whole formal structure.

There are, of course, esthetically satisfying plays without the logic of plot-structure; such plays are theatrical rather than literary, using music and dance or stylized movements, and depend largely on the performers. Their esthetic satisfaction comes primarily from the structural principle of harmony, the textural relationships of the parts (music, dancing, stylized movements as well as language) to each other and to their sum, rather than from the structural principle of narrative unity that has concerned us so far. What takes primacy in such theater is not our usual first phase of artistic apprehension that the work is "*one* thing" but our feeling that is is "a *thing*," in Joyce's words. We "apprehend it as complex, multiple, divisible, separable, made up of its parts, the result of its parts, and their sum, harmonious."[2] Such theatrical plays dominate the Japanese and Chinese theaters and performances are commonly made up of parts of different plays.

While music and choreographed movement are expressive of experience outside the limits of language, the logic that exists in language and in the formal cause and consequence of actions is outside the limits of music or movement. Artaud wrote that "it is not a question of whether the physical language of theater . . . is able to express feelings and passions as well as words can, but whether there are not attitudes in the realm of thought and intelligence that words are incapable of grasping and that gestures and everything partaking of a spatial language attain with more precision than they."

Of course, harmony *and* unity are both necessary principles of structure. The question at issue in analyzing a play for its meaning, is whether or not one of these principles may take precedence, not whether one may be ignored. I shall from now on use "structure" for the principle of unity and "texture" for the principle of harmony, following John Crowe Ransom, for his terms serve more distinctly in drama criticism. Critics have written valuably on texture, or harmony, as a structural principle of drama in which language is the essential medium, and it is well to listen to their "spatial" (not in Artaud's physical meaning of the word) concept. G. Wilson Knight, for whom a play is an "expanded metaphor," considers that a "Shakespearean tragedy is set spatially as well as temporally in the mind. By this I mean that there are throughout the play a set of correspondences which relate to each other independently of the time-sequence which is the story: such are the intuition-intelligence opposition active within *Troilus and Cressida,* the death-theme in *Hamlet,* the nightmare evil of *Macbeth.* This I have sometimes called the play's 'atmosphere.' " L. C. Knights criticized Wilson Knight for being too preoccupied with imagery and symbols. However, he also gives precedence to textural criticism for a "Shakespeare play is a dramatic poem," by which he means "We have to elucidate the meaning (using Dr. Richard's four-fold definition [in his book *Practical Criticism*]) and to unravel ambiguities; we have to estimate the kind and quality of the imagery and determine the precise degree of evocation of particular figures; we have to allow full weight to each word, exploring its 'tentacular roots,' and to determine how it controls and is controlled by the rhythmic movement of the passage in which it occurs. In short, we have to decide exactly why the lines 'are so and not otherwise'. As we read other factors come into play. . . . 'Plot,' aspects of 'character,' recurrent 'themes' and 'symbols'—all 'precipitates from the memory'—help to determine our reaction at a given point." For Una Ellis-Fermor the Jacobeans offer a "highly interesting structural characteristic, that of a play which contains two types of experience simultaneously." One is *temporal,* "plot, story, and the casual connection of event." The other is *spatial* and "regards the play as a grouping of moods, characters, forms of diction or of prosody and looks for form in the inter-relations of these." Again, a critic may contrast "linear" form, which is *plot-oriented,* to "contextual" form, that is, *non-sequential presentations* of psychological states or of static situations. (Sanskrit drama for its unique purpose of creating *rasa,* which is a sentiment induced in the mind of the spectator, always uses states and situations but also always has a "linear" form.) The spatial elements—which are texture, or harmony—must of course be apprehended for fullness of meaning. In *Richard II* it is the textural elements of "iterative symbolism and imagery," Richard Altick has said, that effect the "impression of harmony," as "each image motif represents one of the dominant ideas of the play" and "the coalescing of these images emphasizes the complex relation existing between the ideas themselves."[3]

As the highly developed techniques of poetic criticism are used for textural matters, spatial, or textural, criticism is more accessible to critics than temporal criticism. This study aims to define a better working knowledge than now exists for the criticism of temporal structure. Something may be said about the limitations of spatial criticism. It assumes that a reader can hold the whole spatial design of a play in his mind; but as Carl Jung says in *Analytical Psychology,* "The conscious mind . . . can hold only a few simultaneous contents at a given moment . . . we only get a sort of continuation of a general understanding or awareness of a conscious world through the *succession* of conscious moments." The temporal structure takes precedence over spatial, or textural, structure esthetically as well as psychologically. For texture (as Joyce said) corresponds to the second phase of artistic apprehension which, in Western drama with rare exceptions, is dependent on the first phase, the apprehension of the structural whole. I say "rare" despite the fact that many great plays in the history of Western drama are pronounced plotless by scholars and critics. Plotlessness, for example, is said to be characteristic of the drama of the absurd. But I shall later show that such pronouncements (perhaps a result of an inaccurate understanding of the nature of dramatic action) are not true. Now let us turn to plays that do not need a logically unified plot-structure to be fully satisfying.

5/JAPANESE DRAMA

Noh and Kabuki Plays

We may first consider the Noh drama of Japan, which has the longest living theatrical tradition, a tradition that has changed little since the maturity of the Noh in the late fourteenth century. It is a subtle and sophisticated art form that takes place in its own self-existent world and time. If its human values and dramatic modes are not always those of Western drama, we nonetheless accept them as premises and can sympathetically respond as the premises flower in a perfect formal structure. *Noh* means "accomplishment," that is, of the performer, and although according to Noh's greatest practitioner, Zeami Motokio (in his treatise *Kwadensho*), the "composition of Noh texts is the life of this art" and although the words (partly in verse and partly in prose) may have remarkable literary value, it is the performance that is the significant art form, for dance and music and especially miming (which is "to imitate well all beings," according to Zeami) are of its essence. The mimetic actions are choreographed; most of the words are intoned, and those that are not are recited in a highly stylized way; there are relatively long dance passages ("relatively long" because this austere formal structure rarely contains more than a few hundred lines, and the culmination of the play is likely to be a dance). In our time a program consists of three Noh plays with two *kyogen* (farcical, basically dialogue, plays of everyday life) separating them; a Noh play takes about an hour to perform. In the time of Noh's greatest public success centuries ago, there were five Noh and three or four *kyogen* in a program. (In like manner, during the golden age of Spanish drama, two little farces, or *entremeses,* originally perhaps of a quasi-religious nature at Church festivals, were presented between the acts of a play. The Japanese *kyogen* were also originally presented during religious ceremonies.) There are about two hundred fifty Noh plays still being performed in the repertories of the five principal Noh schools. They may not be the best of the more than two thousand Noh plays extant.

The architecture of Noh was developed by Zeami, sometimes spelled Seami (1363-1443); his father is credited with having invented the modern form. Zeami also wrote treatises on the composition and performance of Noh plays, the most important being the *Kwadensho,* the *Book of the Flower,* also known more properly as *Fûshi Kwaden, the Flower in Form,* that is, the form of the art. The title is an allusion to Zen, in which Noh esthetic principles are rooted. The symbolic "true flower" of Zen had its origin on a day when a great congregation had gathered to hear the first Buddha, Siddhartha Gautama, preach. He silently held a flower in his hand, twisting it, mystifying the multitude and his disciples, except for one disciple who smiled. The Buddha saw that Kashyapa understood "that which goes beyond the word," and the disciple handed on the "flower thought." The "true flower" of Noh, "that which goes beyond the word," is the *yugen,* a supreme beauty or grace (attended, as it were, by a mysterious power) of which the drama makes the spectator conscious, and which, although so elusive it can only be suggested, is meaningfully experienced. (The original meaning of *yugen* was "immutable essence.") In the service of *yugen* the action, poetry, music and singing "open the ear" of the mind, said Zeami, and the miming and dancing address the spectator's emotions and "open his eyes."[1] The stage is bare of scenery but the costumes are gorgeous and elaborate, having, as Artaud would put it, a "revelational appearance" and making rhythmic color patterns in the carefully worked out mime movements and postures; the stage properties are gems of decorative art (such as a fan, which, according to how it is used, may represent a sword, a lantern, falling snow or other things); and the masks are superbly sculptured.

Since much of Noh has "its own concrete language," in Artaud's words, "intended for the senses and independent of speech," appealing through ear and eye to the intuitive faculty of mind, its dramatic form can dispense with a syllogistic plot-structure. It can, but it does not always do so; for wherever there are a story and a disciplined architectural sense a logical unity may emerge, and Zeami insisted on the importance of founding a play "on a story which is itself beautiful, the theme subtly handled," although he says that performance may make bad plays successful.[2] We may measure the importance of performance by the discipline of the actors: they began their training at the age of seven and did not reach their prime until their thirty-fourth year.

Zeami, like Aeschylus, wrote the music as well as the words and devised the choreography. For the text he used a procedure familiar to Western playwrights. In his words, "The writing of Noh consists of three stages: choice of seed [story], construction and composition." The construction is in five sections: *Jo* (introduction), *Ha* (development), and *Kyu* (climax); the *Ha* is in three sub-sections, sub-Jo, sub-Ha, and sub-Kyu. (*Kyu* is translated as "climax," but it is not a climax in the sense in which we have been using the word, as part of a plot-structure; it is, rather, a culmination, usually a dance.) There are two main characters and their attendants, who are costumed, and a chorus, usually of eight to ten, in ordinary dress. There is also a Man of the Place (i.e., of the locale of the play) who, between the usual two parts of a play, may tell the legend on which the play is based and who is sometimes used within the play. Originally in the interlude the actor improvised the words; in time they became traditional although with variations. The interludes are not considered a part of the "true Noh"; however, they may be needed to understand the play fully. For the accompanying music the instruments are usually two hand-drums, a stick-drum, and a flute. The principal performer is the

shite, and typically only the *shite* mimes and dances; the secondary character is the *waki.* The five sections of the construction correspond to the following: (1) the entrance of the *waki*
until the *shite*'s first chant; (2) the *shite*'s entrance; (3) the
dialogue between *shite* and *waki,* and the first unison (either
of the two characters or of actor and chorus); (4) a dance
in which the dancer mimes or a chant; (5) dance, action,
and quick-dance or cut-beat ("finale"). What the remarks
on construction do not reveal is that the technique of narration is always significantly used in the composition of the
play. I give the complete text of a Noh play at the end of
this book.

In a program of five plays, although the content of the
plays is not connected, the whole program as well as each
play has its introduction, development and climax; it is an
emotional and esthetic movement in the service of the *yugen*
mood. A word on the farces between the Noh plays: *Kyogen*
translates as "wild words." The *kyogen* at first were secular
entertainments during long religious ceremonies. Behind the
farces was the thought that the wild words would be transformed by Buddha into a hymn of praise, even while their
immediate purpose was refreshment against the strain of
the long ceremonies. In a Noh program their comic refreshment, while no doubt at end it itself, allowed the audience
to re-gather its powers of response for each disciplined,
intense Noh performance; and the ordinary world of the
kyogen, was transformed, as it were, into a more perfect
flowering in the Noh.

Sometimes a Noh play scarcely presents a story. *Tamura,*
by Zeami,[3] in Part One celebrates a temple and in Part Two
narrates the occasion of its founding, a vow to the Goddess
Kwannon for her help to the *shite* in subduing demons.
Takasago, also by Zeami, is again celebrative, of the moral
and esthetic principles of poetry that are instruments for
the well-being of the state and of the happiness enjoyed under
the Imperial rule at the time of the play.

In Part One, scene 1, Tomonarai, a priest, donning his travel-

ling dress, announces himself and his journey to Takasago, where
we are taken via the travelling song (the *michiyuki*), which ends,

And Takasago Bay is reached at last,
And Takasago Bay is reached at last.

Even if we are unaware of the importance to the Japanese of place
where signal things have happened, Takasago is significant in our
consciousness. Scene 2: The Old Man and the Old Woman are
sweeping away the needles of the Takasago Pine while the thoughts
of their hearts come up in verse. Scene 3: The priest asks how
it is that the Takasago Pine and the Sumiyoshi Pine are called
twins when they are in different places. The hearts of man and
wife, he is told, are joined by love and not separated by distance.
The Old Man has come daily from Sumiyoshi these many years.
In answer to the priest's query, he says the pines stand for auspicious
Imperial reigns and their unfading green "for the art of poetry
flourishing as of old." Scene 4: Poetry lights up the mind and
all nature is instinct with poetry. Scene 5: The two old people
are the spirits of the pines in human form. Trees and plants, even
earth and grass, live gratefully in the present reign. The Old Man
will sail to Sumiyoshi and await the priest there. In the interlude
the Man of the Place tells the legend of the Twin Pines and offers
to take the priest to Sumiyoshi in his new boat. In Part Two, scene
1, the priest and his attendants are in Sumiyoshi, singing their
waiting song. Scene 2: The deity of the Shrine (the *shite* of Part
Two, the Old Man being the *shite* of Part One) enters, sings of
the blessings he has poured on the Imperial house and dances
with joyful heart. Scene 3: The chorus is filled with awe to see
the God dance. The last lines of the play are:

The soughing of wind in the Twin Pines
With gladness fills each heart,
With gladness fills each heart!

And the God, in the conventional manner of ending a Noh, stamps
twice at the *shite* seat.

Eguchi by Kwannami (1333-1384), Zeami's father, com-
memorates a courtesan's becoming a Bodhisattva (a being
who is an intermediary between Buddhahood and mankind,
capable of becoming a Buddha but who renounces
Buddhahood to save mankind). Presenting more story than

Tamura or *Takasago*, it has a causal sequence and a climax in our sense of plot-structure although it does not have the unity of a syllogistic plot-structure.

In Part One, when a travelling monk in Eguchi recites a hermit's reprimand of a courtesan who had refused him a night's lodging, a young woman appears summoned by the shaming poem and says that she did not begrudge the hermit shelter, that the monk should also have recited her poem, which explained that what she did was for the sake of the hermit's soul; the monk approves her. She is the ghost of the courtesan, the Lady of Eguchi. In Part Two the monk and his attendants chant a requiem for the ghost, and there appears on the river a pleasure boat with courtesans (the sequence suggests the chant is the cause of their appearance). They sing, "This world is good," and they protest that it is silly to say they belong to the olden days. Nonetheless the Lady of Eguchi and the chorus think upon their sins in former lives and of the transitoriness of earthly beauty and love to which they became attached, their minds deceived by eye and ear; during the mutability passage the Lady dances. The chorus exclaims, "O rapture!", expressive of the Lady's revelation; she then performs another dance, slow and elegant. She chants of Reality and Truth and of vain attachment to the mutable world; as she told the hermit, "take no thought for a temporary lodging." Then the Lady is revealed as a Bodhisattva and ascends across the western sky.

Many of the Noh plays in like manner present a sequence of linked incidents that do not have a syllogistic plot-structure.

There are Noh plays whose texts alone are deeply moving, such as *Izutsu* (the famous *Well*   ♭) and *Sanemori*, both by Zeami.

In Part One of *Izutsu* the priest, who has visited the seven great temples of Nara, as he stands on the site of the Ariwari Temple where famous lovers once lived, can "feel the transitoriness of human life" and for the sake of the lovers' twin souls performs religious rites. The Maiden (as though in response to the rites) comes to the well, as she comes each morning, and prays that Buddha will lead her to Paradise, for in this world

Vain dreams deceive our minds.

What call will have the power to waken us,
What call will have the power to waken us!

Her deepest feelings, however, are still for her husband and she has come a perilous road back to the well for the paradise that was there. She tells the priest of their early marriage, when her selfless love won her husband back from infidelity, and of their childhood near the well they used to look into together. She reveals who she was and fades away. In Part Two the priest falls asleep, wishing to dream of times gone by. The Ghost of the Wife appears (the Maiden of Part One) and dances slowly, elegantly. Wearing her husband's robe and headgear, she looks into the well as she and her husband used to, and sees a dear face, his living image, but it is not his, it is hers: the momentary happiness is a dream deceiving her mind, and she fades as the Temple's bells toll. The priest's dream is shattered.

The main emotion of the play is her sorrow, and we experience a correlative pity; but there is fear in us also (or perhaps only sorrow) because of the knowledge we experience of what life may be.

Sanemori is a play with a logical plot-structure and seemingly with an ambiguous end.

In Part One, scene 1, the Man of the Place tells us of a priest's moving sermons to grateful multitudes, but at noon each day the priest seems to talk to himself. The Man of the Place, who waits upon the priest, has been asked to question the priest about it, and says to the audience, "If any of you happen to hear him talking to himself, please let me know." Scene 2: The priest sings of Amida (Buddha) and his Western Paradise. Scene 3: An old man comes to listen outside the temple and invokes Amida. Scene 4: The priest, who alone can see the old man, asks him for his name. The man is loath to utter the name he bore in the world of attachment and transmigration, but the priest says that he must if he would confess and be converted to the Buddhism that can save him by Invocation of the Name. The old man is the ghost of Sanemori, who has been unsaved for two hundred years; he fades from sight, not wanting rumor to cause him shame. In the interlude the Man of the Place, after he tells the story of Sanemori's last battle at the priest's request, learns that the priest has been speaking not to himself but to Sanemori's ghost; the priest will pray for the salvation of Sanemori, and the Man of the Place exhorts the people not to fail to attend the prayers. In Part Two, scene 1, the priest invokes the Name: Namu Amida Butsu. (The invocation translates as "I put all my faith in Amida Buddha.") Scene 2: The ghost appears in a smiling mask, blessed hope within him, and says the invocation, which signifies surrender to Amida and good deeds. Scene 3: The priest sees the old man in armor, who has been dwelling among the *Asuras*. (Inhabiting another world of transmigration, the *Asuras* are possessed by hatred and are always fighting each other, their punishment for the violence they committed in a previous life. By invocation of Amida they can be enlightened and be reborn in the Western Paradise.) The warrior is assured that the often repeated golden words, Namu Amida Butsu, will bear him safely to Paradise. Scene 4: By way of confession Sanemori—though he may seem attachment-bound, he says—tells of his last battle, when he dyed his hair and beard to seem young. Favored by his Commander, he wore brocade to meet his death in, and won undying memory for his valor. Scene 5: He is not altogether free of attachment to this world of transmigration, because he regrets not having met in combat the leader of the opposing clan. Spent with fighting, he was killed. The chorus sings these final lines for him as he dances,

Namu Amida Butsu!
O say for me the holy prayers,
O say for me the holy prayers.

The plot-structure is worth examining.

The beginning of change: Knowing of the new teaching, and having invoked Buddha fruitlessly, Sanemori gives his name to the priest so that he may confess and be converted.

The middle: The ghost, now smiling with hope, again makes his invocation and is assured that he will be saved.

To be settled by the end: Will he indeed be saved?

Climax: He makes his confession.

The play ends with the climax.

If theologically his salvation is certain by virtue of the special prayers of the priest and his own confession, which will give repose to his tormented spirit and enable him to be reborn into the Western Paradise, as the translators maintain in their introduction, there is nothing further to say. But another interpretation is possible. In a fifteenth century Noh play, *Kumasaka,* the ghost of Kumasaka, a bandit leader, begs a priest for prayers to be saved: he is attached to the earth and cannot get free to go to the Western Paradise. Even as the priest chants his prayer, Kumasaka, seeing that the moon will not rise until dawn, orders an assault, forgetting that he is a ghost. *That command is the climax:* he cannot let go of the world and so he is doomed. Then he tells the priest the story of his death, how he ordered an assault and was killed by the stripling Ushiwaka, the boyhood name of the hero Yoshitsune. In like manner, even as he confesses, Sanemori in Zeami's play cannot let go of his regret at not having met in combat the leader of the opposing clan. The last images in the play, before the final lines already given which are addressed to the priest, are of Sanemori's death.

Although in this case, analysis of the plot-structure perhaps does not settle the issue of interpretation (to me it seems that the ambiguity may be deliberate), the analysis makes clear that there is an issue and what that issue is. If we are to undertake investigation, whether in scientific work or in literary criticism, we must be able to state the problem clearly.

When we turn from Noh drama to the Kabuki theater, which developed in the seventeenth century, we face a play that exists for the actor and uses scenic spectacle unsurpassed anywhere in the world (there were elevator stages and revolving stages in eighteenth century Kabuki theater). The actors, however, are cardinal; they do not connect themselves to the scenery, playing directly to the audience. They begin in childhood to learn their expressive stylized movements, which are traditional, extensive and complex, and the actors reach complete mastery, if they do, some thirty or thirty-five years later. As in Noh there are miming and dancing, which may reach consummation in an expressive immobile posture (the *mie*). The actor's movements—he is as much a dancer as an actor—lead and interact with the orchestra, whose instruments are usually voices, samisens (played with a plectrum), and three kinds of drums. The rhythms are intricate and changing physical statements. The dancing is not the continuous movement of Western dancing; rather, it is more like a sequence of images.

The words and story in the Kabuki theater are typically so little a matter of literary value that a stable of playwrights could compose separate scenes and the actor, not the chief playwright, would select what scenes of the story to put together for performance. Toward the end of the nineteenth century programs began to be made piecemeal, and still today parts of plays, even parts of acts, are performed on the same program although the audience may not know the stories the various parts come from.

Chushingura, a story the audiences know well (the original version was a puppet play in 1748), is a drama that Paul Claudel thought one of the great works of mankind. In 1960 and again in 1969 the Kabuki company visiting New York gave only four scenes from *Chushingura*'s first part; the complete drama is day-long. The performance was nonetheless expressive of strong tragic emotion. The four scenes, although without the structural unity and completeness of Western tragedies, presented a story with a causal sequence.

Scene 1: At the inauguration ceremonies of a shrine in Kamakura celebrating a victory, the Lady Kaoyo, wife of the noble Enya Hangan, is called upon, because the emperor's helmet was in her care, to identify his helmet, which was worn by a slain rebel lord; it is to be given to the shrine's treasury. She is thus seen by the arrogant Governor of Kamakura, who detains her when the others leave; he gives her a knotted love letter, which she throws back. He warns her that her husband's success depends on him.

Scene 2: In the palace, where it is a capital offense to draw a sword, the Governor baits Hangan. Hangan does all he can to restrain himself but finally erupts when the Governor piles insults on him, and he wounds the Governor with his sword.

Scene 3: Hangan, preparing for the official suicide which has been ordered, regrets that he is not able to see Yuranosuke, his chief councillor, once again. In the presence of the Shogun's commissioners, who are there to witness the suicide ordered by the Shogun, he plunges the short sword into his left side and draws it across his bowels, the *seppuku* ordained. Even then the councillor comes.

Hangan. Is it you, Yuranosuke?
Yuranosuke. Yes, my lord.
Hangan. How I've waited for you.
Yuranosuke. And how grateful I am that I am able to see my lord's face in life.
Hangan. I, too, am happy.

Hangan gives the sword to Yuranosuke as a pledge, who understands the intention. The young Lady Kaoyo shears her tresses, thereby renouncing the world. Yuranosuke tries to console her in her grief.

Scene 4: Outside the gate of Enya Hangan's mansion, which has been confiscated because of his crime, his samurai are in a fit of warlike anger. Yuranosuke restrains them by threatening to kill himself. The Governor's man in charge derides the masterless and wretched samurai and his soldiers laugh at them, but the samurai are controlled by Yuranosuke (for otherwise they will forfeit the chance of revenge against the Governor). In the most famous moment of this most famous play in the Kabuki repertory, Yuranosuke looks at the blood-stained sword, tears of sorrow and passion in his eyes. He gazes at the gate, takes its lantern and rips away the family crest, which he puts in his bosom. The gate moves slowly away from him.

Chorus. The misery of Hangan's last words reach the depths of both his body and soul. It is at this very moment that within him rise the sentiments of an unfaltering loyalty that have made his name eternally renowned.

In deep thought, Yuranosuke leaves.

Of the 1960 Kabuki performances in New York (which I preferred to those of 1969) the audience liked best this final scene and the *seppuku* scene of *Chushingura* and all of *Kanjincho*, whose first performance was said to be "one of the finest of this century." But it was not the excellence of the performance, I venture, that made the New York audience respond most fully to *Kanjincho*; it was, rather, the excellence of the construction and composition of the story presented. (The words of the play were translated as they were spoken and were broadcast to small transistor receivers distributed among the audience for a fee.) For *Kanjincho*, originally a Noh play, the Kabuki company used a version made in 1840 by Namiki Gohei III (the performance cut only the Buddhist liturgy).

Togashi, a samurai, is guarding a barricade gate against the escape of the Shogun's brother, Yoshitsune, said to be disguised as a priest. Three priests have already been hanged. The chorus of eight singers, flute and drum accompaniment, tells of Yoshitsune's wanderings. Yoshitsune, Benkei, and retainers see the road blocked to the North. The retainers want to fight their way through, but Benkei, disguised as a Buddhist priest, argues that even if they succeed the news will travel ahead of them to stop their passage. Yoshitsune is disguised as a porter. They approach the barrier and are stopped by Togashi. Benkei learns that no priest can pass. He calls it monstrous, says that they shall at least die with honor if they must fail in their religious mission, and pretends to perform last rites, calling on the wrath of the Gods. Togashi, suspicious, tests Benkei's story of going for contributions for a temple; he asks to hear the list of contributors. Benkei fakes it, reading from a blank scroll. But Togashi, because Benkei whirls the scroll away from him, now is fairly certain that it is Yoshitsune's party. He puts questions about Buddhism to Benkei, who invents plausible answers. Although he was once a priest, the final question is too difficult for Bankei and he hesitates. Benkei is a great warrior who could kill Togashi, but restrains himself for his lord's sake. Then he brilliantly improvises an answer, deeply impressing the barrier guards. Togashi, although now certain, is so impressed by the defense that he decides to let them pass, going through the form of offering gifts for the temple. But as they are leaving, the barrier guards think they recognize Yoshitsune and Togashi must stop the disguised men. There is a tense moment, the guards and the retainers readying for combat, but Benkei succeeds in averting the collision. To prove that the porter is not his lord, he strikes Yoshitsune twice, an unthinkable act in feudal Japan, pretending that he, the porter, is hateful because he is an impediment to the religious mission. (Benkei must restrain his tears for having struck his lord, but his face shows his grief.) Togashi hesitates. Benkei cries that he will kill the porter to convince him, so that the mission is not blocked. Deeply impressed by Benkei's devotion and moral stature, Togashi decides to let them pass; nor can he show what he knows, for he has failed his own master. A little distance away Yoshitsune forgives Benkei, whose grief for having struck his lord and threatened to kill him is overwhelming.

Togashi comes after them with sake. Benkei understands the gesture. Benkei, good naturedly, drinks enormously and there is a bit of farcical comedy. He speaks ambiguous words and dances his gratitude to Togashi; both words and dance reveal that he understands Togashi's sacrifice. Each now knows that his opposite knows, although no acknowledgment has been made that anybody else recognizes. As Benkei and his party leave, he looks back to where Togashi has stood in a climactic pose. He thinks of Togashi's sacrifice, then of his own difficulties still ahead, and dances off in prodigious leaps and bounds.

It is unified and whole narrative eminent for its literary as well as for its stage merit.

The third classical Japanese theater, the puppet theater,* had an enormous popularity in the eighteenth century and some of Japan's greatest playwrights wrote for its troupes, which came into their own in the seventeenth century. Both the Kabuki and puppet theaters attracted audiences of town merchants, while the Noh was essentially aristocratic. The present form of the puppets, dating from the second quarter of the eighteenth century, is half life-size. Each puppet is manipulated in full view of the audience, by three men who are long and carefully trained. The two performers are a chanter, who narrates and takes all the roles, and a samisen player. The puppeteers' movements are paced by the samisen music and by the chanter and are synchronized with each other. It was the puppet theater that first used scenery, producing spectacular effects with elevator stages and revolving stages, all in the eighteenth century. Nonetheless, the puppet theater, unlike the Kabuki, flourished with literary values; the puppets, although the visual cynosure, were after all not actors and could not usurp attention or decide that only certain scenes should be played. Indeed, the man generally considered Japan's greatest playwright, Chikamatsu Monzaemon (1653-1725), wrote chiefly for the puppet theater, perhaps because only there could the words themselves transmit true emotional power (he insisted on the words of a

* Or *ningyo-joruri.*

play having such power). It should go without saying that
being a professional playwright Chikamatsu exploited, and
was masterly in doing so, the resources of the puppets and
their stage in his time (when one man manipulated a puppet
and there were no elevator or revolving stages). Although
Chikamatsu wrote for the theater and not for the private
reader, he consciously wrote with literary values and apparently thought his fame would endure in books rather than
on the stage. He composed history plays and domestic plays.
The history plays are loosely structured, as is typical of chronicle plays; but his domestic tragedies evolve logically; they
have a unified, even a tight, logical structure. The only point
of unique structural interest in his plays is the textural function of his *michiyuki* (in the Noh a travel song, here the *michiyuki*
is the lovers' suicide journey). As Donald Keene has pointed
out, its expressiveness lends tragic stature to the ordinary
people in his domestic plays and by its dreamlike atmosphere
gives another dimension to the ordinary world.[5]

6/ CHINESE DRAMA   The Ming Tradition

In China the *ching hsi* theater, or Peking opera, like the Kabuki is an art form in service of the performer, an actor-singer for whom the audience comes. Unlike the Kabuki, it uses no scenery; rather, as in the Noh, stage properties may signify a mountain, a river, towers and walls, a gate, a well, and so on. Unlike the Noh and Kabuki, the *ching hsi* does not use abstract dance as an essential expressive element of the formal structure. There is, however, a whole vocabulary of conventional movements (understood of course by the audiences) which signify meanings, often emotional, as words do, and also signify actions (as riding a horse); the stage music is synchronized with the actor's movements as well as with his words, and when he sings or speaks his movements rhythmically accord with his words. Dance elements also survive in the formalized fighting scenes and in the acrobatics of performance.

The dramatic entertainment which is Peking opera has its ancient origins in the song and dance of ceremonial occasions. Dancing in those ancient days, both in China and Japan, always accompanied narrative verse or song, as did instrumental music. The earliest records of dance as entertainment in China go back to the first millennium B.C. In the Tang period (A.D. 618-906) the founding of the Academy of the Pear Orchard to train singers and actors for Court entertainments was an important development. Meanwhile storytelling developed and gave impetus to the growth of drama. But it was not until Yuan times (1280-1368) that a fully formed drama emerged. The Yuan, or Mongol dynasty (founded by Kublai Khan), expelled the scholarly and educated from government positions and a number of these people trained in letters turned to the theater. The *tsa chü* drama they devised almost always had four acts (but typically they were short plays) with song and dialogue; sometimes a play had an extra act, which in *Snow in Midsummer* (analyzed in chapter 10) serves as a prologue. *The Romance of the Western Chamber*, a fourteenth century play which some think the Yuan master-piece but which others think dull, is an exceptional case which presents its story in four sections, each with four acts, and with a Continuation of another four acts. The works of that period are still studied for their literary merit in Chinese universities. It is not known how Yuan drama was performed. There are two excellent translations from this little known drama in the *Anthology of Chinese Literature*.[1]

Most interesting to this study is a play in the theatrical tradition of the Ming dynasty (1368-1644). The *ch'uan* style of opera of that period flourished for four centuries. These plays had a varying number of acts, up to fifty; there was singing of verse as aria, recitative and dialogue, and the sing-ing was always accompanied by dancing and pantomime. Out of other styles that later emerged came the *ching hsi*. But, whereas what literary merit a Peking opera may have is acci-dental, the men of letters who wrote in the Ming period aimed at a reading as well as a theatrical public for their long plays. Hung Sheng after ten years and three rewritings brought to the stage in 1688 *The Palace of Eternal Youth*, an historical romance about the Emperor Ming Huang of the Tang dynasty (he was the emperor who founded the Academy of the Pear Orchard) and his favorite concubine Yang Yu-huan. The story, a thousand years old, was one of China's most popular. Hung's opera was an immediate success both on the boards and in the literary world.

It is the structure of the long plays in the Ming tradition that demands attention. While carefully plotted, the construc-

tion of *The Palace of Eternal Youth* is novelistic, and to illustrate
that I shall give a detailed account of the play. Its success
on the boards is proof enough of its theatricality; it is a play,
not a novel. Because such a construction for a play is rare
in the West, its one great example, the long Spanish *La Celestina* (its traditional English title is *The Spanish Bawd*) written
by Fernando de Rojas and published in its final form in
1502, is generally said to be a novel in dialogue form. Gerald
Brenan, in his justly admired *Literature of the Spanish People*,
says that it "is the first European novel" and the greatest
Spanish work of its period. *La Celestina* has likely never been
produced uncut, but abridged versions have been produced
successfully. There are, of course, modern novels in dialogue
form which are not plays; the difference is stageworthiness
or, in the reading, the sense of drama's technical values (e.g.,
a "dramatic" moment in a novel can be compressed and swift;
in a play its tension will be extended). Although the novelistic
construction can work in short plays, as in short four-act
Yuan plays so constructed, it is fullest and best in the long
play, as in *The Palace of Eternal Youth*. It may be added that
novelistic techniques were not invented by the Chinese playwrights. The Chinese novel made its appearance in the thir-
teenth century and reached its apex in the eighteenth with
Hung Lou Mêng, or *The Dream of the Red Chamber*, which was
first printed in 1792 (a shorter version appeared for sale
at markets in manuscript form nearly forty years earlier).
It has a complex plot in which the chief thread is love, as
in our play; other threads are ambition and intrigue, wealth
and poverty, which are also in our play.

The Palace of Eternal Youth[2] begins with a prologue:

      we shall now
Take music and the tale of Lady Yang
To offer a new play in praise of love!

The prologue then gives an epitome of the story.
    Scene 1: "The Pledge." The Emperor makes Yang Yu-huan
his concubine. A musical passage celebrates:

Maids. All the emperor's love will be hers,
In a chamber of gold to live,
In a tower of jade to sing,
For ever and ever to hand him a brimming goblet of wine.
   All. May love reign as long as the earth endures!
   Eunuchs. The sun shines upon dragon scales carved on the pillars,
And the pheasant feathers move like coloured clouds;
The emperor smiles as he looks at his new lady . . .
   All. May love reign as long as the earth endures!

And in a song that they all sing walking to the west palace is a line fusing the real and the ideal (as in English Romanticism): "Every moment is the best of this clear spring night." As a pledge of their love the Emperor gives her two gifts: a jewelled pin for hair, with two phoenixes always flying together; and a jewel box with a love-knot on it, two hearts as one.

   Scene 2: "The Bribe." An Lu-shan, who believes himself destined for greatness, has lost a battle against tribesmen and is in danger of losing his head. He succeeds in bribing the prime minister, a cousin of Lady Yang, and the prime minister will use a Military Governor's recommendation of An's knowledge of barbarian languages and military skill to sway the Emperor to clemency, although An is only a junior frontier officer.

   Scene 3: "The Spring Siesta." The Lady Yang is full of lassitude, having spent the night with the Emperor who is now always in the west palace with her. After a sophisticated morning toilette, she falls asleep again. She pleads her excuse when the Emperor finds her sleeping at noon, and he, laughing, says, "So the fault is mine, is it?" (This is the first comic tone.) At the end of the scene we learn that Yang, the prime minister, has tested An at the Emperor's command; the Emperor pardons An and appoints him to a post in the capital. The scene closes with the lovers going to see the peonies in bloom and with the Emperor sending for a poet to celebrate the flowers and the lady.

   Scene 4: "The Spring Festival." The eunuch Kao has become a great favorite of the Emperor, enjoying greater power than any minister (he remains always loyal and full of care). An is also a favorite. "It is lucky that I was born with such a big belly, reaching nearly to my knees. His Majesty asked me, laughing, what was in it; and I answered 'Only my loyal heart!' The Emperor was pleased with my reply . . ." An sees Lady Yang's three sisters, now duchesses, and envies the Emperor. The prime minister is enraged

by An's presumption in staring at the duchesses. Then follows
an incident with a countrywoman, a plain girl, and a country gentleman; not only is the scene comic, it gives a sense of the ordinary
world to root the play in. The scene ends with the Duchess of
Kuai, a sister of Lady Yang, being summoned to the Emperor.

Scene 5: "The Mystery." The lovers have quarreled over the
Duchess of Kuai. Lady Yang had praised her sister's beauty and
after three cups of wine had tied the Duchess and the Emperor
together in a love knot; then, afraid of what she had done to create
a rival, offended the Duchess and so made the Emperor angry.
A few days earlier she had insisted that her rival Lady Plum Blossom
be moved to the east pavilion.

Scene 6: "The Sisters Gossip." After a night with the Emperor
the Duchess of Huai was taunted by Lady Yang. Kuai speaks with
her sister Han, revealing anger and bitterness but hiding their
cause. Kuai and Han learn that their sister, the Lady Yang, has
been ordered to the house of their cousin, the prime minister,
and they go off to her out of interest and self-interest.

Scene 7: "A Lock of Hair." The eunuch Kao tells the prime
minister that Lady Yang is inclined to be self-willed and unduly
jealous. The Lady weeps for having lost the Emperor's love. Kao,
who has seen the Emperor sighing, suggests that Lady Yang send
something to move his heart. With a golden scissors she cuts a
lock of hair (everything else she has is a gift from the Emperor;
we learn later that "Fate uses a golden scissors"). Her two sisters
come. Kuai mocks her, singing, "I thought you could laugh or
sulk just as you pleased; I thought however badly you behaved,
the Emperor would never take offence." Han wants to know what
happened. Lady Yang pretends not to hear them and then, saying
she will keep her sorrows to herself, walks out. Han exclaims, "We
came especially to see her, but she flies off in a passion. Next
time *you* go to the pleasure palace, sister, be sure you don't behave
like that! (*The Duchess of Kuai blushes and pretends to be angry.*)"—which
is the end of the scene. (While this passage of comic satire is not
intrinsic to the play, the vignette is at one with the fundamental
strategy of the play: story is presented continuously.)

Scene 8: "The Recall." The Emperor sent Lady Yang away
in a fit of anger over her jealousy; now he wants to recall her
but is ashamed to give the order. When solicitous eunuchs come
to ask him to dinner and to music, he has one and then the other
given a hundred lashes and demoted to menial work. Kao brings
the lock of hair and message of repentance; he suggests that to

recall her now would show the divine mercy of the Son of Heaven, and besides, nobody will know what happened. In the reconciliation each professes having acted wrongly. "A taste of sorrow has increased our love tenfold," sings the Emperor.

Scene 9: "The Writing on the Wall." Kuo Tze-yi, who has mastered the military arts in the hope of becoming a hero who will bring peace to the empire, laments what is happening: the prime minister Yang is taking all power, and An is the Emperor's favorite. At a tavern Kuo drinks moderately in "This country of drunkards." The waiter (in satire that is comic) talks of the competition of families to outdo each other. "When one family sees their neighbor's house is better than theirs, they pull theirs down and rebuild, until they have one exactly the same. This way, one single hall may cost millions." Kuo says of the new palaces built for the prime minister and the duchesses:

>   none dare tell the emperor
> That these vermilion roofs and brilliant tiles
> Are stained with the people's blood!

On the wall he reads a poetic prophecy whose sinister significance he does not understand. There is a hubbub outside. An is riding by robed as a prince. Shocked and angry, Kuo says, "He has the face of a rebel; he will certainly bring ruin to the empire." A prey to doubt, he reflects that "Heaven's will is unfathomable." Then a bulletin arrives with his military commission. He will "support the tottering throne."

Scene 10: "Dream Music." Chang-ngo, the goddess of the moon, will send a fairy to summon the spirit of Yang Yu-huan, who was a fairy in her previous life and used to visit the goddess. She will let Lady Yang's spirit hear the music for the Dance of the Rainbow and Feathery Garments, for she knows the Emperor is fond of music, and will teach the lady the immortal dance. The fairy messenger lyrically sings of the earth, the heavens, and her passage. (The lyrical is an important tone in the drama, justified by the taste of the audience as well as by the operatic form.) Lady Yang learns the dance music, but the time "has not yet come" for her to see the mistress of the moon. The fairy messenger apologizes for having kept Lady Yang from the Emperor's side.

Scene 11: "Writing the Music." As Lady Yang's maid sets out the brushes and ink in the Lotus Pavilion, she sings as though a narrator:

The newly dusted brush-stand and paper are shining,
And the inkstone is filled with fragrant, fresh-ground ink,
In this green shade and chaste seclusion.

(This technique of narration is used often.) The Lady carefully fits words to the music of the heavenly dance, and uses the song of an oriole to make a harmony of the notes she heard in her dream, doing so happily for the Emperor has often praised her rival Lady Plum Blossom's Frightened Swan Dance. The Emperor returns from the Court, where he has appointed Kuo Tse-yi as the governor of a province.

Scene 12: "A Dispute Among the Mighty." Yang, the prime minister, and An are in conflict. The two go to the Emperor. Yang accuses An of traitorous ambition; An's tears plead his loyalty. Since they will not work together in the capital, the Emperor appoints An as a frontier military governor. Yang can only hope that An will revolt so that the Emperor will see his error.

Scene 13: "Stealing the Music." The orchestra leader, Li Kuei-nien, is to train the court musicians day and night, for the new dance is to be performed soon. Li Mu comes outside the palace wall with his iron flute, eager to learn the music he has heard of, and accompanies the rehearsal as the best way to remember the notes. In this musical interlude the scholar Li Mu is the only person seen; the others are inside the pavilion.

Scene 14: "The Lichee Fruit." From distant provinces envoys are carrying lichee fruit ordered by the Emperor for the pleasure of his concubine. "A thousand miles in the saddle,/ And a hard, rough journey" are the first lines of the scene. They gallop across the peasants' fields to shorten their way, and an old peasant has come out to guard his crops. A blind man with a clapper and a blind woman with a stringed instrument come along. The first envoy rides across the grain and knocks down the blind couple; the second envoy tramples the blind man. The woman crawls along the ground, frightened by her husband's silence, and with her hands discovers that his head has been crushed. Weeping, the peasant and the woman carry the corpse off for burial. At the posting station these last few years the horses have been ridden to death by the envoys bearing tribute fruit. Because there is only one lean horse left, the young groom is beaten by the two envoys. The scene ends with the lament, "Oh, Lady Yang, Lady Yang! This is all because of your lichee fruit."

Scene 15: "The Disc Dance." It is the Lady's birthday, and the lichee fruit has arrived in time for the feast. During the feast the Lady dances on an emerald disk while the Emperor beats the rhythm for the musicians on a drum. He is ravished by her dance and gives her his own jewelled pouch containing ambergris to wear whenever she dances.

Scene 16: "The Hunt." An has got rid of the Chinese generals under him and now has only Tartar generals. He has called them to hunt, their manner of practicing military skills. The scene is a spectacle of fearsomeness. Then they roast the game, warm the wine, and the girls sing and dance for their pleasure. The scene ends with An's laughter:

While in his pleasure palace the emperor feasts
And music is played, a sudden alarm will be heard,
And my brave lads will begin the revolt.

Scene 17: "A Night of Grief." Lady Yang is worried that the Emperor's old favorite Lady Plum Blossom may supplant her. And indeed, her rival is in favor again.

Scene 18: "A Visit to the Pavilion." The eunuch Kao is standing guard outside the east pavilion, where the Emperor has spent the night with Lady Plum Blossom. When Lady Yang comes, jealous, the Emperor comically would hide Lady Plum Blossom in his chamber, but the laughing attendant warns that the love nest will be turned upside down. Kao manages to get Plum Blossom away after Lady Yang, finding an emerald trinket and slippers, gives the Emperor a hard time. By the end of the scene they make up.

Scene 19: "The Report." A scout comes to Kuo Tze-yi with news of the rebellion being plotted. Kuo sets his own army in motion.

Scene 20: "The Bath." The scene opens with a maid singing comically as she prepares the pool in the pleasure palace. There is a fine love scene between the Emperor and Lady Yang, in the bathing pool, which we see in the songs of Lady Yang's maids who are looking on.

Scene 21: "The Secret Vow." The Heavenly Weaving Maid (the star Vega) and the Heavenly Cowherd (the star Altair) are meeting this day. Because those lovers once neglected their tasks, the Heavenly Emperor permits them to meet only once a year. The fairies pity the transiency of mortal love. In the palace of eternal youth Lady Yang is praying for happiness; the Emperor joins her there. The Lady, afraid that his love will end, begs that he vow with her to make their love eternal, in life and in death. The Weaving Maid and the Cowherd witness the vow. They say that, although the mortal lovers are soon to be separated by death, if they remain true they will be brought together again.

Scene 22: "Storming the Pass." The Court army inspector, a bad appointment, has insisted that the general and his troops guarding the Pass march out against An instead of holding their strong defensive position in the Pass, and so the battle is lost. The Tartar generals sing with pleasure of the destruction they will effect with their army of a million picked men.

Scene 23: "The Alarm." At the end of a happy feast, Lady Yang drunk, the Emperor hears the sound of rebel drums. The news of An's victories makes him quake with fear. The Emperor must leave the capital and is distressed to think of his concubine taking the road with her flowerlike beauty.

Scene 24: "Death at the Post Station." The imperial guards, learning that the prime minister was secretly negotiating with the western tribesmen, have killed him, and demand the death of his cousin Lady Yang. The Emperor would rather lose his empire, even die himself, than let her die. But the Lady begs him to permit her death to save the empire, and he yields to her insistence. She asks Kao to bury the phoenix hairpin and the jewel box, the Emperor's gifts, with her, and hangs herself with a silken belt. In tears, the Emperor does not care whether or not he reaches safety.

Scene 25: "The Gift of Food." During the escape march a peasant brings the Emperor oatmeal, which he can scarcely swallow. The peasant blames the prime minister's corruption for the Emperor's troubles, and blames the Emperor for putting to death a man who had informed against An. The Emperor accepts the blame and summons his guards to dismiss them from hardship and send them home, offering them his only wealth, silk. They will not desert him.

Scene 26: "The Spirit Follows." Her love unchanged, Lady Yang would follow the Emperor, but her spirit is light as a leaf and cannot; dusty winds hide the way from her. She sees the spirits of her sister the Duchess of Kuai, and of her cousin the prime minister, both killed by the troops, being taken by devils to hell; and she reflects, "Life is nothing but a fleeting dream." Unable to go on, she returns to the place where she died. There a tutelary god has been instructed to watch over her and save her from hell, but cannot say whether she will ever meet the Emperor again.

Scene 27: "The Patriot and the Rebel." A lute player, Lei, once an imperial musician, is disgusted by the turncoat officials who are fawning on An. When An hears Lei crying during his victory celebration, he hales him in. Lei accuses him of being a criminal with no right to talk of victory and throws his lute at An. When he is killed the officials mock, "Where did your loyalty land you?"

Scene 28: "Hearing the Bells." The Emperor has ceded the throne to the crown prince. Thinking of the tragic end of Lady Yang, he is sick at heart and has no desire to live on.

Scene 29: "Lady Yang's Spirit Repents." The lady confesses her crimes (her love of earthly splendor and her indulgence) and asks heaven's pardon; only her love of the Emperor she can never repent. The tutelary god cheers her, gratified that she has wakened from her dream, and allows her to wander freely. She will drift with the wind at night to find her love.

Scene 30: "Suppressing the Rebellion." Kuo defeats two of An's armies and advances on the capital.

Scene 31: "Mourning Before the Image." The Emperor is full of remorse that he did not protect Lady Yang with his own body. He has had a temple built and a sandalwood lifesize image made of her, which he has had placed on a throne in the temple, where he pours libations. As he suffers, tears appear on the face of the image.

Scene 32: "The God's Report." The Weaving Maid, seeing gloom on earth, summons the tutelary god, who is comically made nervous by the angels shouting for him and weeps for fear that he will be dismissed from his humble post by the Weaving Maid. She questions him about the gloom over his post and learns how Lady Yang died. The tears and sighs of her repentance make the gloom. The Weaving Maid will have her restored to heaven.

Scene 33: "Assassination of a Rebel." An wants to make the son of his favorite concubine his heir, and so neither Pigsy, whom An has always treated as a son and who has imperial hopes, nor the crown prince, his legitimate son, has a chance of wearing the crown. The crown prince has plotted with Pigsy who will assassinate An; Pigsy gives An's own rebellion as a justifying precedent. There are nervous moments when Pigsy is almost caught. An has been indulging too heavily in women and wine, and stays alone to rest. The murder is done, and the crown prince blames Kuo Tze-yi.

Scene 34: "Recovering the Capital." Kuo restores the empire, his generals reflecting that the working out of the prophecy on the wall shows how all things are predestined by fate.

Scene 35: "Lady Yang's Stocking." Mistress Wang, an innkeeper, found a silk stocking under the pear tree where Lady Yang died; the stocking makes her business flourish. The young scholar Li Mu (of the iron flute) and an abbess admire the stocking. The peasant who gave oatmeal to the Emperor, and confronted him with blame, feels his blood boil at the suffering of the people caused by the Emperor's spending all his time in pleasure with Lady Yang and neglecting the governance of the empire. Li Mu wants to buy the stocking so that the abbess can dedicate it to the gods in her nunnery. The peasant growls, "Why pay for this stinking thing?" It's not for sale, says the innkeeper.

Scene 36: "The Resurrection." Lady Yang has not found the Emperor. The pavilions and palaces where she loved are decaying. Against her will the wind blows her to the place of her burial. There the Weaving Maid has come to take her to Paradise. Because she had loved earthly splendor, she suffered heavy punishment, but because of her repentance the Heavenly Emperor has pardoned her and she is to be resurrected. When her spirit sees her corpse moving toward her, her frightened spirit says, "If that Lady Yang is alive, what is to become of me?" Her corpse pursues her. The unifying is accomplished. Lady Yang leaves behind the scented pouch that the Emperor gave her when she danced on the emerald disk, and goes to the fairy mountain.

Scene 37: "The Rhapsody." The old imperial orchestra leader now wanders the streets, a beggar playing his instrument. Li Mu, the scholar with the iron flute, is looking for him.Some merchants wanting to hear the old man take Li along. It is a scene of the ordinary world after the supernatural. After the old musician sings of the Emperor and his concubine, there is a pleasurable comic reaction by one of the merchants and there is also talk of the blame attaching to the Emperor's infatuation and his bad political and military appointments. After the performance:

First Merchant. He sang of fortune which ended in disaster.
Second Merchant. And we, who heard his song, were moved to tears.

Li Mu takes the old orchestra leader home with him. The old man will teach him to perfect his knowledge of the score of the Rainbow dance so that he can hand it down to posterity.

Scene 38: "Sacrifice at the Nunnery." Lady Yang's palace maids are now nuns. They reflect, "If she had studied the truth early, she would not have died as she did." They will dedicate a peony, her favorite flower, to her. The old musician, taking shelter from the rain, sees the shrine to Lady Yang. The three lament together and talk about those who have died, the old man saying that the loyalty of the musician who died cursing An shames the tears he is now shedding.

Scene 39: "A Fairy Visits." A fairy comes from the goddess of the moon to Yang Yu-huan, now herself a fairy, to request her score for the Rainbow dance.

Scene 40: "Looking at the Moon." The Emperor, welcomed by citizens, returns to the capital. Mourning and sorrow possess him always. Alone under the moonlight, he asks the Moon to find the Weaving Maid and the Cowherd, who witnessed their pledge of eternal love in the palace of eternal youth, to help make it come true.

Scene 41: "Preparations at the Station." The station master where Lady Yang died is worried by the coming of the Emperor. If anything goes wrong, he will lose his head. It's a hard life, but he steals from the tributes that pass through, squeezes something out of the workers' food, exacts bribes from those who want to avoid conscription. In order that Lady Yang's body may not be seen by a man, four hundred women have been conscripted to build a new grave in time for the reburial. In a small piece of comedy, one turns out to be a man because there are only 399 women in the town. Mistress Wang, who has come with the silk stocking and an eye on reward, takes his place.

Scene 42: "The Reburial." The Emperor discovers that only the scented pouch is in the grave. The pouch alone is buried in garments of pearl and silk in a marble casket. Mistress Wang gives the Emperor the silk stocking and is richly rewarded. The victorious Kuo comes to the station to journey the rest of the way to the capital with the Emperor.

Scene 43: "The Gods Pity the Lovers." The Cowherd persuades the Weaving Maid during their night's meeting that the Emperor may deserve to be rejoined with his love. At the end of the scene the heavenly cock crows, and even as we think it the Cowherd says to the Weaving Maid, "Ah, Emperor Ming Huang and Lady Yang, do you know that we have wasted a whole night because of you," the one night a year they can meet.

Scene 44: "A Rainy Night." The Emperor dreams: Two attendants wearing swords awaken him and say Lady Yang is still alive and longing for him. Going with them, he is confronted by the commander who forced her suicide. When the commander threatens another rebellion, the Emperor has the attendants kill him. They reach the station where the lady died and the attendants vanish. The station changes to a flooding river and from the water emerges a monster with the body of a dragon and the head of a pig (An while drunk once imagined he was such a monster, and as the dragon is royal, took it as prophetic); the frightened Emperor runs back to his couch, and two gods with gold maces beat off the monster. The fright awakens him. He thinks that Lady Yang's spirit caused the dream and sends for a necromancer to summon her spirit.

Scene 45: "The Search for Lady Yang's Spirit." The necromancer speaks of the mystical attributes of his altar, a symbol of Primary Truth, built with inner force and in no time at the center of the universe and which can contain the whole universe. The necromancer cannot find Lady Yang's spirit on earth or in hell or in heaven. But he meets the Weaving Maid on the way to the Heavenly Emperor, tells her of the Emperor's grief and evokes her pity. She sends the necromancer to the world where the fairy mountain is, and decides to weave together the broken threads of the love of Lady Yang and the Emperor.

Scene 46: "Making Amends." The Weaving Maid speaks of matters we already know (such recapitulations are common in Chinese plays; in this play the repetitions are never dull), and then promises Lady Yang—who is so far from bearing ill will toward the Emperor for her tragic death that she would gladly give up heaven for punishment on earth could she be his lover again—to ask the Heavenly Emperor to put them both in the highest heaven forever.

Scene 47: "A Message of Love." Lady Yang gives the necromancer the message that the Emperor can meet her again in the moon on the night of the autumn festival, when the Rainbow Garment Dance will be performed in the moon; if he misses that chance he will never have another.

Scene 48: "The Message is Received." The Emperor is doubtful at first that what he hears is true, but words that only Lady Yang could have spoken persuade him. With the prospect of the reunion the sickness he has been suffering disappears.

Scene 49: "The Lovers' Reunion." The Emperor crosses a fairy bridge to the moon. The lovers each take the blame for the Lady's tragic death. The edict from the Heavenly Emperor brings a happy end to their sorrow. The Rainbow Garment Dance is performed to Lady Yang's music, and with that music the lovers, who have discarded earthly passions, are escorted to the highest heaven.

The Palace of Eternal Youth would take four evenings, about sixteen hours, to perform. Greek dramatic festivals (at which many plays were performed, of course) took four consecutive days before and after the Peloponnesian War, although only three during the war, and held an attentive audience of as many as fifteen thousand; the English medieval cycles in some towns took from dawn to dusk and in others ran for three whole days (they tell the sequential story of universal history); the most famous of the French passion plays, Arnoul Greban's *Le Mystère de la Passion*, a fifteenth century literary and musical composition of over thirty thousand lines, was divided into days rather than acts, and although production took four days it was performed over a hundred times in various cities of France; and the French *Passion Play* at Le Mons in 1501 took eight days. Two hours' traffic on the stage is hardly the limit for an audience. It should be added, however, that modern productions of *The Palace of Eternal Youth* present at most only one evening's portion of the play; it can be done in the Ming mode of performance, which is known. More often a program will present selected acts, or only one act, of this play along with excerpts from other plays.

The novelistic techniques in *The Palace of Eternal Youth* are apparent enough. There is a freer movement in time and in space than is typical of drama; and the story line is more intricate, much more of the story being molded to the syllogistic armature of the plot-structure than is typical of drama. The scenes are like chapters and are used to follow the courses of various characters, as the scene-chapters in which the stories of An and Kuo are followed. There are many minor characters who have their own moments in the foreground, giving a much fuller, ramified sense of ongoing life than is typical of the more contained world of a play (Brecht's epic plays, e.g., do not have the same novelistic effect, either because a single character is more dominant all the way through or because the play is more limited in its activity). And narration is used often, as though a passage from a novel were being delivered in the third person. But there are all kinds of ways, of course, to write novels. We need only conclude that because of its novelistic techniques *The Palace of Eternal Youth* is a dramatic experience different from that of other formal structures of drama, and that nonetheless this play has logically unified plot-structures, Lady Yang having the main one and the Emperor a subordinate one.

7/SANSKRIT DRAMA Three Classics and Wilder's *Our Town*

In Sanskrit drama we find yet another kind of dramatic experience. Sanskrit drama, although it used mimetic dance, a code of stylized gestures, song, and instrumental music, is primarily a literary art. In Indian esthetic theory there is no essential difference between the esthetic experience of drama and of other forms of poetry. Indeed, the Sanskrit drama is considered "the highest product of Indian poetry." In the plays elaborate stage directions were given not only for the actor but for the reader. And although the poets, of course, wrote for public performance, their plays depended for their reputation on being read rather than seen, according to the eminent Sanskrit scholar A. Berriedale Keith.[1] The Sanskrit is a unique body of drama in that, although it is primarily a literary art, it does not use logically unified plot-structures; rather, it uses narratives with causal sequences that are not syllogistic.

Why is it that Indian dramatists did not use the syllogistic plot-structure although it has everywhere else been the practice to do so in the construction of plays of which language is the essential medium? The question may seem even more puzzling when we consider that Indian dramatists were not indifferent to the construction of a plot; indeed, The *Natyasastra*,[2] the manual that governed Indian dramaturgy and histrionics, gives careful directions for plot construction.

Moreover, the protagonist of an Indian play functions very much like the central character of a plot-structure; as Keith says, "The hero owes his name, Nayaka, to the fact that it is he who leads (ni) the events to the conclusion." But those events were not unified because the aim of Sanskrit drama to create *rasa* in the minds of the audience ruled the playwright, and a unified plot-structure would not do well for that aim. It is doubtful that *rasa* can be experienced in English translation for, as philologists believe, Sanskrit poetic thought and feeling are not communicable in European languages; but it can be talked about. The *Natyasastra* gives the meaning of *rasa* as "capable of being tasted." It is thus sometimes translated as "flavor," which is a metaphor for what the spectator or reader experiences: a fully satisfying state of mind, even joyful in its fulfillment, in which esthetically induced generic or idealized feelings, conjoined with a happiness that comes from insight into reality, participate both in the completeness of experience and the unity of perfection, reconciling, say, disgust with love or sorrow with mirth. As *rasa* is a state of mind, "mood" is also used for its translation. Now, while *rasa* is in its perfection a single and ineffable sentiment ("sentiment" is the rendering we shall use for *rasa*, which is so rendered in the English translation of *Natyasastra*), it is eightfold in esthetic experience, and there are eight dominant emotions that evoke it. The eightfold sentiments, or forms of *rasa*, are in the minds of the audience; the emotions are in the language and situations and actions of the play, in the representations by the actors and also in the music, makeup, and costumes. The immediacy of a theatrical performance, its visual and aural power, may intensify the experiencing of *rasa*, but the play experienced as a poem is all that is needed for the infusion of sentiment, for the creation of the state of mind that is the play's aim. The eight emotions are love, mirth, compassion, anger, energy, fear, disgust, and astonishment. The corresponding sentiments are the erotic, the comic, the pathetic, the furious, the heroic, the terrible, the odious, and the wonderful.

The *Natyasastra* defines the kinds of plays in Sanskrit drama, the most important being the Nataka, or heroic

drama, for which the main sentiments are the erotic and
the heroic and to which are also especially appropriate the
pathetic and the wonderful. The *Sastra* states explicitly that
the ideal Nataka should create "many Sentiments." That
injunction is at odds with a logical unity of plot-structure,
whose actions are part of a single action, the change in the
central character. *Rasa* has its sources not so much in actions
as in situations or conditions of being. The main definition
of drama in the *Sastra* is a "mimicry of actions and conducts
of people, which is rich in various emotions, and which depicts
different situations;" the "actions and conducts," we must
note, are defined as that which depicts situations and are
chosen for their emotional richness. They are not of the
nature of dramatic action defined as that which has a consequence. Elsewhere the *Sastra* says that the representation of
"human nature with its joys and sorrows . . . is also called
a drama" and that a "mimicry of the past exploits of gods,
sages, and human beings should be also called a drama"
("human beings" is later in the manual changed to "kings
as well as of householders in this world,") and finally, "When
human character with all its different States is represented
with Gestures it is called the drama." In no case is there
any reference to an Aristotelean "imitation of an action that
is complete in itself"—such was the imitation in Greek drama
and everywhere else in the world, except in India, in drama
using language as its sufficient medium. There was unquestionably Greek influence in India when the Sanskrit drama
came into being, which was no later than the second century
B.C., but the Indian mind went its own way in evolving dramatic form.

The *Natyasastra* in its present form may have existed by
the second century A.D.; it was based on a body of dramatic
literature now lost. Although there is no certain evidence
to determine when it reached its present form, the *Sastra*
clearly exeɪcised a binding authority on dramatists by the
time of Kalidasa, who wrote probably late in the fourth century, and Bhavabhuti, who wrote around 700 A.D. The earliest
extant dramatist, Bhasa, is generally placed in the third century A.D. (he is also placed in the fourth century B.C.). Some

scholars think the *Natyasastra* followed him, that a *Natyasastra* he refers to was an earlier version, because by showing death and violence on stage he violates rules that bound the others.

Keith, after considering the *Natyasastra* and treatises on drama written long after the great playwrights, concludes that the Indian conception of drama "is the imitation or representation of the conditions or situations in which the personages who form the subject of treatment are placed from time to time, by means of gesture, speech, costume, and expression," these means of representation distinguishing drama from other kinds of poems; it must be remembered, however, that "poetry is the dominant element," the poetry of the words taking artistic precedence even over the narrative.

To consider the nature of Sanskrit plot and its relation to *rasa* we shall first turn to Kalidasa's *Sakuntala*,[3] often spoken of as the masterpiece of Sanskrit drama. The play, translated by the English orientalist Sir William Jones in 1789, was praised extravagently by Goethe. The play's heroine has enchanted India for over fifteen hundred years.

After a benediction on the audience the stage manager in a prologue announces the play and tells an actress to sing a song. The intention of the prologue is to make the audience receptive.

Act I. King Dushyanta and his charioteer are in pursuit of an antelope; their speed is incredible. A hermit's voice cries out to the king not to kill the hermitage's animal. Because of the king's restraint the hermits pray that he be rewarded with a world-commanding son. The great saint of the hermitage, Kanva, is absent, but the king will tell the saint's daughter of his homage. The king lays aside his ornaments, as is right on entering a penance grove, and, hearing hermit maidens, conceals himself to watch them. Sakuntala asks one of her two friends, her attendants, to loosen her dress; the king admires her beauty. She shows a sisterly love for the flowers, her favorite the jasmine, "now by her own choice the bride of the mango tree." Her friends reflect that she thinks, "As the jasmine is united to a suitable tree, so may I also have a husband worthy of me." The king wishes that she were not of the priestly caste, but considers, "She can be a warrior's bride—Since my truest soul desires her." When a bee attacks the girl, the king thinks her very repulse is charming, and envies the bee. (The king's descent from his chariot, Sakuntala's watering of the plants, and her escaping from the attacks of the bee are all signified by stylized movements.) The king steps forth. Not knowing him yet, they extend courtesy; Sakuntala feels "an emotion unsuited to this holy grove." The two friends in an aside encourage her to think of the stranger as a husband. The king wonders how she can be the daughter of a holy man and is told that Kanva is her foster father; she is the daughter of a royal sage and a nymph (and so she and the king are of the same caste). The act ends as the king hastens away to protect the holy grove from an invading element. Sakuntala pretends that her garment has been caught by a bush so that she can look at the king another moment (it is done charmingly and amusingly; there are other touches in the act that evoke smiles). In the first act, then, the state of love is dominant, the erotic sentiment being leavened by the comic.

Act II. This act begins with mirth (the emotion corresponding to the comic *rasa*) in the complaints of the *vidushaka*, or jester, who is a Brahmin; and the love motif is treated comically also. The jester does not like the life in the forest, not the chase, not the heat, not the water tasting bad from leaves, not the food; and the king, having caught sight of Sakuntala, does not want to return to the city. The *vidushaka* and the general of the forces debate whether the king should hunt; the king calls off the hunt in order not to disturb the sacred grove, he says, but actually because his mind can think only of Sakuntala. He speaks to the *vidushaka*, as to a friend, about her; he wants the jester to contrive a device for visiting the hermitage. Hermits arriving that moment present him with a device, and the comic sentiment gives place to the heroic as the young hermits praise the king's majesty, goodness, and prowess. Let the king come to the grove for a few nights to protect them against demons disturbing their sacrifices. The jester is not eager to go where there are demons. A message comes from the king's mother requesting his presence at a sacrifice for his welfare. Torn between the obligations to the hermits and to his mother, he sends the jester, received in the past as a son by the queen mother, to discharge the part of a son. The jester, delighted, asks for suitable appurtenances. The king gives him a retinue and, thinking him lightheaded enough to talk too much, says that he spoke only in sport about loving the hermit girl.

Prelude to Act III, or entr'acte. With King Dushyanta in the grove the demons are gone, so great is his power. But Sakuntala, the life of the hermitage, is ill; it is thought she is ill from exposure to the sun.

Act III. The third act belongs almost entirely to the erotic senti-ment. Distracted with love, the king comes upon the three girls in a bower and thinks that not the noonday sun but love is the cause of Sakuntala's illness; and he overhears his thought confirmed by her in a confession to her friends. If they can find no way to make the king pity her, she will die. They suggest that she write a love letter, which they will give him hidden in a flower. The king, hearing her lover's verse, steps out of concealment into the bower. One of her friends says that, as it is the king's duty to free anybody in the realm who is distressed, he must restore the maiden who is suffering out of love for him. But Sakuntala says he must not be detained, for he must long for the ladies of his court. He declares that of his consorts only two will be his glory, his realm (which he thinks of as a consort) and this girl. When her two friends leave the bower, Sakuntala confesses her love but begs the king to observe decorum. Fearful of his lovemak-ing, she hides in an amaranth hedge, but hearing him speak his love, she shows herself again. The king wishes to kiss her. The girl in confusion puts him off by saying the matron of the hermitage is approaching; the king hides at her request. The matron nun of the hermitage being present, the girl complains in an aside, "Oh, my heart, when your happiness was within reach you feared to enjoy it. Troubled and regretful, what anguish will now be yours?" Seemingly to the bower, but really to the hidden king, she says, "Soother of my suffering! Until another blissful hour, I bid you farewell." The king regrets that he played a cowardly lover. A voice in the distance speaks of the flames of the evening sacrifice and the demons stalking like red masses of clouds and shadowing the sky, evoking the sentiment of terror.

Prelude to Act IV. The king has married Sakuntala in a Gandharva ceremony, or declaration of mutual acceptance, which is secret, and has returned to the city. One of her dear friends wonders, "Will he remember what has happened or not?" Behind the scenes the loud voice of an angered saint not honored by Sakun-tala, who was absorbed in thinking of the absent king, brings down the curse that the king shall forget her. Her friends intercede. The saint cannot recall his words but offers this much mercy: "At the sight of the ring of recognition, the spell shall cease." They will spare their friend knowledge of what has happened. The remaining sequences of the plot depend on this curse, with one possible exception in the links of cause and effect, the king's heroic battle with the demons. It is never made clear whether Indra reunites him with Sakuntala as a reward for his heroic battle fought in defense of the God.

Act IV. It is the pathetic sentiment that dominates this act. Kanva has returned from his pilgrimage, there has been no word from the king, and Sakuntala is soon to have a child. A voice from the sky chanted to Kanva knowledge of the child and its father; the saint will send her, splendidly robed and ornamented by supernatural means, to her husband. Although unused to such ornaments, her friends can array her well because of their skill in painting. Kanva performs religious rites, purifying his child; and the trees and flowers of the sacred grove, and kindred nymphs, make their farewells, while deer and creepers and peacocks are saddened by the separation. Kanva gives some words of advice.

Though he offend you never show
An angered mind before your lord.

Her two dear friends, who have spared her knowledge of the curse, tell her to show the king his ring if he is slow to recognize her, a misgiving that makes her tremble. Kanva prophesies that after she and the king have ruled for many years, they will return to this grove. Since the prophecy of so holy a sage makes facts, we may think that the play will end well for her.

Act V. Love and sorrow are the dominant emotions in the fifth act. We also see the king as a monarch who is admirable in that role. Hearing a wife complain delicately in a song that he no longer favors her, the king accepts her censure and feels, somehow, that he has been separated from a being he loved, like a memory of affection in a former life. The emissaries from Kanva arrive. The king admires the beauty of Sakuntala, but reflects that it is improper to gaze on another man's wife; the girl feels bad omens. The emissaries announce that she is about to be the mother of his child, that it is time for the king to receive her for the "joint performance of holy rites." With no memory of their marriage the king reflects, echoing an image of their first meeting,

I cannot taste, nor yet forsake,
Her sweetness, like the bee that flies
Around the dewy bud at dawn.

The girl appeals for justice and thinks to confirm her claim with his ring, but she has lost the ring, perhaps when offering homage to the Ganges. The king speaks of her devices as cunning, making her indignant: this man had "honey on his lips, but poison in his heart." After their first reproaches the angry emissaries will waste no more words, adding only this to the king:

She is your bride! Receive her, you,
Or cast her off; for absolute
Is the husband's power over the wife.

Nor will they let the girl, who wants to leave, act wrongly; her duty is to stay. A priest advises the king to let the lady live in his house until the child is born; if the child has the royal birthmark in his hand, or if the sign is wanting, the truth will be known. The king agrees and the lady follows the priest out. The priest returns in a state of astonishment, which the court shares: a shining apparition has borne the lady away. (It is a taste of the wonderful, like the voice that spoke to Kanva.) The king will hear no more of the matter, although he is troubled in his soul.

Prelude to Act VI. The prelude evokes the comic sentiment, although its matter is the wonderful recovery of the ring. A fisherman has been apprehended by constables, in a scene of low comedy, for trying to sell the king's ring, which he claims he cut out of the mouth of a carp. The Chief of Police enters the palace—the constables think he is taking a long time (there are only a few lines of dialogue before he returns)—and learns the fisherman is innocent. The king, the Chief tells the others, broke down for a moment when he saw the recovered ring, and the king has given the fisherman a purse for the full value of the ring. The fisherman gives half to the constables to buy the funeral flowers they were itching to fix on him. They all go to a wineshop together.

Act VI. For the sake of her friendship to Sakuntala's mother, a nymph descends in a celestial car to observe the sainted king, and is surprised to find that there have been no preparations for the Vernal Festival. The reason is, we learn, the king's agony; the ring has made him remember. His pain of separation sustains the love motif. The observing, invisible nymph responds sympathetically to him. The jester finds it all very touching, but *he* is being devoured by hunger. The queen's portrait, painted by the king, is brought at the earlier suggestion of the jester, and the nymph praises the king as a real artist. As the king gazes at the picture, the jester observes in an aside, "Surely, like a madman he has forsaken the reality for a mere shadow." The jester sees that the lady in the picture is frightened; a bee is flying against her face.

The king threatens to shut the bee within a lotus cup. When he
reacts to the picture as though it were a reality, his near madness
and sorrow persuade the nymph that he has atoned for his wrong.
Then in a matter brought to him concerning the right of succession
to a man's inheritance, we see in the king's understanding and
justice that his private despair has made him a better ruler, closer
to his subjects. After the incident the king unhappily reflects that
at his death the fortunes of his race will be lost, "as the seed planted
in the soil at the wrong season." The nymph thinks to relieve his
mind, but restrains herself as the gods have already made a promise
to Sakuntala. Suddenly there are screams of distress from the jester
elsewhere in the palace, which call into being the furious sentiment
as the king grasps his bow against a threatening demon, only to
face Indra's charioteer, who chose to rouse the king's energy (the
state that evokes the heroic sentiment) in this manner. His private
despair must not enervate his royal energy and duty. Indra, who
cannot destroy the race of giants, calls upon the king and his bow
to destroy them. The king leaves for his heroic task.

   Act VII. The king, who has destroyed the giants, thinks himself
unworthy of the honor of having been seated in a throne at Indra's
side in the presence of all the celestial beings. With stylized movements to represent passage through the sky, the king and his
charioteer go through a region once purified by Vishnu for supreme
bliss, where the king experiences profound repose. (Such sublime
tranquillity was in later centuries characterized as a ninth *rasa*.)
As they approach earth's beauty, the king requests to be taken
to the Golden Peak where dwells Kasyapa, the holy sire of gods
and demons. As the king waits in a sacred grove, an extraordinary
child comes his way dragging a lion's cub; when hermit women
warn the child against the lioness, he laughs fearlessly. The king
thinks it his own childlessness that draws his heart to this unruly
boy. At a hermit woman's request the king frees the young lion
from the child's hand; the woman expresses amazement over the
resemblance between the child and the man. By an accident the
king learns that the child's mother is named Sakuntala; yet the
king, afraid of bitter disappointment, will think only that it is a
common name. The king picks up an amulet that the child dropped
in playing with the lion, an amulet of supernatural powers given
to the child by Kasyapa at the natal rites. The women are astonished
at King Dushyanta's impunity, for only the child or his mother
or father can touch the amulet, called the Invincible, without suffering harm. The king feels blessed. Sakuntala, hearing of the wonder-

evoking incident, comes clothed as an ascetic, not daring to believe her fortune. At first she does not recognize her revered husband, so pale is he. He falls at her feet, asking her to banish the bitterness of his act from her soul. She ascribes what happened to her sins in a previous life. Indra's charioteer, after telling the king that Indra is aware of the reunion, announces that the divine Kasyapa will vouchsafe a meeting with Dushyanta, who advances with his wife and child. Kasyapa explains that Sakuntala's mother (a nymph) brought her here to Aditi, his wife; and that the repudiation was a consequence of a curse. Thus the king is freed from reproach and there is no blemish upon the king's and queen's state of love. Kasyapa promises that the child will be the ruler of the earth. King Dushyanta, his wife and their child return to the royal city. They are, Kasyapa says, a trinity to bless the world. The king prays that rulers ever seek their subjects' good, that the goddess of arts and literature be honored by poets, and that the self-existent god Siva save him from being born again on earth.

In a play that represents an action that is complete in itself, each part of the action—that is, the beginning, the middle, and the end, and the climax—is shown happening. If the playwright fails to present any part of the logically unified action on the stage, he weakens his play because the essential power of his imitation is in the immediate visual perception of what happens. The Sanskrit drama could allow itself to *narrate* crucial actions because the esthetic effect of the play did not depend on the imitation of a complete action. (The "complete action" is synonymous with plot-structure; "action" signifies each separate act that I have defined as a dramatic action—that which has a consequence.) In *Sakuntala* we do not see the girl (absorbed in thinking of the king) fail to honor the ascetic, an action that brings on the irascible saint's curse. Indeed, we do not even see the saint, we only hear his voice behind the scenes, for the *Natyasastra* rules that "pronouncing a curse . . . shall not be made directly visible in an Act." The saint's softening of the curse is narrated after Sakuntala's friend intercedes. The esthetic effect of the incident, then, comes from the poetry of the words in the way of narration. The crucial finding of the ring not only is narrated, it happens as a lucky accident to a character who comes into the play for that purpose only; and the king's recognition of the ring and his consequent remembering of the marriage are also narrated. But to say "lucky accident" is perhaps to interpret unfairly. The recovery of the ring is doubtless meant as a marvel, and the use of marvel is in accord with the statement of the *Sastra* that in resolving the plot of a Nataka, or heroic play, "experts should always introduce the Marvelous [or Wonderful] Sentiment." As for the action of recognition being *narrated* rather than *shown,* the playwright was obviously most interested at that juncture in portraying the state of sorrow, which evokes the pathetic sentiment, and did not want to lessen the single effect of that portrayal by showing the complex emotional state of the shock of recognition.

When a marvel resolves what happens in the end, there is no climax, no action of the central character that determines how the question raised by the middle will be answered. As he is beyond reproach, Dushyanta never has to make himself worthy of a reunion. Otherwise his conquest of the giants could be a climax. However, it is not a climax. We are told only that Indra knows of the reunion, not that he allowed or caused it. Nor does Sakuntala do anything to make the reunion possible. Her neglect of the holy sage is the play's most crucial action, and she is actually the principal character, for it is her happiness that is at issue, not the king's. Her loss of the ring may be interpreted as a climax, the consequences of which are reversed by a marvel. But the marvel of the ring explains only the king's return of memory, not the event of the reunion. Although Sakuntala has an action interpretable as a climax, she does not have a unified plot-structure because her beginning and middle actions are divided. Her beginning action is that, having fallen in love with the king, she marries him in a secret ceremony. Her middle action is her neglect of the irascible saint, which throws her future happiness into doubt. For the plot-structure to be unified, the beginning and the middle must involve the same characters. We may note, too, that the marriage as well as the neglect is never presented. The playwright was apparently more interested in the situations consequent upon the actions than he was in the actions—the consequent situations being what he needed for *rasa*.

Although the esthetic effect of Sanskrit drama depends on the production of *rasa* rather than on the imitation of a complete action, we must not underplay the plot, which is distinguished from "plot-structure:" a plot has causal sequences of actions or events but not a logical unity. "The plot and its elaboration," says the *Natyasastra*, are "the basis of the Sentiments," that is, the plot brings into being the conditions and states that evoke *rasa*. The only structural necessity is continuity. The *bindu*, or prominent point, is "that which sustains the continuity"; the *Sastra* says that the *bindu* "should again and again (literally, always) be made to occur (literally, pervade) in the plot." According to the *Sastra* there are five stages to the plot in a Nataka and other types of plays, and these stages have five corresponding elements and five corresponding junctures. The stages and junctures do correspond, but the elements do not although they do deal with technically related matters. The five stages describe the "exertion of the Hero (literally, one who strives) towards the result to be attained." The junctures carry each corresponding stage to a close.

STAGES	JUNCTURES
Beginning	*The Opening*
That part of the play which merely records eagerness about the final attainment of the result with reference to the Germ [the first of the "elements," defined as "that which expands itself in various ways and ends in fruition," i.e., it is the seed of the action; the *bindu* is another element.] The desire leads to effort.	That part of the play in which the creation of the Germ as the source of many objects and Sentiments takes place.
Effort	*The Progression*
[Hero's] striving towards an attainment of the Result when the same is not in view, and showing further eagerness.	Uncovering of the Germ placed at the Opening after it has sometimes been perceptible and sometimes been lost.

Possibility of Attainment

When the attainment of the object is slightly suggested by an idea [i.e., usually with regard to the means and obstacles].

The Development

The sprouting of the Germ, its attainment or non-attainment and search for it.

Certainty of Attainment

When one visualizes in idea the sure attainment of the result [i.e., if the obstacles can be surmounted].

The Pause

One's pause (literally, deliberation) over the Germ that has sprouted in the Development on account of some temptation, anger, or distress.

Attainment of Result

When the intended result appears in full at the end of events [of a play].

The Conclusion

Bringing together the objects [of the Junctures] such as the Opening, etc., along with the Germ, when they have attained fruition.

The *Sastra* goes on to say that there are types of plays that are to have only four junctures (no pause); others are to have three (no development and no pause); and still others are to have only two (only the opening and the conclusion). Thus in a Sanskrit drama there is continuity always insisted on but there is no need for logical unity. We may add, as is apparent from the stages and junctures, the *Sastra* also legislates that the structure of a plot must always end well from the point of view of the main character. Towards unity of impression, which is quite different from unity of action, the *Sastra* suggests the presence of an important character in each act; it also provides for unity of time by ruling that each act must take place in one day, although fairly long intervals may separate the acts.

Keith analyzes the stages and junctures of *Sakuntala* in a way worth following. Let us align them again:

STAGES	JUNCTURES
Beginning	*The Opening*
"the king's first anticipation of seeing the heroine"	"extends from Act I to the point where the General departs" after the debate with the jester on the merits of hunting
Effort	*The Progression*
the king's "eagerness to find a device to meet her again"	"begins with the king's confession to the Vidushaka [jester] of his deep love and extends to the close of Act III"
Possibility of Attainment	*The Development*
in the prelude to Act IV "we learn that the anger of the sage [saint] has in some measure been appeased, and the possibility of the reunion of the king and Sakuntala now exists"	"occupies Act IV and V up to the point" when Sakuntala is shown to Dushyanta who fails to recognize her although moved by sight of her, because "the curse darkens the mind of the king, who, instead of rejoicing in reunion with his wife, pauses in reflection"
Certainty of Attainment	*The Pause*
"in Act VI the discovery of the ring brings back to the king remembrance, and the way for a reunion is paved . . .	"this pause in the action extends to the close of Act VI"
Attainment of Result	*The Conclusion*
to be attained in the following act"	"is achieved in the last act"

(Unlike my analysis, Keith's makes the king the principal character and interprets the discovery of the ring as a determining cause of the reunion.)

Some Indian scholars give Bhavabhuti's *Uttararamacarita* pride of place over *Sakuntala;* the drama tells the story of Rama after his defeat of the ten-headed demon Ravana, who

was working evil in the world, and his freeing of his wife
Sita whom Ravana had captured. It is based on the last book
of the *Ramayana*. (Rama was an incarnation of Vishnu.)
In Bhavabhuti's play on Rama's earlier career, the *Maha-
viracarita*, the playwright uses dialogue not in the way of
presenting actions but to narrate the main events of the
Ramayana, lending dramatic tension to his story by making
the feud between Ravana and Rama the center of gravity.
In that play Rama and Sita spend a banishment in a forest
which is a central setting in the later story of Rama, the
Uttararamacarita.

It is worth giving the preliminaries of the play.[4] The
benediction is brief: "Having made an obeisance to former
poets, we pray for this, that we may obtain the immortal
goddess Speech, who is a phase of the Supreme Soul."
Whereupon the stage manager exclaims, "Enough of prolix-
ity!" (Such a reaction by the stage manager to the benediction
is typical of Sanskrit drama.) The immediate amusing tone
is sustained as the stage manager goes on talking, prolixly.
The amusing tone of the preliminary, like the song in the
prologue to *Sakuntala*, is intended to put the audience in
good humor to see the play. (The early Spanish playwrights
of the golden age also followed such a practice in their form
of a prologue, the *loa*.) We learn at the end of the prologue
that the "very wicked" people distrust the fire ordeal that
Sita underwent in order to prove her purity after her captiv-
ity.

　　Manager. If the scandal were to reach the great king, then
it would be very painful.
　　Actor. The sages and gods will by all means bring about what
is good.

And so we know that there will be pain but that the end
will be good.

　　Act I. Rama, as guardian of the world's welfare, must please
his subjects, as his spiritual guide commands. After a passage expressive of his sensitive and overwhelming love for Sita, and after his
pregnant queen falls asleep, a Brahmin comes to say that the people

distrust Sita's purity (the fire ordeal was performed on an island far away). The Brahmin is shocked at the reaction of Rama who lets his royal obligation take precedence over his private feelings because, like the whole solar race he descends from, he must propitiate the world. Banishing Sita, Rama knows "the purpose of Rama's life is at an end today. The earth is now a sterile wilderness; worldly life is without interest; the body is full of worry. I have no refuge left. What can I do?" It is a potentially tragic beginning. When Sita awakens alone (Rama has been called out to deal with a demon), she speaks of her evil dream of separation from her lord—all "separations . . . cause anguish," we heard earlier—and touchingly goes on, "My lord has gone away leaving me alone fast asleep; what can this be? Well, I will get angry with him, if I am master of myself when I see him." (Even before the banishment Rama prayed to holy Ganga, the goddess of the Ganges river and tutelary goddess of Rama's family, to protect Sita and prayed also that his invincible supernatural weapons reveal themselves to his unborn sons for their mastery; and after the banishment he prays to Earth, the mother of Sita, to care for her. These prayers have their consequences.)

Act II. In the prologue to the act there are two characters in a forest who appear nowhere else in the play and who are here only for narrative exposition. We learn that two wonderful boys, twelve years old, were raised by the sage Valmiki who has composed the story of Rama's life; that nothing is known of Sita who was abandoned twelve years ago; and that Rama must root out an impiety in this forest. There is a description of the beauty of these woods, where Rama and Sita once lived during a banishment and where now Rama's grief is intense. The physical beauty of the world is, indeed, described in several places in the play in epical detail. The conventions of the Indian theater allowed for such passages as the audience, it is said, were connoisseurs who delighted in the texture of narrative and descriptive poetry.

Act III. Ganga, having heard of Rama's coming to the forest, has brought Sita there on the pretext of performing a domestic rite in the Godavari river. Sita emerges from a pool of the river, beautiful but pale and emaciated, as though she were the incarnation of Pathos; a river goddess is her companion. Made invisible by the power of Ganga, she comes upon Rama and, seeing him pale and attenuated, faints; and Rama, too, remembering the time of his happiness with Sita in these woods, faints. (Swooning as a consequence of strong emotion is frequent in the play.) Sita,

coming to herself, is encouraged by her companion to revive Rama
by the touch of her hand, for dear is the touch in which he takes
delight. Rama, arising, thinks the touch of Sita has gladdened him
although he cannot see her, and Sita, hearing the depth of his
affection and delight, prizes her existence once more although
the unjust banishment still rankles. Here the erotic sentiment is
evoked, as it can be according to the *Sastra,* by love in separation
rather than by love in union; it is not, by the same authority, the
pathetic sentiment that is evoked in such circumstances, although
the circumstances include a condition available for the pathetic
sentiment. Vasanti, the guardian deity of the wood and a dear
friend of Sita's, although compassionate for Rama, rebukes him
for his "unworthy act"—"fame, they say, is dear to thee, but can
any infamy be more terrible than this?" Rama in his uncontrollable
agitation and distraction again faints. Sita thinks she is cursed;
because of her he has suffered a change in condition which puts
his life in danger—he who is the support of the world's welfare.
Again her touch revives him, and Rama feels the joy of her presence.
Sita in turn, because of his unchanged affection, experiences an
assuaging of her long and terrible sorrow (she has also suffered
the pain of separation from her sons, whom she has not seen since
their birth). So it is that Rama's expressions of the depth of his
love are dramatic actions, for there have been consequences. To
repeat: after her first touch and his responsive joy, she could prize
her existence again; and now after her second touch a further
change takes place in her, her sorrow being assuaged. Rama speaks.
As a wife must be present in the ceremony of the horse-sacrifice
(marking his taking possession of the world), Rama, rather than
marrying again, will have a golden statue of Sita in the ceremony.
Sita, hearing, breathes calmly again and in tears says, "Thou art
now indeed my noble lord; my lord has plucked out the dart of
the shame of my repudiation." Thus the reconciliation becomes
possible of attainment (the third "stage" of a Sanskrit plot), which
measures what happens in the act. More obviously the act presents
the state of anguished separation which evokes dominantly not
the pathetic but the erotic sentiment, although we also experience
pity for the pain. At the end of the act the river goddess makes
an explicit statement of pity as being an essential *rasa* of the play:
"Oh wonderful is the arrangement of incidents! The pathetic sentiment, though one in itself, being modified by various occasions,
seems to assume different forms as it were, as water assumes the
various modifications of eddies, bubbles, and waves and it is all

nevertheless but only water." (The prologue to Act VII says that wonder is the other chief *rasa.)*

Act IV. The prologue, expository as usual, has attractive mirth in it (there was a touch of humor toward the end of the third act, the playwright knowing how to harmonize tones). Two ascetic boys are talking, and one is glad to welcome the gray-bearded elders to Valmiki's hermitage in the forest because of the holiday they have brought; the other laughs, saying, "Your reason for showing regard is peculiar!" The elders are Janaka, father of Sita, Kausalya, mother of Rama (their arrivals are managed so as not to seem contrived). Once seeming the goddess of prosperity, Kausalya is now compacted of grief; once a feast to Janaka's eyes, she is now intolerable salt to the wound of his loss. He sarcastically asks, "Is the mother of the king, who protects his subjects, well?" But then he is moved to compassion by her sorrow. The act is expressive of the state of sorrow of the elders, evoking the pathetic sentiment. Their grief is somewhat allayed when they catch sight of Rama's son Lava; for although they do not know who he is, they seem to recognize their own children in the boy. (The meaning and value of family are important thematic elements in the play.) When Lava recites the passage from *Ramayana,* composed by Valmiki who has raised him and his brother, on the banishment of Sita, Janaka broods: "Oh, the wickedness of the citizens. Oh, the precipitate action of king Rama . . . it seems to me the time has come for my wrath to blaze forth either with a curse or a bow" (he is both a saint and a king). For a moment the tension of tragic potentiality seems to tighten, but Janaka is calmed almost at once, extending "peace to both." The act ends with Lava irritated by the insolence of a voice proclaiming the "valor of the only hero of the seven worlds," and he prepares to engage the royal guard of the sacrificial horse. For him the phrase "the only hero" insults the whole warrior caste of which he is a member.

Act V. When Lava and the prince Candraketu (Rama's nephew, who is commanding the army of the royal guard) face each other, they say, speaking with one voice as with one mind, "Oh, how noble-looking this prince is. Can it be our chance meeting, can it be the excellence of his qualities, or an ancient acquaintance intimately formed in some previous life, or some relationship between us two unknown by the power of fate? My heart becomes all attention on beholding him." And an onlooker reflects—reflection is a characteristic convention of Sanskrit drama—"Generally this is the way of living beings, that one person feels an ardent

affection for some other person, which worldly people call friendship of the planets and love at first sight; wise men say that love
is indescribable and without apparent cause. There is no preventing
that liking which is causeless, for that is a thread composed of
affection knitting together beings internally." But in confronting
each other they come to anger out of pride—anger is the emotion
corresponding to the *rasa* of fury—and the onlooker uses another
characteristic convention, detailed description of emotion: "Their
anger has blazed forth. Tremor produced by intense feeling agitates
their knots of hair fastened up on their head; their eyes, which
are naturally red like the leaf of the pink lotus, spontaneously
assume a fiery glow; their faces, from the knitting of the eyebrows
suddenly dancing, wear the beauty of the moon with its spots made
prominent, or of a lotus over which bees are hovering."

Act VI. Two spirits narrate the engagement of the princes:
"the marvellous combat goes on terrible to the worlds," and the
marvels are detailed. Rama comes and quiets the contenders. In
Lava's presence Rama suddenly feels rest from his grief; and when
Rama embraces Lava's brother, he is so struck by his own feelings
as to wonder whether the boy could be his son. He begins to recognize himself and Sita in them, but regrets his hope when, weeping,
he realizes he has become an object of pity to the boys who have
been talking indifferently. Thinking on Sita's beauty and their
lovemaking, Rama knows that "the world is a withered desert when
one's wife is dead." When Sita's father and Rama's mother come,
terrified at having heard of the combat, they swoon on seeing
Rama's emanciated state. Rama says their pity is thrown away on
him who showed no pity to Sita.

Act VII. In the theater on the bank of the Ganges the power
of the sage Valmiki has placed the "whole world of creatures,"
including gods, demons, animals, and people. The prologue commands the world's attention to the play, composed full of the sentiments of pathos and wonder, because of the "importance of the
matter." The prologue ends with the shock of the unexpected:
the audience hears that Sita, even while in the throes of childbirth,
is throwing herself into the Ganges. (Rama reacts as though it
were actually happening, and is calmed by his brother.) Ganga
reflects, "common to all is this thread of life, which has the knot
of infatuation of mind, and which is a source of misfortune to
sentient being." The play goes on. There is a tumult in the heavens
and the presiding deities of Rama's invincible weapons announce
that they are destined for Sita's sons, newly born, as Rama promised;

and Ganga will entrust the boys to Valmiki. (Rama is overwhelmed, realizing that Lava and his brother are his sons; Lava used the weapons in the combat with Candraketu.) Sita nonetheless wants to die, unable to endure her terrible humiliation. (Rama swoons.) A voice announces a holy miracle, the Ganges churns, the sky is crowded with divine beings, and Sita and the goddesses Ganga and Earth rise from the water. Now Sita leaves the play and revives Rama with a touch. In joy Rama awakens. The goddesses say they responded to his prayers before and after the banishment for their protection of Sita. The people are scolded for having doubted their queen, who sprang from sacrificial ground, and the people do obeisance to her. Rama will appoint the living Sita rather than the golden image as his fellow worshipper in the horse sacrifice. Her sons are presented to Sita for the first time by Valmiki, and her father too is present for her happiness. Rama delivers the play's closing benediction, saying, "This story purifies from sins and increases blessings"; the play is "Brahma revealed in the form of words, while its nature is brought out by acting."

As the prologue of Valmiki's play within the play states, the sentiments of pathos and wonder dominate. These *rasas* are clearly what Bhavabhuti was most interested to evoke, although the erotic and heroic sentiments (usually dominant in a Nataka) are strong. The fourth and fifth acts have little to do with the story of Rama and Sita, the fourth evoking pathos for characters incidental to the story and the fifth evoking wonder with incidents way out of proportion to the needs of the plot. Pathos and wonder are evoked, of course, in several situations outside the fourth and fifth acts, and the fifth act also evokes the heroic *rasa*.

The main materials for a plot-structure, which are in the first, third, and last acts, *contain a beginning (the banishment), a middle (Rama's expression of love which makes reconciliation possible) and an end (the reunion); but these do not comprise a unified plot-structure because there is no climax,* no act of Rama's that determines a solution to the linked problems of his finding happiness with Sita and ruling well (which includes keeping his subjects contented). Although there is no unified plot-structure, in performance the music, dancing, and stylization allow the play to have a satisfying formal architecture; and the satisfac-

tion of *rasa*, presumably, allows the absence of syllogistic unity
in the literary experience. But to those who cannot experience
rasa, not knowing Sanskrit, the play's construction limits
the pleasure offered.

More appealing to the Western mind than *Sakuntala* and
Uttararamacarita, although these are the best of the extant
heroic plays, is *Mrcchakatika*, the *Little Clay Cart*, if we judge
from the relative number of performances. Who the playwright of the *Little Clay Cart* was, or when he wrote, is not
known; the play gives the legendary King Sudraka as its
author. The first four acts closely follow what remains of
Carudatta in Poverty by Bhasa, the earliest of the great Sanskrit
dramatists whose works are extant.

Sudraka's play has been adversely criticized by Indian wri-
ters on poetics for being neither elaborate nor ingenious in
its descriptive stanzas, but the mind nourished on Western
drama prefers Sudraka's dramatic liveliness and relative pithi-
ness of style. The *Little Clay Cart*[5] has ten acts. It is really
two plays, a five-act comedy and its sequel of a five act melodrama.

Untypical of Sanskrit drama, the comedy has a logically
unified plot-structure. The central character is a charming
and intelligent courtesan of the first rank, Vasantasena, who
performs the actions of the beginning, middle, and end, and
of the climax, the complete action being directed toward
her happy conquest of Carudatta, whom she loves. The
melodramatic sequel has a causal sequence of actions but
not a unified plot-structure. Carudatta, accused of the supposed murder of Vasantasena, is the main character; but
he does not have the climax. The climax is an act of his
loyal friend, the *vidushaka*, who in beating the villainous
accuser drops Vasantasena's jewels; the possession of the
jewels (entrusted to him) condemns Carudatta. The reversal
at the end of the play is brought about in a way to satisfy
the sentiment of wonder. A Buddhist friar taking Vasantasena to the house of Carudatta must choose between two
roads, and his fortunate choice of the royal highway takes

them to the place of execution—in time to save Carudatta because the executioner's raised sword leaps inexplicably out of his grip and falls to earth, delaying the beheading. In a melodrama all that is required of a plot is an exciting sequence of incidents, and the sequel has that. If the premise of the wonderful is accepted, the resolution works well. We may add that the ten acts successfully blend a political story with the love story. The rightful king is a focus for goodness in the play; and the political story, skillfully connected to the love story, makes possible the triumph of the good.

Thornton Wilder's stylized *Our Town* (1938) bears formal likenesses to Sanskrit drama. It actually is a play and a sequel. Although language is *Our Town*'s sufficient medium, the play (i.e., the first two acts, the third act being the sequel) does not have a unified plot-structure; like Sanskrit drama it has a causal sequence, especially in the story of George and Emily. The two young people grow up caring for each other. Early on George tells her, as they are walking in the town, that he is to have his uncle's farm; and in the next scene Emily wants her mother to tell her whether she is pretty enough to attract anyone. George and Emily also talk to each other from their bedroom windows on a moonlit night—with choir practice going on in the distance—mainly about an algebra problem. Later on, because of a misunderstanding they have, their feelings are released in a talk; and when Emily doubts that her letters from their town, Grover's Corners, would interest him off at Agricultural College, he makes up his mind not to go. The scene, meant to make the audience, as the stage manager says, "remember what it was like when you were young," creates a state of feeling which is a happy sadness. It is George's mother who decides that he would be better off getting married and going directly to the farm than he would be with any other alternative. The play (i.e., the first two acts) ends with the wedding. *As in the* Uttararamacarita *there are a beginning, middle and end–the action is George's–but George, like Rama, has no climax, and so the play cannot be said to have a unified plot-structure.* (It is his mother's decision that determines the end.) The play moves through situations and moods with various of the people living in Grover's Corners,

New Hampshire, in 1901, the situations designed to evoke states of feeling in the audience; it is akin to the Sanskrit aim of evoking *rasa.* Wilder wrote of his play, in *Three Plays,* "It is an attempt to find a value above all price for the smallest events in our daily life," and value is a matter of feeling. As Jung says, "Feeling informs you through its feeling-tones of the *values* of things . . . what a thing is worth to you." In Sanskrit drama a stage manager in the preliminaries introduces the play. *Our Town* uses a stage manager who does that and who does a lot more: he fills in the little world of Grover's Corners with things, places, incidents, people, themes—freely narrating, describing, and reflecting, which techniques are typical of Sanskrit drama. Wilder's stage manager, however, directly addresses the audience. (In *Sakuntala,* for example, the stage manager in a prologue speaks to an actress about the audience and the new play by the famous Kalidasa.) It is Wilder's stage manager who entitles the acts of the play, "Daily Life" and "Love and Marriage." The acts of Sanskrit plays typically have titles (although they probably were not given by the playwrights, according to Keith).

The sequel, whose subject is death, takes place nine years later. Emily is now the protagonist (there was also a change of protagonist, as the reader will recall, in play and sequel in *The Caucasian Chalk Circle* and in the *Little Clay Cart),* and she has a unified plot-structure.

The beginning of change: Emily joins the dead, whose desire is to be weaned away from earth so that their eternal part can come out clear.

The middle: Despite their advice, she decides to return to earth, for life is all she knows, all she had.

To be settled by the end: How will she respond?

Climax: She learns that life is too little lived.

In the end, among the dead again, she will let herself be weaned away from what she knew on earth.

8/A TRUE PLOTLESS PLAY

Carroll's *Trumpets of the Lord*

In the best Western drama a dramatic formal structure without a syllogistic armature is unusual. One excellent American play that shows that a dramatic formal structure can exist without even a causal sequence for the whole (which the Eastern plays do have) is the *Trumpets of the Lord* (1963),[1] a musical adaptation by Vinnette Carroll of James Weldon Johnson's *God's Trombones*. The formal structure of this play, which is a serious and moving entertainment, imitates a gospel service, and in that imitation is its wholeness.

The performance begins with a processional, the entire company singing "So glad I'm here! So glad I'm here! So glad I'm here in Jesus' name . . . " Then the pastor of the church prays:

O Lord, we come this evening
Knee-bowed and body-bent
Before thy throne of grace
O Lord—this evening—
Bow our hearts beneath our knees,
And our knees in some lonesome valley.
We come this evening—
Like empty pitchers to a full fountain,
With no merits of our own.
O Lord—open up a window of heaven,
And lean out far over the battlements of glory,
And listen this evening . . .

Let the Lord make the words of the men of God (who will speak to the congregation this evening) "sledge hammers of truth/ Beating on the iron heart of sin." And the *amens* ring out.

Sister Pinkston speaks of the presence of the visiting preachers, "mighty dynamos of the gospel," and invites the congregation (i.e., the theater audience) to have a good time, to enjoy themselves, and shout and sing when they like. In fact, why don't they join in singing the hymn "In His Care"? After the hymn comes the high point of the service—the trumpets of the Lord. Their own pastor will break the ice.

The Reverend Parham rhythmically tells of the creation, and his movements have the effect of choreography in creating emotional meaning.

And God stepped out on space,
And he looked around and said:
I'm lonely—
I'll make me a world.

The darkness everywhere was blacker than midnight in a cypress swamp.

Then God smiled,
And the light broke,
And the darkness rolled up on one side,
And the light stood shining on the other,
And God said: That's good!

Then God reached out and took the light in his hands,
And God rolled the light around in his hands
Until he made the sun . . .

In a long passage the account of the creation goes on, told in familiar and bold imagery. After God makes man, Sister Pinkston sings "God leads us along."

Then the Reverend Sister Marion Alexander, one of the visiting preachers, tells of the fall of Adam and Eve. The musical accompaniment and the acting successfully fuse formal and colloquial expressions:

And God called Adam before him, And he said to him:
Listen now, Adam, Of all the fruit in the garden you can eat,

Except of the tree of knowledge; For the day thou eatest of that
      tree
Thou shalt surely die.

Then pretty soon along came Satan.
Old Satan came like a snake in the grass
To try out his tricks on the woman.
I imagine I can see Old Satan now a-sidling up to the woman.
I imagine the first word Satan said was:
Eve, you're surely good-looking.
I imagine he brought her a present, too—
And, if there was such a thing in those ancient days,
He brought her a looking-glass.

      Back there, six thousand years ago,
Man first fell by woman—Lord, and he's doing the same today.

"And that's how sin got into this world." Sister Marion tells
of the earth becoming "corrupt and rotten with flesh,/ An
abomination in God's sight," and then chants the story of
Noah. When Noah preaches,

Sinners, oh, sinners, Repent, for the judgment is at hand,

the entire company sings a hymn on the theme "Run sinner
run, God's wrath is gathering in the sky." The narration
goes on, ending with God's warning, "Next time I'll rain
down fire" (and it is difficult not to think of an atomic
holocaust). The entire company sings "Didn't it rain, children . . ."

The Reverend Ridgeley Washington begins by saying that
the rain of fire will happen on Judgment Day. (Like the
other two ministers, he makes effective use of movement.)
God tells Gabriel to blow his silver trumpet, first blowing
"calm and easy" to wake the living nations, and then blowing
like "seven peals of thunder," for which the archangel puts
one foot on the battlements of heaven and the other on
the steps of hell.

The preacher offers a vision of the Judgment, of those
walking on the golden streets of heaven and those falling
like lumps of lead for seven days and nights into hell, "their
cries like howling, yelping dogs," and then:

I hear a voice, crying, crying:
Time shall be no more! Time shall be no more!
Time shall be no more!
And the sun will go out like a candle in the wind,
The moon will turn to dripping blood, the stars will fall like cinders,
And the sea will burn like tar;
And the earth shall melt away and be dissolved,
And the sky will roll up like a scroll.
With a wave of his hand God will blot out time,
And start the wheel of eternity.

The chorus sings strongly in a long passage about "that great gittin' up mornin'," alternating with the preacher. They warn the long-tongued liar, the midnight rider, the gambler and the backbiter. God will cut them down. They sing of Samson. They warn the man who goes to church "to make a date with the neighbor's wife"—one day, when he thinks the neighbor has gone to work, the neighbor will be there and that will be the sinner's end.

Then follows a moving passage on the coming of death, "a man goin' round taking names"; the entire company alternates with single voices. The longest section is a preacher's account of God taking pity on Sister Caroline and sending Death to Savannah, Georgia. Death's journey on his pale horse is cosmic and terrifying, but to the dying woman he looked "like a welcome friend . . . And Death took her up like a baby" and brought her to rest in the bosom of Jesus, who rocked and comforted her.

Sister Pinkston sings of Jesus who will say "Well done" if you give the best of your service although men don't believe you when you say the Savior is come, the chorus joining her. Then she sings of Jesus in the garden of Gethsemane, his capture, and the crucifixion. The Reverend Alexander laments:

Jesus, my lamb-like Jesus,
Shivering as the nails go through his hands;
Jesus, my lamb-like Jesus, Shivering as the nails go through his feet.
Jesus, my darling Jesus,
Groaning as the Roman spear plunged in his side . . .

Female voices wail, and the Reverend Alexander concludes with a passage having this theme:

I'm telling you brother just keep on fightin'.
You gonna reap just what you sow.

And then the whole company exultantly sings "We shall not, we shall not be moved. . . . Till we have love and freedom, we shall not be moved . . . King Jesus is my captain, we shall not be moved . . . I woke up this morning with my mind stayed on freedom . . . I'm singin' and shouting with my mind stayed on freedom. Hallelu Hallelu Hallelu."

The last episode is the Reverend Washington's account of the dramatic story of Moses, the dialogue here as earlier acted out. It ends with a powerful contemporary pertinence:

Listen!—Listen! All you sons of Pharoah.
Who do you think can hold God's people
When the Lord God himself has said, Let my people go?

The performance ends with the entire company singing "We shall overcome." The audience joined in the singing.

While it is the theatrical presentation of a gospel service which gives the play its formal design, it is obviously a play, not a service, for the design is an artifice acted out for an audience. The formal design has no plot-structure at all for the whole; although separate narratives in the play have plots by virtue of their being skillfully told stories, they do not together form a single logical whole as do the plots in *Phaedra,* for example, or, as we shall see, in *The Plough and the Stars.* Moreover, the stories are narrated in the past tense, not shown happening in the present as is the mode of drama, although the narrators do considerable acting in telling the stories. (The technique resembles early forms of Eastern drama in which narratives were chanted along with instrumental accompaniment and the performer acted out the various roles, dancing and miming. Such performances are still very much alive in Eastern dance-drama.)

Although there is no cause-and-effect sequence of actions for the various parts of the play, there is another kind of logical design. The theme in the beginning is that the preachers' words

be "sledge hammers of Truth/ Beating on the heart of sin."
There is logic, then, in beginning with the creation and the
coming of sin into the world, in following that with the
increase of evil, and in culminating with the flood. We may
observe, too, that the choruses emerge from and lead into
narrative passages. The flood passage ends with God's saying
"Next time I'll rain down fire" and the next narration is
of Judgment Day and its rain of fire. The chorus then sings
of events in daily life as given perspective by the vision of
the Last Judgment, and includes a narrative scene of salvation. Again what follows is a direct emergence: the determination in song to have love and freeedom on earth; and from
the freedom theme in turn emerges the story of Moses, ending with its contemporary pertinence, the gospel service itself
ending with "We shall overcome."

For the audience, white and black, it was a powerful theatrical experience. Some—including reviewers—thought the play
outdated. It is unfortunate that the militancy of the times
made it seem so to them. Perhaps the religious experience
the play presents made some think it, to use the old metaphor,
an opiate. Others no doubt reacted against the colloquial
language which they misconceived as "Uncle Tom" language—God's saying "I'll make me a world" or a narrator's
speaking of "Old Satan now a-sidling up to the woman"—not
realizing that such language is perfectly legitimate, equal in
value to any other colloquial language, and that the fusion
of colloquial and formal language in the play (the poetry
of the play being given expression in both kinds of language)
is a considerable esthetic success.

It seemed to others that passages in the play had burning
contemporary relevance, that the whole play as a theatrical
experience can be responded to as a metaphor rather than
as an actual gospel service, and, most fundamentally, that
like all important art it takes place in its own timeless world.
Be that as it may, the play was, as I have said, a powerful
theatrical experience—perhaps owing chiefly to its fusion
of music and stylized movements with the narrative poetry,
all set in a formal design—and it is a genuinely American
version of those Eastern forms whose music and dance or

stylized movement make reading the words much less of an experience than seeing and hearing the performance. Along with the play, the director and actors of the Broadway production in 1969 deserve praise, for their excellence was crucial in giving the words a bodily existence and a rich life.[2]

9/ SO-CALLED "PLOTLESS" PLAYS
Euripides' *The Trojan Women*

That plays without plot-structures are rare and are completely successful only when there are music and either dancing or miming and stylized movement completing the words is a critical premise that can be validated only if the great plays that are said to be plotless can be shown to have plots—and not simply a causal sequence of actions but a unified plot-structure which defines the change in the protagonist and therefore what is central to the play as narrative. We may begin with the first great body of drama in the world's literature.

In the plays of Aeschylus, Sophocles, and Euripides, dancing and stylized gesture and music were important, but because of their literary merit the plays are sufficient without the dancing and music; they have been produced successfully without dancing and music. On occasion a modern production with choreographed movement and music can be enthralling, such as Katina Paxinou's production of *Medea*. Even those in the large audience of the Odeon of Herodes Atticus in Athens in 1956 who could not understand the Greek could understand the emotions, particularly of the chorus who had the largest share of choreographed movement. But we cannot reproduce ancient Greek music (the article in the *Oxford Classical Dictionary* gives an excellent brief account of what is known) and, although we know that gesture was important

120

as a manifestation of feeling, we do not know the degree of stylization of gesture. Certain it is that there were Greeks, Aristotle among them, who believed that the plays could be experienced by reading only. Plays had a reading public in Athens in the fifth century and scholars say that copies of plays were in wide circulation in the fourth century. The Greek theater was different from the Chinese Peking opera and the Japanese Kabuki theater not only in the primacy of words over dancing and music but also in the primacy of the play over the actors. Not until the great age was passed do we hear "that the actors are now more important than the poets," which Aristotle stated in his *Rhetoric* in the middle of the fourth century.

The primacy of the words notwithstanding, dancing and song and instrumental music were important to the Greeks, pervasive in their daily lives. Dancing then signified rhythmic movement generally and included juggling, tumbling (tumblers whirl a measure to music in the *Odyssey*), and the gestures of the chorus in a play. The choruses sang in unison; their music was predominantly melodic and subservient to the words; the rhythms were much the same as the meters of the verse. Sometimes, as Aristotle recorded in the *Poetics,* "Rhythm alone without tune is employed by dancers [in a play], for by means of rhythmical gestures they represent both character and experiences and actions." Juggling, tumbling and acrobatics the world over have been connected to the early history of drama; acrobatics are still sometimes part of the dancing in Eastern drama and are a survival of dancing in Peking opera. In the West as late as Elizabethan times there are records praising the dancing and acrobatics of English actors on the Continent. Originally, as Gilbert Murray says, "The ancient dance . . . was religious: it was a form of prayer. It consisted in the use of the whole body, every limb and every muscle, to express somehow that overflow of emotion for which a man has no words." In Greece there were *molpai* ("dance-and-song"), the bard-harpist singing a narrative while young men danced, "for sowing and harvest; for rain or for sun; for fertility in man, beast, and fruit; for the averting of pestilence, and for most of the other things people pray for."[1] Similarly, in ancient China and Japan dancing was always combined with song or chanted verse and instrumental accompaniment, as it still is in Southeast Asia and Indonesia.

When dancing in Greece became secular, the Greeks "danced" poetry, the dancer using his hands and arms, his face and head, his body, his legs and feet to represent the verses delivered either by himself or a chanter or singer. For this kind of dancing they developed *cheironomia,* an extensive and complex vocabulary of gestures and movements, perhaps like the classical gesture-language of dancers in India (where dance has always been closely associated with theater) who can carry on fully expressive conversation by means of their gestures. Greek tragic dancing had *cheironomia.* Ancient sources say that Telestes (a dancer-choreographer of that name worked with Aeschylus) could represent clearly the whole story of Aeschylus' *Seven Against Thebes* by dancing and gesture alone. In the mimed drama of Malabar the dancer represents the story with hand pantomime for the expression of ideas and facial pantomime for the expression of emotion while men in the orchestra chant the narrative. That the Malabar performances can run for thirty-six hours indicates the complexity of the narrative represented by dance.

Dramatic pantomime in the classical world reached its zenith in Rome, in a form matured by Bathyllus and Pylades, slaves who became freedmen, the first perhaps of Maecenas and the latter of the Emperor Augustus. Using *cheironomia* they portrayed Greek legends and myths, Bathyllus dancing the comic or satiric and Pylades the tragic. One dancer played all the roles, usually, costumed spendidly and masked. A herald opened the performance, giving a brief version of the story. Singers, not on the stage, perhaps sang the appropriate portion of the libretto before each episode (during these interludes the dancer changed costume). Notable poets wrote the libretti. There were usually four or five scenes. The accompanying instruments were lyre, double flute and Pan pipes, and, for percussion, hand drums, cymbals, castanets, metal rattles, and a loud foot-operated instrument made of wood and metal. The rivalry of Bathyllus and Pylades set off frequent factional broils between Roman citizens in the public streets. A passion everywhere in the Graeco-Roman world, dramatic pantomime became corruptly erotic and horrifying.

Of the various dance-dramas that still flourish, those of Bali are perhaps the most impressive. It was to Balinese dance-drama that Antonin Artaud responded crucially.

In fifth-century Greece the first generation of dramatists wrote the music as well as the words, and Aeschylus, at least, choreographed many dances, his most famous being the "lyreless" binding dance of the Furies in *Eumenides*. (Like Aeschylus, the highly admired Yuan dramatist Kuan Han-ching was skilled in music and dancing and, as Aeschylus probably did, sometimes acted in his own plays.) Although we know that Sophocles was an accomplished dancer, we know nothing of the dances in his plays; nor do we know anything of the dances in Euripides' plays. These dramatists also taught their actors and choruses. It remains only to say that Greek dancing in the tragedies was imitative, as were Zeami's dances. The quotation from the *Poetics* suggested as much ("by means of rhythmical gestures they represent both character and experiences and actions"), and Plato, in the *Laws,* defined dancing as "the representation, by means of gestures, of things told."

Although the drama as a theatrical representation cannot be neglected, the bias of this study is toward drama as literature, and so music and dancing and histrionics are talked about only as they are pertinent to the main premises. Since we are about to examine Greek plays outside the theater, and since the question of whether plays can have an autonomous existence outside the theater was first commented on by Aristotle, we may now consider the two kinds of experience of drama, the communal and the private, in the theater and in a book. Aristotle declared in the *Poetics,* "Indeed the effect of tragedy does not depend on its performance by actors" and repeated in a later chapter, "tragedy fulfills its function even without acting." But we cannot forget that the private experience of reading lacks the "urgent immediacy in the playhouse," as Allardyce Nicoll puts it, for that immediacy is the consequence of the visual power of performance; nor

can we forget the communal emotional experience in the
theater, for as Jane Harrison writes, "Emotion socialized,
felt collectively, is emotion intensified and rendered permanent"; and finally, as Susanne Langer observes, spectacle
(costume as well as stage sets) can "raise feeling, whatever
the feeling is."[2] It is in the first of these grounds that most
proponents of the superiority of the theatrical over the literary experience root themselves, although the second may
have equal value to the audience.

J. L. Styan flatly says, "The play as it is seen in any theatre,
with its effect and response in the theatre, is what really
matters" and that "quality is to be measured by the only
test—performance in the theatre, and when we read a play
critically, we are first and foremost making this test of stageworthiness in our imagination." Presumably he means that
a play is not worth a bean outside the theater and that any
performance, no matter how bad, shows what the play is
and what it is worth. Allardyce Nicoll, whose own predilection
is for the theater, nonetheless grants the "drama . . . extends
in depth beyond the theatre's range," that, for example, "no
performance, however finely conceived and executed, can
give us the whole" of *Hamlet*'s content; and when L. C. Knights
says that because *Macbeth* is poetry "the apprehension of the
whole can only be obtained by a lively attention to the parts,"
Nicoll also grants that such attention "goes beyond what can
be secured in watching a performance." But, he insists, "since
a play is primarily intended for the stage, the perusal of
its text must be bound by thought of the theatre." Alan
Reynolds Thompson is of like mind on perusal: "A printed
play is not a complete artistic creation in the sense that a
printed novel is, and the reader must learn the art of imaginative production in his mind's eye." Much earlier Molière put
it succinctly, that we should read with eyes that "uncover
all the stage action."[2]

G. Wilson Knight, although he has acted and directed,
takes a different stand. "Nor will a sound knowledge of the
stage and the special theatrical technique of Shakespeare's
work render up its imaginative secret. True, the plays were
written as plays, and meant to be acted. But that tells us

nothing relevant to our purpose. It explains why certain things cannot be found in Shakespeare: it does not explain why the finest things, the fascination of *Hamlet,* the rich music of *Othello,* the gripping evil of *Macbeth,* the pathos of *King Lear,* and the gigantic architecture of *Timon of Athens* come to birth."[2] Knight has more deeply influenced Shakespearean criticism than any other critic of the last fifty years.

Plays have always been read with pleasure, in ancient Greece, in medieval Europe, in Asia, in the modern world, and by innumerably more people in the long run than see them. That they have been read as imagined stage productions, except by theatrical people reading for professional purposes, is at least dubious. Indeed, it is a misconception of those with a predilection for the acted play to think that the reader should direct the play in the stage of his mind, which is necessarily a poorer experience than watching the play well acted. It is a richer experience to read the play as one reads a novel, letting it take place in its fictive (and real) world rather than on an imagined stage. Nor is there any difficulty in doing so, for as Henri Ghéon says in his *The Art of the Theatre* (although for other purposes), the dramatist's "very words must of themselves evoke image, gesture, movement, action, life" and, we may add, the look of the persons as well as their characters. Obviously the more literary merit a play has, the more it will lend itself to reading. To say, as some do, that literary merit decreases theatrical merit (as though the two together can add up only to a limited sum of merit) is to be blind to Shakespeare and Sophocles. The historical certainty is that plays last beyond their own time not because they are excellent theatrical pieces but because they are excellent literature (except when there is a long continuous tradition as in the Noh and Kabuki theaters and when the performance—of the dancing, the miming, the music—is essential to the formal structure; and even in such a theater the better the text the more assured the success of the performance, as Zeami pointed out). The literary bias of this study, then, answers to common experience the world over ever since there have been theaters. Moreover, plays are read before they are staged, and therefore the critical instrument used in this study to determine narrative meaning is a telling advantage to theatrical people as well as to critics and readers. As a precedent for the use of literary criticism by theatrical people, there is Stanislavski, that supremely theatrical person; he welcomed the interpretive guidance of the literary critic and dramatist Nemrovich-Danchenko, who was no great shakes as a playwright but was a good critic. Stanislavski believed that "one must have a wide literary education" as well as complete practical knowledge of the theater; "one must understand art . . . as a critic" and as a *"litterateur,"* not only as an actor and director. His "plan was to realize all the intentions of the dramatists, to create a literary theatre," observed Jerzy Grotowski; but nobody has ever questioned the theatricality of Stanislavski's productions.

It is true that when *The Trojan Women* was presented in New York some years ago, it was a powerful experience for the audience. But it is also true that by doing violence to the text—nearly all of the prologue was cut—the stage production changed the meaning of the play; there was a collaboration with Euripides, which he, being dead, had to consent to. Aside from the change effected by the collaboration, it is dubious that the production could reveal qualities that an informed and intelligent reading of the play could not (although reading is a more difficult experience than seeing a play, for a stage production interprets the text). Despite the mistaken change, it was a fine production and for the impact of a "fine production . . . no substitute may be found," again to quote Allardyce Nicoll. That is perfectly true, but it says only that one kind of experience cannot be substituted for another, not that one is necessarily better.

That watching and reading a play are different kinds of experience is self-evident. One is communal, the other private, and each has its own pleasures. When a production is good, to watch is a more powerful, immediate experience; it can be more transforming, more exciting. To read is, of course, a more reflective experience, an experience with subtler response to the textural qualities of the play, and for these reasons is perhaps a deeper experience. It is needful only to recognize the differences between the two kinds of experiences, not to judge between them. Nor need we say, each to his own taste. One taste does not exclude the other.

In any case the stage production is not before us and so, if we are to go on, we must assume the value of literary experience for the human mind and accept the common judgment of mankind for two millennia that *The Trojan Women* (415 B.C.) is a literary masterpiece. If it is plotless, as is universally declared, it follows that plays with great literary merit and with a long history of stage success need no plot. Here are judgments of admirable classicists. Edith Hamilton: "There is no plot in *The Trojan Women* and almost no action." Richmond Lattimore: "The general shapelessness is perhaps permitted partly because the play was one member of a trilogy; no piece which stood by itself could pass with so little dramatic action . . . " (but there is no evidence that Euripides ever wrote a trilogy). And again, G. M. A. Grube: There is "no action or plot in the Aristotelian sense." D. J. Conacher, as though offering another kind of plot: "Those [readers] who like the play praise it for its final and total impact"—therefore, it must have "an organic dramatic structure," which Conacher finds is a "rhythm of hope and desolation," for in the *"Troades* . . . the time for action has passed."[3] (A rhythm of hope and desolation can make a lyric structure but not a dramatic structure.)

Well, here is what happens in the play,[4] which begins with Poseidon speaking: "I am the sea god. I have come/ up from the salt sea depths of the Aegean . . . " Troy is "smoke only;" the Greeks "wait now for a fair wind for home,/ the joyful sight of wife and child again," while they load their ships with Trojan treasure. Poseidon, too, must take leave of glorious Troy, the city of his favor, and forsake his altars. "When a town is turned/ into a desert, things divine fall sick." In huts outside the city are the Trojan women, Helen with them. Hecuba lies upon the ground, not knowing that her daughter Polyxena has just been killed upon Achilles' grave, and that Agamemnon will force Cassandra upon his bed although

Apollo spared "her wild virginity." Three times Poseidon
speaks of Athena's agency in the destruction of the city; and
as he turns to go the Goddess who had been Troy's great
enemy comes to him for his help to "give the Greeks a bitter
home-coming." For they outraged her: when Ajax dragged
Cassandra out of Athena's temple, not one Greek blamed
the man. (In their exchange Poseidon appears the better
of the two.) Athena says, "Whenever the ships sail,/ Zeus
shall send rain, unending rain, and sleet,/ and darkness blown
from heaven" and he has promised his thunderbolts "to strike
the ships with fire." Let Poseidon make his "sea-roads
roar—/wild waves and whirlwinds,/ while dead men choke
the windy bay." The sea God grants the favor, saying he
will stir "the wide Aegean. Shores and reefs and cliffs/ will
hold dead men, bodies of many dead," and with irony, "When
a fair wind sends the Greeks to sea,/ watch the ships sail."
The men are fools "who lay a city waste,/ giving to desolation
temples, tombs,/ the sanctuaries of the dead—so soon/ to
die themselves."

This grim knowledge, like the sleet and darkness of Zeus,
hangs over the play, balancing in our minds the grief of
the Trojan women. That knowledge has the dimension of
tragic continuity, the warning of Clytemnestra in *Agamemnon*
on the night the Greeks were sacking Troy:

And if they reverence the gods who hold the city
and all the holy temples of the captured land,
they, the despoilers, might not be despoiled in turn.
Let not their passion overwhelm them; let no lust
seize on these men to violate what they must not.[5]

The imagery of wind and storm in the prologue, expressive
of the Greek fate, is woven with the thought of Hecuba,
who lifts her head from the ground as the day dawns (the
Gods are no longer there). She pronounces, "Endure. The
ways of fate are the ways of the wind." And again, "No use
to turn the prow to breast the waves./ Let the boat go as
it chances." Hecuba's *Endure,* an action of her mind, is crucial
to the careful structure of the play, for the change in the
play, which the syllogism articulates, is Hecuba's; she is

central. Her mind, which in the beginning of the play wills
endurance, changes when her cup of life and grief seems
full with rising sorrows culminating with the knowledge that
Hector's child must die. In the plot-structure's middle she
exclaims,

Troy lost, now you [the child]—all lost.
The cup is full. Why wait? For what?
Hasten on—swiftly on to death.

The end must say whether she will reach that consummation
or not. The climax, as we shall see, is her burial of the child.
But to return to Hecuba's beginning.

Even as her mind acts to endure, Hecuba believes, "What
sorrow is there that is not mine,/ grief to weep for," and
believes too, since so much was lost, "All was nothing—nothing always." The Greek ships came for what? "A woman?
A thing of loathing, of shame." Poseidon spoke of Helen
being in the huts with the Trojan women, and six more iterations of Helen's name are made before Greek soldiers drag
her out of the hut; in that scene, which is important both
structurally and thematically, we learn the symbolic value
of the iterations.

Hecuba's lamentation brings the Trojan women out of their
huts, and their fears measure the widening grief in the play.
With the coming of the Greek herald comes the reality of
what they only feared until now, their dispersal. Hecuba
learns that Agamemnon, loving Cassandra for her "strange
purity"—the girl is "God's, a virgin,"—has chosen her for
his own bed. The compassionate herald puts off Hecuba's
questions about her other daughter, Polyxena, who has been
sacrificed on Achilles' tomb, but tells Hecuba she is to be
the property of Odysseus. To her mind Odysseus is a vile
man—"There is nothing good he does not hurt"—and slavery
in his house is "a lot the hardest of all."

The herald will answer none of the other women: the soldiers must be quick to give Cassandra to the chief. A flash
of light among the huts makes the herald think that the
women are choosing to die by fire rather than sail to
Greece—"as well for them perhaps," he thinks. This thought

and Hecuba's "a lot the hardest of all" give tragic dimension, in the play's values, to her failure to die. But nothing is burning. It is Cassandra bearing a torch, lifted up for her bridal. The girl dances and sings a marriage song, blessing Agamemnon and herself that she will lie in the king's bed. We miss the emotional value of the choreography and music, but much remains in the words. The Trojan women think her frenzied in her joy, and Hecuba grievously reflects, "Your sufferings, my child,/ have never taught you wisdom." (That truth is in lives of tragic protagonists also, those critics notwithstanding who think the tragic hero always learns wisdom.) Cassandra exults, prophetically knowing of the murders of Agamemnon and of Clytemnestra: "All, all because he married me and so/ pulled his house down." The Greeks have had the worst of it these years of the war. The allusion to Agamemnon may make us remember the herald speaking of the hard years of the war in *Agamemnon*.

Were I to tell you of the hard work done, the nights
exposed, the cramped sea-quarters, the foul beds—what part
of day's disposal did we not cry out loud?
Ashore, the horror stayed with us and grew. We lay
against the ramparts of our enemies, and from
the sky, and from the ground, the meadow dews came out
to soak our clothes and fill our hair with lice. And if
I were to tell of winter time, when all birds died,
the snows of Ida past endurance she sent down,
or summer heat, when in the lazy noon the sea
fell level and asleep under a windless sky—
but why live such grief over again?

Yet the lust of war was inescapable, and we may remember also Aeschylus' account of the Greeks' terrible lot in the aftermath of the war.

For they, of old the deepest enemies, sea and fire,
made a conspiracy and gave the oath of hand
to blast in ruin our unhappy Argive army.
At night the sea began to rise in waves of death.
Ship against ship the Thracian stormwind shattered us,
and gored and split, our vessels, swept in violence

of storm and whirlwind, beaten by the breaking rain,
drove on in darkness, spun by the wicked shepherd's hand.
But when the sun came up again to light the dawn,
we saw the Aegaean Sea blossoming with dead men,
the men of Achaea, and the wreckage of their ships.

That there is nothing arbitrary in Euripides' play makes the
world of his play and the values conferred on the events
in that world the truer. Against Aeschylus' account we hear
Cassandra. (The *Agamemnon* was produced forty-three years
earlier, but Aeschylus' plays were read and revived in the
fifth century, and at least the "wiser sort" of spectators watching *The Trojan Women* would profit from knowledge of the
earlier play.) I give a long passage from Cassandra's speech
because of its importance thematically in the play, because
it goes into the balance against the pain.

> This town now, yes, Mother,
> is happier than the Greeks. I know that I am mad,
> but Mother, dearest, now, for this one time
> I do not rave.
> One woman they came hunting, and one love,
> Helen, and men by tens of thousands died.
> Their king, so wise, to get what most he hated
> destroyed what most he loved,
> his joy at home, his daughter, killing her
> for a brother's sake, to get him back a woman
> who had fled because she wished—not forced to go.
> And when they came to the banks of the Scamander
> those thousands died. And why?
> No man had moved their landmarks
> or laid siege to their high-walled towns.
> But those whom war took never saw their children.
> No wife with gentle hands shrouded them for their grave.
> They lie in a strange land. And in their homes
> are sorrows, too, the very same.
> Lonely women who died, old men who waited
> for sons that never came—no son left to them
> to make the offering at their graves.
> That was the glorious victory they won.
> But we—we Trojans died to save our people,

no glory greater. All those the spear slew,
friends bore them home and wrapped them in their shroud
with dutiful hands. The earth of their own land
covered them. The rest, through the long days they fought,
had wife and child at hand, not like the Greeks,
whose joys were far away.
And Hector's pain—your Hector. Mother, hear me.
This is the truth: he died, the best, a hero.
Because the Greeks came, he died thus.
Had they stayed home, we never would have known him.
This truth stands firm: the wise will fly from war.
But if war comes, to die well is to win
the victor's crown.
The only shame is not to die like that.
So, Mother, do not pity Troy,
or me upon my bridal bed.

The Greek herald would pay her for those "evil words,
bad omens" against his people were she not mad. To Hecuba
the herald says, "Follow quietly when Odysseus' men come,"
and Cassandra in surprise reflects, "You say my mother goes
to serve Odysseus?" Her next lines I give literally, somewhat
changed from Edith Hamilton's translation:

Where then are Apollo's words
which with me interpreting say
that she will die here?

Apollo can say what a person's *moira,* or portion, is; but no
Necessity, at least in this play, is at work. A person's portion
is not necessarily the limit of his destiny; it is the given circumstances. Hecuba's action swerves her from her portion, and
that swerving goes into the making of her tragedy. She will
later want to die, but by her act of burying the dead child
will preclude her own physical death. The death that will
find her here is the dying of her spirit, and yet there is
a measure of restoration for her in the traditional rite of
burial.

Cassandra's scene is important not only thematically but
also structurally. Under its emotional burden Hecuba collapses; that collapse is the first action in the change from her

will to endure to her desire for death. The women lift up
their fallen queen, who ends her lamentation saying,

Why lift me up? What hope is there to hold to?
    This slave that once went delicately in Troy,
take her and cast her on her bed of clay,
rocks for her pillow, there to fall and die,
wasted with tears. Count no one happy,
however fortunate, before he dies.

The shift to the third person is curiously like a technique
in Noh drama (at least as such passages are commonly interpreted in translation) for creating esthetic distance between
the sufferer and the audience. And her last sentence makes
us remember Aeschylus and Sophocles, as though their common wisdom here expressed were axiomatic in human existence. First in Aeschylus' play, Agamemnon, ignorant of near
and violent death: "Call that man only blest who has in sweet
tranquillity brought his life to close." Then the chorus ending
Oedipus the King: "We must call no man happy who is of
mortal race, until he has crossed life's border, free from
pain." Now, after Hecuba expresses that condition of life,
the chorus sings a marvellous ode of the rejoicing of young
and old in Troy the night they brought the wooden horse
through the gates of the city as a gift for Athena, who had
devised their overthrow, and of the slaughter.
    After the choral ode, as though out of the sacked city,
Hector's wife Andromache comes, sobbing, with her child
and Hector's bronze armor, the spoil of the Greeks.

Hecuba. Oh, our sorrow—our sorrow.
Andromache. Why should you weep? The sorrow is mine.
Hecuba. O God—
Andromache. What has come to me is mine.
Hecuba. My children—
Andromache. Once we lived, not now.
Hecuba. Gone—gone—happiness—Troy—
Andromache. And you bear it.

Andromache does not let Hecuba claim any part of her sorrow
and judges against the older woman for enduring the great

loss. The two women contend in crying out to Hector,
Andromache wanting the dead hero to defend her, Hecuba
saying, "come to me, lead me to death," a desire that
Andromache understands: "Death—oh, how deep a desire."
But Hecuba means her cry to her son as an expression of
pain for the loss of Hector, not as an act to be wished for.
For when Andromache tells Hecuba of the death of her
daughter Polyxena, saying, "She has died her death, and
happier by far dying than I alive," Hecuba replies, "Life
cannot be what death is, child./ Death is empty—life has hope."
Then Andromache prepares thematically for the change in
Hecuba:

Mother, O Mother, hear a truer word.
Now let me bring joy to your heart. '
I say to die is only not to be,
and rather death than life with bitter grief.
They have no pain . . .
She is dead, your daughter—to her the same
as if she never had been born.
She does not know the wickedness that killed her.

Hecuba would still have Andromache endure, beginning her
persuasion with the storm images of the Gods, herself con-
quered by the "great wave from God." If Andromache honors
her master, perhaps she will be able to rear her son to man-
hood, who will build another Troy. That hope is terribly
short-lived. The Greek herald comes to say that Odysseus
persuaded the Greeks to kill the child, and he cautions
Andromache not to say words that will make the army angry,
for they would pitilessly deny burial for the child. In her
pitiful farewell to the child, she breaks out in anger against
Helen, "no child of Zeus, as people say," but of "whatever
poison/ the earth brings forth—not child of Zeus,/ but Greece's
curse and all the world's." (For Aeschylus Helen was a name
for death: "that name/ for the bride of spears and blood,/
Helen, which is death." Probably not Andromache's cry but
what Hecuba says later is a clearer statement of Helen's meaning in the mind of Euripides.) The herald feels pity and
shame but has the soldiers take the child to his death.

It is at this juncture that Hecuba decides to die.

As though commenting on the course of human existence, the chorus sings of the earlier destruction of Troy by Heracles because the Trojan king broke his word to give two immortal horses to the hero. Nor is Troy blameless for its present fall: at least in Andromache's mind it was "the anger of God against Paris . . . / who laid Troy's towers low/ to win an evil love." Contrasted to that love, in the song of the chorus, is the love that once exalted Troy, "binding her fast to the gods, by a union," the love of the goddess Dawn for Tithonus, brother of Priam; but the "love of the gods has gone from Troy." After their ode—the choruses in this play are always linked emotionally or thematically with the structure—comes the scene with Helen.

Menelaus approaching exults in the bright sunlight this day, as though it were celebrating the delivery of Helen into his power. Hecuba overhears his intent to take Helen to Greece and there "give her to those to kill/ whose dearest died because of her." Queen Hecuba prays to whatever power upholds the world in justice, "God, or Necessity of what must be,/ or Reason of our reason." "A queer prayer," thinks Menelaus, an ordinary man in his emotions and understanding. Out of a passion to expose Helen for the "evil she did in Troy," that the justice of her death be wholly known, Hecuba suspends her own will to die swiftly and persuades Menelaus that Helen should not die unheard. Helen's defense matches her beauty, a cunning femininity of mind that makes a Trojan woman say, "Her soft persuasive words are deadly." We do not know whether Hecuba can worst Helen, whom she hates for what Helen is, but her mind remains admirable and clear. Her arraignment gives the meaning of the iterated allusions to Helen. Not Aphrodite as a power having its own existence different from the minds of men was the cause of Helen's betrayal.

Men's follies—they are Aphrodite.
She rose up from the sea-foam; where the froth
and foam of life are, there she is.

Helen, then, is a symbol of men's follies, of the froth and

foam of life they indulge in with disastrous consequences.

Hecuba has her victory; the scene ends with the knowledge that Helen will die. But Hecuba pays an extreme price for her victory: her freedom to die. Her exposure of Helen is, as it were, the prelude of the climax. Following the scene the chorus does not celebrate the fate of Helen; they lament their own. Our last vivid image of Helen is of "froth and foam," when the chorus wish for her death along with Menelaus' by the thunder of God at sea (the image again recalling the terrible journeys the Greeks are about to embark on):

And Helen, too, with her mirrors of gold,
looking and wondering at herself,
as pleased as a girl.

Imagining her so on the ship, the chorus seem to think that Helen will always have her way with men.

During Hecuba's defeat of Helen, Andromache's child was flung from a tower of Troy and Andromache taken away by Achilles' son who had to sail hastily because of bad news in his own country. Andromache begged that the herald take the body of the child and Hector's bronze shield to Hecuba for burial, which Achilles' son granted. The herald, moved by tears, washed the body and will dig the grave in the hard earth. Out of love and pity Hecuba buries the child with due ceremony, although she believes "those that are gone care little how they are buried. It is we, the living, our vanity." Her burying the child is the climax of the play, for the time the burial takes makes it too late for Hecuba to die. The Greeks are now upon her, and when she exclaims,

O God—What makes me say that word?
The gods—I prayed, they never listened.
Quick, into the fire—Troy, I will die with you.
Death then—oh, beautiful,

the herald commands,

Lead her away—Hold her, don't be too gentle.
She must be taken to Odysseus.
Give her into his hands. She is his—

For Hecuba, as we have seen, there is no viler end than to

become the property of that vile man. But there was some recompense of mind during the burial of the child whose life was taken by a "woman whom God hates" (we again hear in this last allusion to Helen her symbolic meaning as men's follies). The recompense to a mind like Hecuba's is knowledge of glory:

And yet—had God not bowed us down,
not laid us low in dust,
none would have sung of us or told our wrongs
in stories men will listen to forever.

As the Trojan women hear Troy collapsing in the fire, Hecuba speaks her final words,

Trembling body—old weak limbs,
You must carry me on to the new day of slavery,

and the women go down to the Greek ships.

That Hecuba's will to endure changes to the will to die and that her will to die is frustrated by a harder lot are what happens in the play, its essential dramatic action, and it is a very considerable action. (There are, in the light of my account of the play and in the light of what dramatic action is, many other actions.) The plot-structure has a logical form:

The beginning of change: Hecuba, who has told herself "Endure . . . drift with fate," discovers that she is to be slave to the vile Odysseus, which is "a lot the hardest of all."

The middle of change: When her "cup is full"—after Cassandra, Polyxena, and Andromache meet their destiny—Hecuba determines, "Why wait? For what? Hasten on—swiftly to death."

To be settled by the end: Will she die, not wait, not endure?

Climax: She buries Astyanax, who was condemned by Odysseus. (The Menelaus-Helen episode is also important structurally, giving Hecuba reason to delay the burial and her death; but until she undertakes the burial, she has time to die. It is the burial, then, which is the crucial action determining the end.)

With the return of the herald Talthybius and the soldiers of Odysseus she loses her chance to die, and the play ends with her having to endure a tragic lot.

10/ THE TRILOGY AS A DRAMATIC FORM
Aeschylus' *Oresteia*
Kuan Han-ching's *Snow in Midsummer*

There remains in considering plot-structure in Greek drama the matter of the trilogies. None by Sophocles or Euripides exist; we do not know whether or not they wrote any. That it was Aeschylus' practice to write trilogies is common knowledge, but only one trilogy exists, and so we can say nothing general about the construction of his trilogies as a formal whole. Albin Lesky thinks that as Aeschylus' first extant play, *The Persians* (472 B.C.), is not part of a trilogy, he only later developed that form. Aeschylus wrote his trilogy the *Oresteia* (458 B.C.)[1] in his last years, long after Sophocles had perfected the construction of the single play, the supreme example being *Oedipus the King* (which Aristotle used pre-eminently in the *Poetics*, and which may therefore be said to have fixed the logical form of unity of plot-structure in Western dramaturgy). There is no saying how Aeschylus constructed the individual plays in his other trilogies. There may have been only a causal sequence within each play (which we have seen in Eastern drama, and as there is from play to play in the *Oresteia*), or there may have been syllogistic structures for each play (we have also seen such structures in the works of Eastern playwrights who never knew anything of the West, let alone of Sophocles).

Although only the *Oresteia* trilogy is extant, C. M. Bowra writes of Aeschylus that "his massive trilogies are built on an architectural plan, on an idea which permeates the whole and can be abstracted from the particular presentation." It is misleading critically to equate an "idea" with an "architectural plan." In like vein Werner Jaeger writes of the *Oresteia* that it must be treated as a single whole, which is certainly true thematically. He declares, "It is impossible to separate *Agamemnon* from the two tragedies which follow it. Strictly speaking, it is barbarous to treat it as an independent play—to say nothing of *The Eumenides,* which cannot be understood except as a colossal finale to the whole trilogy." But there is structural unity and therefore *a* complete meaning in each play standing alone, as is objectively demonstrable. No single play, it goes without saying, has the full meaning of the trilogy.

Agamemnon

1. The beginning of change: Clytemnestra, in the ambiguous lines 341-344 and 349-350 (the line numbers refer to Lattimore's translation), reveals her intention (to the audience, who know the end of the story, not to the chorus, who do not), warning that Agamemnon, who has violated what a man must not violate, has still to make his run to safety, and expressing the wish that she will win through. Her intention is ambiguously revealed again in lines 912-913, this time to Agamemnon.

2. The middle of change: Having succeeded in making Agamemnon walk on the purple tapestry and thus cross the will of the Gods (an act that strengthens her psychology in two ways: she has imposed her will, she has the Gods on her side), she prays to Zeus for success, which includes not only her husband's death but rule with Aegisthus, the "master" of line 972.

3. To be settled by the end: Will she succeed?

Climax: She catches Agamemnon in the net, which in lines 355-361 is used as an image for the destructive will of Zeus.

Thus she can kill the king, and the death of the king, scattering the purpose and will of the chorus, enables her to impose her will on the city. That Zeus had a part in what happened is stated by the chorus:

For what thing without Zeus is done among mortals?
What here is without God's blessing? (1487-1488)

The Libation Bearers

*1. Orestes at the grave of his father prays for success in executing
vengeance against his mother who (together with Aegisthus, the nomi-
nal head of state) rules the power of Argos, having only his sister
Electra and the chorus to help him. (They are the libation bearers,
the libation being made at the command of Clytemnestra who dreamed
that a snake drew blood as well as milk from her nipple; Orestes
interprets himself as the snake.)*

*2. Proceeding with the assurance that he is doing the will of
the gods, he deceives his mother with the story that Orestes is dead
and is admitted to the stronghold.*

3. Will he succeed?

*Climax: He kills Aegisthus, which removes the power that stands
between him and his mother.*

After the killing of the tyrant, a Follower (a man-at-arms)
of Aegisthus says that there is no use fighting for one who
is dead. Clytemnestra had sent Orestes' old nurse to summon
Aegisthus with a bodyguard of men-at-arms back from the
fields, but the chorus persuaded her to tell him to hurry
back without a bodyguard. (Thinking Orestes dead, the nurse
gave to the chorus a realistic account of her care of Orestes,
even to his voiding; the meaning of Orestes to her establishes
her motive for disobeying the queen.) The scene in lines
891-930 extends the drama of the act of killing Clytemnestra,
at the end of which Orestes and Pylades force the queen
inside and the act is done by Orestes. The chorus in its humanity says, "I have sorrow even for this pair in their twofold
downfall." Although the plot-structure ends with Orestes'
successful vengeance, it is an unhappy pass for him. "I have
won"; he says, "but my victory is soiled, and has no pride,"
and he is conscious of what he must face, "I go, an outcast
wanderer from this land." The Furies come, seen only by
him, and drive him away. There are terror and pain in his
experience, and in us, perhaps, sympathetically.

The Eumenides

1. Given authority by the Furies who are set against Orestes, Athene establishes a court of mortal citizens to try Orestes.

2. Although the Furies convinced of their right in the matter threatened her land if the vote goes against them, she decides to vote for the acquittal of Orestes in the event of an even vote and does so.

3. Will she be able to placate the Furies?

Climax: She does not weary of offering good things to the Furies (line 881).

The Furies have a subordinate plot-structure; the end of their plot-structure is a reversal of their climax, the reversal being caused by Athene's climactic action (such reversals are a technique typical of melodrama, in which the emotional tension of the audience is tightened by violence or the threat of violence and near the end is suddenly released). The exciting opening scene in Delphi presents issues of the play. A priestess discovers the sleeping but terrifying Furies surrounding Orestes in the Temple; Apollo directs the suffering man to Athens for a trial. The ghost of Clytemnestra awakens the Furies, spurring them on to their vengeful work; and there is a confrontation between the Furies and Apollo.

1. The Furies, shamed by having let Orestes slip through their net, go to hunt him down in Athens, where he has been sent to Athene for judgment, and to win their right of vengeance for matricide.

2. Convinced of their right in the matter, they give authority to Athene to try the case.

3. Will they get satisfaction?

Climax: Having lost Orestes, they determine to poison Attica (lines 780-783) for satisfaction of their ancient rights.

But they reverse themselves in the end, persuaded to accept honor and new powers and to become benefactors of Athens.

It needs only to be added that Aeschylus' plot-structures are looser, or perhaps it is better to say more submerged, than a plot-structure in a single play such as *Oedipus the King*, a condition dictated by the causal connections from play to play in the *Oresteia*.

Trilogies in the West since Aeschylus, having his for precedent, cannot be said to have a formal structure that emerges
from the nature of drama; but that the trilogy is a potential
inherent form, not one absolutely invented by Aeschylus'
genius, is suggested by the Yuan play *Snow in Midsummer*
(late 13th century) by Kuan Han-ching, whom I have already
likened to Aeshylus. The play is not set up as a trilogy; rather,
it is written in four fairly short acts, as Yuan plays usually
were. Nonetheless its sequence of actions is trilogical in the
way of the *Oresteia*: each "play" or Part has a different protagonist and its own plot, and the Parts are connected causally.

Snow in Midsummer
Part One

Prologue. In scene 1 the widow Mistress Tsai, who is owed
money by the scholar Tou, in lieu of payment takes his young
daughter Tuan-yun for future marriage to her eight-year-old son.
Tou leaves the child he loves to go to the capital to take the examination for an official post.

Act I. In scene 1 we meet Dr. Lu, an apothecary, who owes
Mrs. Tsai twice as much money as Tou did; he is confronted by
her. (With each appearance characters announce themselves and
narrate exposition. "I am Mrs. Tsai. Thirteen years ago Mr. Tou
Tien-chang left his daughter Tuan-yun with me to marry my son,
and I changed her name to Tou Ngo. But after their marriage
my son died . . ." With stylized movements and rhythmic patterns
on the musical instruments the conventional iterations of name-
saying can work as a leitmotif.) When she demands her money,
Dr. Lu says that he has no money at home and that they must
go to the village. They start walking, and on the road with no
one about Lu tries to strangle the widow with a rope he has with
him for the purpose, but Lu is put to flight by Old Chang and
his son Donkey who turn up. Old Chang revives the widow. When
she tells them her circumstances, Donkey proposes that his father
take her as a wife and that he take her daughter-in-law Tou Ngo,
the former Tuan-yun. When Mrs. Tsai offers money instead, Donkey threatens to strangle her and so she agrees to the proposal.

Part Two

In scene 2 Tou Ngo presents herself. At three years old, she tells us, she lost her mother; at seven she had to leave her father. She is now twenty; her husband died three years ago. She is awaiting the return of her mother-in-law from the collection of the debt. It is Tou Ngo who has the singing role, and she sings of her grief, wondering whether it is her fate to be wretched all her life. When her mother-in-law, returning, announces to Tou Ngo that Old Chang is going to marry her (Mrs. Tsai), the girl upbraids the woman, who will make people split their sides with laughter at seeing a sixty-year-old woman take a fancy to another man and paint her eyebrows. But Mrs. Tsai responds only that the girl had better take a husband too, and that the wedding can be today. Tou Ngo scorns the old yokel Chang and his ruffian son. Donkey, going to drink with his father and Mrs. Tsai, says that he won't let Tou Ngo get away.

Act II. In scene 1 Donkey goes to Dr. Lu's shop for a poison to kill Mrs. Tsai, who is ill, for he thinks that once she is dead Tou Ngo will have to be his wife. Lu refuses at first but gives the ruffian the drug when Donkey threatens to expose him for having tried to murder Mrs. Tsai. Lu decides to go to Chuchow, the main city in the district, to avoid trouble. In scene 2 Old Chang, put out by the ill luck of his prospect of losing his rich wife-to-be, encourages her to eat; she would like mutton tripe soup. Chang sends Donkey for the soup. In scene 3 Tou Ngo, who has made the soup, sings of the virtuous women of earlier times and the unfaithful, wanton wives of the present. Donkey comes for the bowl of soup, says it is tasteless, and sends her for salt and vinegar, which gives him a chance to poison the soup. Chang calls for the nourishment. Mrs. Tsai insists that Chang drink some first, which he·does. Tou Ngo sings in anger over Mrs. Tsai's trying to please Chang. When Chang, dizzy, falls to the ground, Mrs. Tsai wails over him. Tou Ngo sings that she has no business grieving over the death of Chang, who has been here only a few days. Donkey accuses her of poisoning his father, and Mrs. Tsai says that she had better marry Donkey now, but Tou Ngo knows Donkey has done the poisoning and is not frightened. Donkey drags the two women off to court.

Act III. The prefect of Chuchow in making his vaunt boasts that he profits corruptly out of the lawsuits in his court and stays at home in bed, pretending illness, when his superiors come to investigate. The prefect, at Donkey's accusing Tou Ngo of having poisoned his father, has the girl beaten with a bastinado to make her confess, but she sustains the terrible beating. Only when the

prefect orders the mother-in-law beaten does the girl say she
poisoned Old Chang. The prefect orders her execution on the
morrow and calls for his horse to go home to drink. Mrs. Tsai
laments that she is the cause of the girl's death. Tou Ngo declares
that when she is a headless ghost she will not spare that scoundrel.
In the next scene, before she is beheaded, she reproaches both
Earth and Heaven for not saving her from injustice. She sings,

> The sun and moon give light by day and by night,
> Mountains and rivers watch over the world of men;
> Yet Heaven cannot tell the innocent from the guilty,
> And confuses the wicked with the good!
> The good are poor, and die before their time;
> The wicked are rich, and live to a great old age.
> The gods are afraid of the mighty and bully the weak;
> They let evil take its course.

Tou Ngo tells her mother-in-law that she confessed to murder
only to save her from suffering, that it was Donkey Chang who
poisoned the mutton tripe soup thinking to kill *her,* not his father;
and she asks that her mother-in-law perform rites for her. Mrs.
Tsai laments for the third time, "Ah, this will be the death of
me!" Tou Ngo declares to the executioner that although it is the
hottest time of summer, as evidence of the injustice three feet
of snow will cover her dead body, and the district will suffer from
drought for three years. The snow begins to fall even before the
beheading. The last line of the act is the executioner's "A fine
stroke! Now let us go and have a drink!"

Part Three

Act IV. Tou Tien-chang, now an Inspector with the responsibility for seeing that justice is done and with authority to punish
corrupt officials, has come to Chuchow. He wonders why the district
has had no rain for three years. In examining the court's cases,
he comes upon Tou Ngo's but, since it has been dealt with, puts
it at the bottom of the pile after remarking that the culprit's surname
is the same as his. Tired after travelling, he naps. The ghost of
Tou Ngo enters to visit her father in his dreams. Tou wakes, remembers that he saw his daughter in a dream, and finds the case of
Tou Ngo again on the top of the pile. When he returns it to the
bottom, the ghost makes his lamp flicker; as he trims it, she turns
over the file of cases. He wonders whether there are ghosts present.

Again he puts the case at the bottom, and again the lamp dims. Then he sees the ghost and is scared. When Tou learns who she is, he says that she, condemned for a heinous crime, has disgraced her ancestors. Let her tell him the whole truth, or the tutelary god will keep her a hungry ghost forever, never to re-enter human form. The ghost tells her father the story we already know, and does so in detail. She asks her father to avenge the wrong. He remembers a similar case in the Han dynasty, when an unjust execution caused a drought for three years. The ghost, knowing that the unjust verdict will be changed, asks that her father care for her mother-in-law, who is old. In the brief final scene Tou orders Donkey Chang executed in public for murder and blackmail, the prefect given a hundred strokes and removed from office, and Lu beheaded for selling poison. Mrs. Tsai will be lodged in Tou's house.

Then let us offer a great sacrifice
So that my daughter's spirit may go to heaven.

In *Part One,* as we have seen, the protagonist is Mistress Tsai, and the effects of her moneylending on her life and character are shown. Her climax is her being threatened with death by Donkey. In *Part Two* the protagonist is Tou Ngo, who has to cope with the consequences in her life that her mother-in-law has caused, and who, in contrast to Mrs. Tsai, sustains her goodness in face of death. Her climax is hearing that her mother-in-law will be beaten. In *Part Three* the protagonist is Inspector Tou, who is responsible for justice in all the districts of the Huai River Area, and who must determine whether his daughter's case was dealt with justly or not. His climax is hearing from his daughter's ghost, under conditions in which one false word would be most terrible for her, the evidence of the injustice.

11/SHAKESPEAREAN STRUCTURES

Henry IV, Part One
Twelfth Night
Macbeth

I have suggested that the logical form of unity of plot-structure in Western dramaturgy descends from Sophocles, whose perfectly constructed *Oedipus the King* Aristotle used pre-eminently in the *Poetics*. We have seen syllogistic plot-structures in the *Oresteia*, written after *Oedipus*, and have seen that *The Trojan Women* is logically unified. Seneca, following Euripides, was the great exemplar of the five-act structure for the Elizabethans, whose critical authority for that structure was Horace. The way that Elizabethan plays take of beginning at the beginning and going on to the end is, of course, medieval and not classical, like the long sweep of the medieval cycles that begin with the creation and end with doomsday. Nonetheless there is a logical unity of action in Elizabethan plays that is, as it were, the bones for the play's body; and the sense of form that came with the five-act structure was possibly instrumental in the fashioning of that logical unity. In any case syllogistic plot-structures are typical of much of Elizabethan drama. Just as Aristotle took Sophocles for his model, we shall (for the while) take Shakespeare and analyze a history, a comedy, and a tragedy.

The First Part of Henry the Fourth,
with the Life and Death of HENRY
Sirnamed HOT-SPURRE[1] (1597)

146

The king catalyzes the rebellion, but it is not he whose actions make the plot-structure of the civil war. *After his provocation of Hotspur, he has no action which moves that plot-structure forward.* It is, rather, Hotspur who is central to the action of the war.

1. The beginning of change: Hotspur is angered by the king, who accuses Mortimer of treason and refuses to ransom him.

2. The middle: Learning that his brother-in-law Mortimer was proclaimed heir to the crown by King Richard, Hotspur joins the plotting rebels in order to pull Henry IV down and put Mortimer on the throne.

3. To be settled by the end: Will he succeed?

The middle of Hotspur's change follows swiftly upon its beginning. It is an unusual construction—the beginning and the middle are almost always separated—but in this play the unusual construction is right as it fits Hotspur's nature. Hotspur is the center of interest and attraction in all his subsequent scenes: in his angry impatience with the letter of the lord who is afraid to pluck the flower safely out of the nettle danger, and in his immediately following high spirits and charm with his lady; in his baiting of superstitious Glendower—to his bargaining in that scene, since it is England they are dividing, our reaction must be at least ambivalent—followed by his jesting with his wife; in his modesty and praise of Douglas who, unlike Hotspur, praises himself; in his not wavering when he learns that his father's army and Glendower's forces are not coming; in his account to Blunt justifying his rebellion, and his prudent willingness to hear the king; in his speeches on the verge of battle which have one kind of manliness, which have dignity, beauty, and warm courtesy, whether or not they are our notions on life, death and war; in his being more modest than the prince in not making a battle boast, although he would be more justified in doing so; and in the tragic loss of his "proud titles," so accepted by the prince whose elegy speaks of Hotspur as a "great heart."

Climax: Although his father's army and Glendower's forces are not coming, and although the king's power enormously outnumbers

his, he, as commander-in-chief of the rebels, decides on battle:
"Doomsday is near. Die all, die merrily."

The fierceness of Hotspur and Douglas succeeds in making
a head against the royal army and it seems as though they
may win as "rebels' arms triumph in massacres," but as Hotspur's "Doomsday is near" showed, they cannot win against
so overpowering a force. It is not the prince's killing of Hotspur that wins the battle. It is perhaps worth adding to this
view of Hotspur as central to the main action of the play
that in 1598 *Henry IV* was regarded as a tragedy by Frances
Meres, a man of representative judgment in that time. Even
if he thought the play a tragedy only because deaths occur,
interest was focussed on Hotspur.

Although the king is not the central character, he does
have a plot-structure; its deuteragonist is Prince Hal, not
Hotspur.

*1. The king, hearing of Hotspur's conquests, laments what his
own son is like.*

*2. The king confronts the prince with his "vile participation,"
rouses him by contrasting him to Hotspur, and, satisfied with his
son's response, gives him "charge [command] and sovereign
trust."*

3. Will his hopes be satisfied?

*Climax: He realizes the prince is his true son when the
prince saves his life.*

In the end it is Hal he chooses to fight by his side against
the devilish Glendower, confirming the "soverign trust" he
gave his son.

For most people Hal is the hero of the play, but he is
not the central character; his plot-structure could not go past
its beginning if it were not for Hotspur's plot-structure.

*1. The prince, whom the world and his father think riotous and
dishonorable, declares that when the time comes he will break through
the clouds of his seemingly dissolute life and be the sun he is.*

*2. Confronted by his father with his "vile participation," accused
of being an enemy to the king, the prince promises that he will
be more himself and redeem his reputation with glory, and for that
promise is given command in the king's forces.*

3. Will he fulfill himself and justify himself to his father?

Climax: He fights successfully showing himself a warlike and true prince by preventing Douglas from killing his father and by winning Hotspur's glory.

These climactic actions, which are two sides of the coin, are very near the end. It would be unusual for a climax of a main plot-structure to be so near the end, but even if Hal is considered central the climax is justifiably so near the end because Part Two is to follow (as implied by the Archbishop of York's action in Act IV, scene iv, which is a preparation against the king should his power defeat Hotspur; the scene exists only to anticipate Part Two, having no causal connection to any of the action of Part One). The play ends with the king dividing his forces to engage the remaining enemies in York and Wales, choosing his son Hal to fight by his side.

If Hal is the hero of the play for most people, Falstaff is the play's greatest creation.

1. Falstaff, whose comic genius and gusto attract the prince, shows the prince that he prefers life to danger and will lie unconscionably.

2. When war erupts, he is given responsibility by the prince for a company of infantry.

3. How will he make out?

Climax: He stabs the dead Hotspur.

He misuses the king's press damnably for his own profit, as he says, but justifies his pitiful infantry to Hal as being able to "fill a pit as well as better." He is no eager fighter and has no use for honor; nonetheless, we find him in the hot places of the battlefield. His company of 150 are nearly all wiped out. Dover Wilson thinks he led them to where they would be killed and then took cover himself in order to collect their pay,[2] but after his company has been nearly wiped out we find him in such dangerous parts of the field as where Hotspur and Hal fight and where he fights with Douglas. When Douglas proves too much of a threat to his life, he "falls down as if he were dead." The prince, after killing Hotspur, "spieth Falstaff on the ground" and says, "I could have better spar'd a better man." That feeling of his prepares us for his reaction to what Falstaff does, his stabbing the dead Hotspur in the thigh and claiming that he killed Hotspur who, like himself, was only down because out of breath. There is something comic in the preposterousness of what he does, but darkly comic, the inverse of the decent. What is likable and admirable in Falstaff is not in his plot-structure.

Not only are there four distinct plot-structures, there are causal connections among actions of the four plot-structures: Hotspur, angered by the king, becomes a rebel. Faced with a war, the king gives his son Hal a high command in the army. Hal, in turn, puts Falstaff in charge of an infantry company. The prince redeems his bad reputation by killing Hotspur and saving his father's life. Falstaff stabs the dead Hotspur and claims reward for having killed him. Thus the four plot-structures are interrelated. The playwright's architectural skill was extraordinary.

Unlike this history play there were many Elizabethan chronicle plays without logically unified plot-structures; they purported to present a sequence of historical actions without dramatic and fictive shaping. Shakespeare, on the other hand, carefully shaped his drama even to the extent of changing the historical facts as narrated in Holinshed, e.g., by making Hotspur (who was killed by a nameless hand) and Hal the same age for dramatic purposes (Hotspur was actually forty and Hal sixteen at the battle of Shrewsbury), and by making Hal save his father's life as the climax of Hal's plot-structure although there was no historical warrant for that. (Hotspur's young age may derive from Samuel Daniel's *The First Fowre Bookes of the Civile Wars Between the Two Houses of Lancaster and Yorke*, 1595; there also Hal saves his father's life, and there it is implied that Hotspur and the prince met in combat on the field but not that Hal killed Hotspur.)

Twelfe Night, Or what you will (1601-2)

Shakespeare may have said "what you will" for the title of this comedy, but he had no such carelessness about its construction. Like *Henry IV, Part One, Twelfth Night* has four interrelated plot-structures.

1. Olivia, wooed by Viola-disguised-as-Cesario for the Duke, is "charm'd" by Viola's "outside."

2. Rejecting the Duke's suit, she declares her love to Viola-Cesario.

3. Will she come to grief?

Climax: She marries Viola's brother Sebastian (an "apple cleft in two is not more twin" than Sebastian and Viola), thinking him Cesario.

The plot-structures for Olivia and Viola overlap, like planes in a Cubist painting.

1. The disguised Viola (who in three days has won extraordinary favor of the Duke) woos Olivia for the sentimental Duke, although she herself is in love with him.

2. She discovers that Olivia has fallen in love with her disguise.

3. Will she be able to make her way through the difficult pass?

Climax: She tells the Duke, "My father had a daughter lov'd a man/ As it might be perhaps, were I a woman,/ I should your lordship."

In the fifth act the Duke, after being rejected harshly by Olivia, says in an anguish he does not wholly understand:

Why should I not, had I the heart to do it,
Like to th' Egyptian thief at point of death,
Kill what I love?—a savage jealousy
That sometimes savors nobly.

The "Egyptian thief" would have killed a captive girl that he loved rather than think anyone else would enjoy her. The Duke's thoughts become "ripe in mischief" to sacrifice the lamb he loves to spite Olivia. The psychology is subtle and true. Viola would "most jocund, apt, and willingly" die a thousand deaths to give him rest. When the Duke learns on the testimony of the priest that Olivia and Viola-Cesario are married, he gives the "dissembling cub" to the Countess, commanding Viola-Cesario never to come near him again. It is at this point that the confusions are set right by Sebastian's appearance. The Duke tells the Countess Olivia, "Be not amazed; right noble is his blood"; and the Duke can recognize his own love for Viola (his passion earlier in the scene purged him of his sentimental love for Olivia) and can understand her climactic declaration of love for him. The Duke embraces the happy Olivia's offer for him to marry Viola in Olivia's house, accepting Olivia "as well a sister as a wife;" and this one day "shall crown th' alliance."

Both these plot-structures are connected to Sir Toby's (Olivia's uncle who lives in her house).

1. Toby persuades the foolish Sir Andrew to send for money to continue his suit of Olivia, the money to be milched by Toby.

2. When Andrew decides to leave because of the favor he saw Olivia bestow on "Cesario," Toby persuades him that it was out of love for him that Olivia so acted and that he should challenge his rival to a duel to show his valor.

3. Will Toby succeed in this device?

Climax: He undertakes Sebastian instead of Viola-Cesario.

The outcome of this plot-structure, thereby, leads to the resolution of Olivia's and Viola's plot-structures, when Sebastian comes to make his apology to Olivia, who is in the presence of the Duke and the seemingly faithless Viola-Cesario, for hurting her kinsman Sir Toby.

Toby is the antagonist in Malvolio's plot-structure. He and Malvolio, Olivia's steward, are temperamentally at odds.

1. Malvolio confronts and threatens Toby, who seizes with delight on the plan of Maria (a gentlewoman in Olivia's service) to make a fool of Malvolio.

2. Malvolio takes the bait, a letter apparently inviting him to undertake a suit to Olivia.

3. Will he suffer in the trap of the conspirators?

Climax: Wooing Olivia as though he were mad, he is put into Toby's charge.

Toby locks him up, and he is tormented by the clever Feste, Olivia's clown, in the guise of a curate for his "madness." At the end Malviolio gets no redress, but is sent after by the Duke to be entreated to peace and for information about the sea-captain who had befriended Viola, "now in durance, at Malvolio's suit." Malvolio's plot-structure is, of course, satirical, one in which the central character is criticized and comes off badly. Malvolio's wooing parallels and contrasts both to Viola-Cesario's wooing of Olivia and to Olivia's wooing of Viola-Cesario-Sebastian. Malvolio, whatever qualities he may possess that commend him to Olivia in his office, is the reverse of being "generous, guiltless, and of free [i.e., noble] disposition," in Olivia's words—the desirability of those qualities in human relations is a main theme of the play.

The Tragedie of Macbeth

If, as in *Henry IV, Part One* and in *Twelfth Night,* Shakespeare is usually Gothic in his multiplicity of structure, he uses, relatively, a classical simplicity of structure in *Macbeth.* Indeed, Richard G. Moulton showed in his *The Ancient Classical Drama* that *Macbeth* could be reconstructed in the form of a classical Greek tragedy.

1. Macbeth, told by the Witches on the heath that he is to be a king of Scotland (their masters know his thoughts, we later learn), wavers between the prompting to murder Duncan and the notion that Chance may crown him.

2. Swayed by his wife's passionate urging, with whom he shared the Weird Sisters' promise of greatness, he murders Duncan to become the king.

3. Will he be able to keep the crown?

Climax: He orders the slaughtering of Macduff's wife and children. That act turns all Scotland against him. Rosse, bringing Macduff the news of the slaughter, says to him, "Your eye in Scotland/ Would create soldiers, make our women fight," and we learn later, as Malcolm says to Macduff near Dunsinane, "Both more and less [i.e., of high and low estate] have given him the revolt,/ And none serve with him but constrained things."

Shakespeare gives Banquo a plot-structure for the sake of fullness of and alignment to his contrast to Macbeth. Both plot-structures begin in the encounter on the heath.

1. Banquo hears the Witches hail Macbeth as king and sees him "start, and seem to fear/ Things that do sound so fair."

2. Asked by Macbeth to cleave to his consent, he says that he will only if he can do so without losing honor and can keep his "bosom franchis'd" (i.e., free from guilt, as Bradley interprets and Muir[3] accepts).

3. Will he survive the jeopardy he has placed himself in?

Climax: although Banquo suspects Macbeth "play'dst most foully" for the crown and knows Macbeth also heard that his posterity and not Macbeth's would be kings of Scotland, he returns from his ride to attend the feast.

The murder of Banquo is one of the "secret murthers" that cause revolts upbraiding Macbeth's "faith-breach."

Banquo's intention at the end of the king's murder scene that the lords investigate the "bloody piece of work" and his taking the lead by saying, "In the great hand of God I stand; and thence/ Against the undivulg'd pretence I fight/ Of Treasonous malice," are forestalled by the flight of Malcolm and Donalbain and the consequent naming of Macbeth as king. There is no breach in his honorableness. When Macbeth requests his presence at the ceremonious supper where Banquo is to be the chief guest, he replies,

> Let your Highness
> Command upon me, to the which my duties
> Are with a most indissoluble tie
> For ever knit.

Although Banquo suspects that Macbeth played foully for the crown, there is no certainty, Macbeth has shown no tyranny yet, nor has he called upon Banquo to lose any honor. The allegiance Banquo promises in his formal and proper words depends on being "clear," as he said earlier, on being unstained. His reply to Macbeth is circumspect. We may accept Macbeth's judgment of him,

> to that dauntless temper of his mind,
> He hath wisdom that doth guide his valor
> To act in safety.

It is that combination of valor and prudence that makes Banquo the only man Macbeth fears. Why Banquo returns from his ride we are not told. If we wish to treat him as a man rather than as a character of whom nothing more can be said than the play shows, we may speculate that he feels he owes allegiance to the elected king so long as that allegiance is clear or that his being the chief guest leads him to think that Macbeth wants his "consent" and he is therefore in no immediate danger.

Although Lady Macbeth has actions crucially affecting Macbeth, her actions do not cohere as a plot-structure. On his arrival at Inverness she asks him to "put/ This night's great business into my dispatch," but he says only, "We will speak further," in Act I, scene v. Two scenes later, after he considers in his soliloquy the consequences of the crime and the reasons not to perform it, he tells his wife "We will proceed no further in this business," but he yields to her passionate and feminine urging. In the next scene, Act II, scene i, he promises Banquo, "If you will cleave to my consent, when 'tis,/ It shall make honour for you"—his mind, that shows, is determined on the murder. After the exchange of words with Banquo, he sees the vision of the dagger which he thinks a reality, so intense in his mind is the act he is ready to commit, and he lets the dagger marshal him to the performance. Duncan's knell rings. Macbeth has taken the deed to himself; he does not act as a result of Lady Macbeth's failing to murder Duncan ("Had he not resembled/ My father as he slept, I had done 't"), that is, her not doing it had no consequence, and therefore the line saying what she would have done does not have a dramatic action as a referent. It is she, however, who returns the daggers to the place of the murder and smears the grooms' faces with blood to make it seem their guilt. In Act III, scene ii, she confirms Macbeth in his mind to kill Banquo. And in the banquet scene she takes control. That is the last we see of her strength and will. She appears only once more, sleepwalking and her mind diseased.

12/ THE MEDIEVAL ACHIEVEMENT

The Wakefield *Second Shepherds' Pageant*
The Brome *Sacrifice of Isaac*
The Hegge *The Woman Taken in Adultery*
The York *Creation* through
The Fall of Man and Others

To say that in Western dramaturgy the syllogistic plot-structure descends from Sophocles is not to say that without his genius such plot-structures might not have been invented. It is truer to say that he was the discoverer of the syllogistic structure rather than its inventor. For logical unity is inherent in dramatic form when language is the essential expressive medium.

Just as there are syllogistic plot-structures in Eastern drama whose playwrights knew nothing of Greek drama, so there are such plot-structures in the medieval English dramatic cycles. Surprisingly (especially as these plays are read mainly in universities) many think the plays of the medieval cycles artless. Hardin Craig, for one, will have it that the medieval "religious drama had no dramatic technique or dramatic purpose, and no artistic self-consciousness"; and again, "When one considers the origin of the mystery plays within the medieval church, an origin without thought of dramatic or histrionic effect, and when one considers also how these plays passed into the hands of very simple medieval people—authors, players, managers, and all—one can see that their technique was inevitably naive and firmly conventional." But there were some four hundred years of development between the origins and maturity of medieval drama; and the plays certainly, as we shall see, are no evidence that the authors were "simple" people.

We can hardly believe the people of the middle ages more simple than people of "primitive" human societies. As Claude Lévi-Strauss observed in the interior of Brazil, the Nambikwara; "little bands of nomads who are among the most genuinely 'primitive' of the world's peoples" have a "lively intelligence." Even a chief, who we might expect would be a man of action, was a man of contemplation "as interested in our own ways, and those of other tribes that I had examined, as I was in his. With him, the anthropologist's work was never one-sided: he saw it as an exchange of information, and always had a cordial welcome for all that I could tell him." Their emotions were no more "primitive" than their intelligence. "There's a delightful gaiety in the spectacle of a mother with her child," and the "relations between father and children are marked by tenderness and solicitude." On another level, "few peoples . . . have so elaborate a system of metaphysics" as the Bororo tribe. "A primitive people," he says flatly elsewhere, "is not a backward or retarded people." Almost all primitive peoples, like the "simple" people of the middle ages, utilize "religious feeling to establish a viable, if not always harmonious, synthesis of individual aspirations and the social order. Nor may we think that the all-pervading magic and religion of primitive life gave those people simple beliefs or simple practices, says Paul Radin: "For aboriginal men, the validity and authenticity of the outside and inward worlds are established by sensory and pragmatic tests." He also tells us that the "vast majority" of aboriginal societies "possess an intricate and, often, a subtle and highly elaborate social, economic and political structure, with secondary developments in the arts, literature, and music, commanding complete respect." As Lévi-Strauss concludes, "man has always been thinking well."[1] He has never been simple.

Many think the medieval plays artless, no doubt, because of medieval conventions that have been almost entirely absent from Western drama since. (The productions being given in England every few years, during summer festivals, may change such notions; for as conventions are concrete to the

physical eye but are thoughts to the mind's eye, they can
seem more real, are more persuasive, in the seeing than in
the reading.) As examples, characters appear anywhere or
anywhen pat as they are needed with no explicable motive
or circumstance; they travel long distances in a few steps;
and most "primitively" they make their vaunt. But such conventions do not make a drama artless or primitive or simplistic; indeed, medieval English plays they appear in are masterly. The conventions we are taking as examples, which
appear in the earliest and latest medieval English plays extant,
are each worth looking at comparatively. They also appear
in acknowledged and sophisticated masterpieces of Greek,
Sanskrit, Japanese, and Chinese drama.

The late play *Everyman* was written towards the end of
the fifteenth century (among the first plays printed for a
reading public, its earliest extant copy dates from 1508). Its
esthetic value as a play is considerable, and it is still both
moving and amusing. Nor is it impaired by the economy
of characters appearing at need. When Everyman learns that
his day of reckoning has come, he thinks only of Fellowship
to turn to, for in him is all of Everyman's trust. No sooner
thought than Everyman can say, "I see him yonder certainly."
When his friend fails him, he believes that his kindred will
give help in his necessity. "Where be you?" he asks, first
of his kinsmen, then of his worldly Goods, then of his Good
Deeds, and they each announce their presence out of
nowhere. When Good Deeds says her sister Knowledge will
help Everyman make his dreadful reckoning, Knowledge
enters. Nor need these appearances trouble anybody; they
are easy to accept in the logic of what unfolds. There is
a similar convention in Aeschylus where, as Kitto observes
in *Form and Meaning in Drama,* the "actors keep their distance
from each other; they do not, in general, explain their com-
ings and goings, like characters who are seen against a more
naturalistic background." There is an exact parallel to the
convention in *Everyman* in the surviving comic masterpiece
of the Sanskrit drama, the *Little Clay Cart.* A character
announces, "I shall go to look for Carudatta. *(He advances,
looking about.)* There he comes now!"

In the sophisticated writing of the *Second Shepherds' Pageant,* from the Wakefield cycle,* in a version composed in the fifteenth century in a complex nine-line stanza with realism, liveliness, and warmth, the Wakefield Master (who composed five of the plays) uses the convention of a character walking a few steps to cover a considerable distance. The thief Mak, having stolen a sheep, makes it home to his wife from the fields in about twenty quick words and then makes it back with equal indifference to space in order to pretend to have slept all the while with the snoring shepherds. We have already met a similar convention in the *michiyuki,* or travelling song, of the Noh drama of Japan. These brief songs descriptive of a journey are sung while the character walks slowly across the stage, and end typically with a line saying "the journey has been so fast that I am already at Miyako" (or whatever the place). We may take another example from the *Little Clay Cart:* "Well, let's go home and see if my wife has prepared any food. *(He walks about.)* Here's my house; let's go in." And again, Carudatta and Vasantasena leave his house to go to hers. He speaks a few lines descriptive of the night. *"(They walk about.)* Lady Vasantasena, we have reached your house. Do you wish to enter?" At an American production of this play the audience never even noticed that it was accepting the conventions once the comedy was a little under way.

In the St. George folk plays a convention appears that seems simplistic by nature—the vaunt.

> *Enter Prince George.* I am Prince George, a worthy knight;
> I'll spend my blood for England's right.
> England's right I will maintain;
> I'll fight for old England once again.
> *Enter Turkish Knight.* I am the Turkish Champion;
> From Turkey's land I come.
> I come to fight the King of England
> And all his noble men.

---

* The cycles are generally named for the city in which they were performed, sometimes for the owner of a manuscript. The plays in a complete cycle are a chronicle of universal history.

The vaunts, of course, prepare us for a strife. George boasts of having killed the fiery dragon; the Turkish Champion taunts him with being a fool for wearing a wooden sword. The Turk is a "dirty dog" for saying so; the sword is made of the best metal. They fight and Prince George is killed. The King of England summons a noble doctor, who revives the prince. It *is* a simple play (as are the other versions of this folk play), but not because of the vaunt as a convention. In the first play of the York cycle, which tells of the creation and of the fall of Lucifer, God vaunts. His opening two lines are in Latin, *I am Alpha and Omega, the life, the way, the truth, the first and the last;* and then in English,

I am gracious and great, God without a beginning;
I am maker unmade, all might is in me . . .

Few are likely to think these lines simplistic. Far different is the vaunt of Herod in the relatively late Coventry *Herod and the Three Kings,* which is artfully used to betray his mania for greatness. The Herald commands the barons, knights, and gentlemen to be quiet and pay deference to their noble king, who is present. (It is easier to assume that the Herald is talking to the audience—an example of making the play intersect contemporary actuality—than to extras in the cast.) Then Herod speaks.

I am the mightiest conqueror that ever walked on ground;
For I am even he that made both heaven and hell
And of my mighty power I hold up this world round.

The true mightiest conqueror, of course, is the child born twelve days earlier. The pre-Christian deity Poseidon begins *The Trojan Women* by saying,

I am the sea god. I have come
up from the salt sea depths of the Aegean . . .

And later in the play King Menelaus vaunts,

                    I am Menelaus,
the man of many wrongs.
I came to Troy and brought with me my army . . .

The brilliant Oedipus concludes the first speech of Sophocles' play with "I ... have come hither myself, I, Oedipus, renowned of all." The greatest of Sanskrit dramatists, Kalidasa, uses the vaunt. In the Noh drama name-saying by a character is so much a convention that the *shite* pillar is also called the "name-saying" pillar because that is where it is always done. And we have seen that characters in Chinese drama may iterate their names again and again, at successive appearances, like a leitmotif. So much, then, for this "primitive" convention of the vaunt.

"The history of the theater shows us," reflects Thornton Wilder, "that in its greatest ages the stage employed the greatest number of conventions. . . .

"The convention has two functions:
1. It provokes the collaborative activity of the spectator's imagination; and
2. It raises the action from the specific to the general.

"This second aspect is of even greater importance than the first."[2]

Disproving the "primitiveness" of conventions which, it may be, have chiefly prevented the medieval cycles from coming into their own as a great body of dramatic literature does not argue that they are therefore great works. There are other matters to consider, e.g., the medieval literary commonplaces in the plays, the characters who are typical, the versification, but with the possible exception of the last on which much work has been done to not enough avail, these matters are not the obstacle that the conventions are. Although the plays are unquestionably uneven, I believe that the play cycles are great works as self-contained and self-sustaining dramas, without reference to their theologic motive. But this is not the place to try critically to demonstrate their literary value. In any case the artifice of the syllogistic plot-structure, although not always used, was quite within the grasp of the medieval playwrights, whose artistry was accomplished.

The maturely formed drama of the Wakefield Master's *Second Shepherds' Pageant*,[3] composed some time earlier than the mid-15th century, came a long way from the simple Latin dialogue presented at Christmas in a church in France four

centuries earlier. Persons at the manger talk with the
shepherds:

Whom do you seek at the manger, shepherds? Speak.

Christ the Savior, the infant Lord wrapped in swaddling
clothes, as the words of the angel say.

The child is here with his mother Mary, of whom the prophet
Isaiah spoke long ago, prophesying, "Behold a virgin shall conceive
and bear a son." Now as you go forth, say that he is born.

Hallelujah, hallelujah! Now we truly know that Christ is born
in the world. Of him let us all sing, saying with the prophet, A
child is born.

Here is the Wakefield play's plot-structure, somewhat
elaborated.

*1. The beginning of change: Having complained of the winter's
cold, of the injustices done against them, and of other disharmony
and discontents, and having sung for some comfort, the three weary
shepherds fall asleep after Mak comes although they know he is
a thief.*

*2. The middle: After awakening, although they find him apparently
asleep and he protests his innocence, they go to their sheep and
find one missing.*

*3. To be settled by the end: Will they secure justice and recover
the lost sheep?*

*Climax: Mak and his wife having fooled the shepherds into believ-
ing that the sheep is a newborn child and the shepherds having
left his house, the youngest shepherd, Daw, returns to give the little
day-star a gift, for, he complains to the other two, "Fair words
there may be" for Mak's innocence, but "love there is none/ This
year./ Gave ye the child anything?"*

The theft discovered, Mak begs for mercy. Daw says let them
not kill or curse or chide Mak, and they only toss him in
a blanket. Tired again by the events of the night, the three
shepherds fall asleep. So ends the first part of the play, and
a second part follows, a kind of sequel. An Angel appears
in their sleep. His speech, announcing the birth and God's
command that they go to Bethlehem, begins, "Rise,
shepherds, have joy," and he marvellously sings a Glorie
(which a shepherd with a poor voice tries to imitate only

to be a comical failure). At the crib they worship the child and give him simple but touching gifts, wrap a cloak around the little cold child, and rejoice, singing as the play ends. It is the morning and springtime of the world. Their capacity for love and mercy, seen in the first part, makes them deserve what happens in the sequel.

The beautiful and poignant Brome *Sacrifice of Isaac* preserved in a fifteenth-century manuscript but composed a century earlier also has a plot-structure.

1. Abraham, who loves nothing except God as much as he loves his son Isaac, and who has prayed to God that no ill come to his child, is told by an Angel that God commands him to sacrifice the child.

2. Although he loves God more than Isaac, his conscience is stirred against God; and when the child expresses fear of his drawn sword, Abraham's heart is torn.

3. Will he kill the child or disobey God?

Climax: He is told by the child that there is no other way but to do God's bidding.

But when Abraham raises his sword, there is a reversal. The Angel suddenly appears and takes the sword in his hand. (God, as we know from the brief prologue in which the Angel speaks to the congregation, has been testing whether Abraham loves God enough more than young Isaac to make the sacrifice.) The Angel provides a ram for the sacrifice, but for a while the boy cannot believe that he has been spared. God promises Abraham and Isaac that he shall multiply their seed and that of them "shall come fruit unknown." The sacrifice of the ram prefigures the sacrifice of Christ and Abraham's willingness to sacrifice his son prefigures God's.

Before giving the plot-structure of *The Woman Taken in Adultery,* from the Hegge cycle (the latest of the medieval cycles), it would be well to tell the story briefly. Jesus preaches to the audience, setting mercy against the law. Against his preaching the scribe and pharisee react with strong passions. The accuser, who takes pleasure in the sport, gives them their game: to take "the fair young queen ... fresh and gay" and the "tall man" who with her "doth mell" even now. The scribe and the pharisee at once see the trap they can lay: either Jesus must not preach mercy and show himself unstable, or he must violate Moses' law that ordains death by stoning for adultery. They break open the door to the woman's house, and the young man comes running out comically, holding up his breeches. Although himself scared, he threatens them with a dagger, and being cowardly they let him go (their cowardice is pertinent at the climax). With powerful and vile language they call out the woman. She begs for mercy; that not granted, she asks to be killed privily so that slander may not shame her friends (thereby revealing a character that makes possible the verity of her repentance later). They say, "Against the law shall we thee kill?" and they take her to Jesus, whom they confront for a judgment for he is a wise prophet. Jesus says nothing, but writes on the ground. The woman asks for mercy—she has great repentance in her heart for her abominable sins—although she knows she deserves death and shame. The three men press Jesus to speak his thought: shall she be stoned, according to the law, or not? Jesus gives his well-known response and goes on writing. The three men separate "as if put to shame." They have seen their own sins written on the ground and are fearful of exposure (what Jesus was writing, the Bible does not say). In shame they leave Jesus and the woman. No man has condemned her, nor will Jesus. She will henceforth "try to be God's true servant."

Here is the plot-structure:

1. Jesus' teaching of mercy against the law makes enemies of the scribe and pharisee.

2. He is confronted by them with a seemingly inescapable trap.

3. Will he have to deny his own teaching of mercy or violate Moses' law?

Climax: He writes the men's sins on the ground.

They are therefore afraid to cast the first stone, and as none has condemned the woman Jesus can grant mercy without violating the law.

The York* *Crucifixion* has no such plot-structure; its events are presented as chronicle. Pilate exonerates Jesus, saying that his examination showed no cause to destroy Jesus; but he has given Jesus to destruction, and Annas and Caiaphas justify their having had him tried and condemned, exulting in their triumph over the false one, the braggart who boasted he was God's son but cannot save himself. Then Jesus speaks from the cross to man, whose bliss he must buy full bitterly. Mary weeps for the doleful death of her Lord, a bright blossom untruly tugged to the tree, hanging there as a thief. Jesus tells her not to weep, for John will be her son in his stead. The thief on the left would have him, if he is God's son, save himself and them. The thief on the right tells the other to stint of his sound; they two are worthy of ill, but no ill did he to die so, who is their Lord. Jesus will take him to paradise that day, since he falls from his folly. Jesus thirsts. A boy prepares him a drink of vinegar of gall. Jesus commends his spirit to his Father and dies. Mary and John leave. Pilate would have the blind Sir Longeus thrust a spear into Jesus' side. But Jesus gives him his sight and he knows that Jesus is God, that he has spilt his blood to bring man bliss, and that his mercy is marked in giving Longeus sight. A centurion says that it is God's very son who died by the law unrightly. Joseph of Arimathea prays that the true Lord may save Pilate and let Pilate give him Jesus' body for burial. Pilate grants the gest. Nichodemus, whom Jesus called to be his, gives Joseph aid to take Jesus down from the cross and has brought myrrh and aloes to anoint the wounded body. They pray to their Savior.

What happened then to Jesus on Calvary is happening again in the present tense of the drama, which seems not a play but a reality to its Yorkshire audience, and its meaning is in that reality rather than in the artifice of fictive shaping, that is to say, its value is wholly religious, and that is why

---

* The one complete manuscript of the York cycle that exists was made about the middle of the fifteenth century, and it shows that the plays, first written about a hundred years earlier, were revised in the course of the century. By 1415, as a contemporary record shows, the York plays were a major cycle.

the structure of the drama is that of a chronicle presenting
the events as they were on Calvary and as they are in York,
with Jesus saying from the cross to the Yorkshiremen that
they mend their mood for the bliss he is purchasing and
Joseph saying that again to the Yorkshiremen in the last
lines.

It is worth a moment's digression to say that the Wakefield
Crucifixion is grimmer. Torturers drag Jesus bearing the cross
to Calvary. There they fasten him to the cross with realistic
detail, mocking him for not being able to save himself, speaking of him on the cross as though he were a king riding
a palfrey in a joust, holding down his knees better than nurse
ever did to fix his legs in place, calling on spectators to help
raise the cross (again the crucifixion seems contemporary
and actual), giving him the crown of thorns and drink of
vinegar. There is similar cruelty, portraying men at their
worst, in the York *Second Trial before Pilate*. At the climax
of that play the wavering Pilate hears that Jesus claims to
be king and so commands that Jesus be scourged for treason.
The knights, in the extended scene of scourging, are brutal
and take pleasure in the brutality. When Jesus loses consciousness, they revive him to torture and taunt him more, with
scorn and contempt and laughter. Our pity and terror are
intense.

There are medieval plays without syllogistic plot-structures
because they are so short they scarcely have time enough
for such a structure, nor do they need one for their unity.
They do little more than present an incident together with
only few matters connected to the incident. The incidents,
of course, were of the greatest moment in the beliefs of their
medieval audience, and still may command interest whether
as religion or literature. Two such plays are the Hegge *Parliament of Heaven; and Annunciation and Conception* and the York
Birth of Christ.

In the *Parliament of Heaven* Contemplation in prologue
prays to God to save mankind. There follows a parliament
of heaven. The four Virtues, daughters of God, are the
pleaders; Truth and Justice accusing Man of having offended
God and therefore deserving of endless punishment, Mercy

setting forth Man's grieving and frailty and God's endless
mercy, Peace wanting the Virtues not to be in dissension nor
God and Man forever in division. Peace advises that they
put the matter to God's high wisdom, and they agree. (The
sisters make vaunts and say their names, as "Lord, I am
thy daughter Truth,/ That shall last without an end" or
"Mercy . . . You know well I am your sister Justice./ God
is righteous and righteousness [justice] loveth.") Gabriel
appears and speaks God's word: Adam died that truth and
righteousness be not violated; to restore mercy and peace
a second Adam must die, and so let the Virtues search for
a man without sin for only such can make the sacrifice. *"Truth,
Justice and Mercy search and return."* They could find neither
a man without sin nor a man with charity and love enough
to die. Peace advises that they beseech God to give himself.
They hear the voices of the Trinity each speak, saying what
will be and how it will be. Which makes a "loveday" for the
four sisters, who leave singing Psalm 85, "Mercy and Truth
are met together." In the next part, a sequel, Gabriel makes
the annunciation to Mary. After the annunciation the passage
has a measure of dramatic tension: Mary does not know
how it can be done, and Gabriel tells her to hasten to a
decision, for the Holy Ghost and all the chosen souls in Limbo
are desiring to hear her answer, desiring her assent to the
Incarnation. She makes her answer, Gabriel gives her thanks,
and the conception is represented. *"Now the Holy Ghost descends
with three beams to our lady; the Son of God next with three beams
to the Holy Ghost; the Godly Father with three beams to the Son;
and so enter all three to her bosom."* In the thirty eight-line stanzas
(there are some variations in the stanzas) there is a causal
sequence but not a syllogistic plot-structure. The parliament
takes its theatrical power from the debate, much as modern
courtroom trial dramas can hold an audience. The dramatic
power in the sequel comes from the audience's realization
that Mary must make a decision, from Gabriel's extended
plea which sustains the tension, and from the representation
of the conception (we do not know how it was done).

   The *Birth of Christ* is even shorter, only 154 lines. Joseph
prays to God for good harbor; they have none in the press

of the town, the walls of the stable they are in have fallen
and the roof is ruined. He turns to Mary, who advises that
it is God's will that they stay where they are for the birth.
It is dark and cold. Joseph wants to get light and warmth,
and while he is out looking for fuel Mary speaks to God
and the child is born. Outside in the terrible cold Joseph
is astonished by a light shining suddenly. He returns to Mary
and sees the sweet child. Mary says that God ordained a
star to be shining at the birth of her son, as the prophet
Balaam foretold. Mary lays the child in a crib between two
beasts; and Joseph marvels at their mild and loving manner,
as though they were men and knew their Lord. Mary says
that they do know him and are worshipping him, and are
warming him with their breath against the cold. Joseph
remembers that the prophet Habakkuk said the Savior would
lie between beasts. Joseph binds himself to God's service,
and then Mary does, beseeching God's blessing on "us all
now here." Again, the chronicle is happening now even as
it did then; the birth is being re-presented rather than represented, and the "us all now here" includes the medieval
audience as well as the holy family. The brief account of
the play can give nothing of its simple beauty and poetry,
which are its appeal and which, together with the momentous-
ness of the birth which can be felt in the play even by many
for whom it is myth and not actuality, can sustain the attention
of the audience. The brevity of the play is artistically right
and precludes a plot-structure, which would have got in the
way of its beautiful simplicity.

Plays so short as these in the York cycle were also constructed to form a larger, more complex whole that does have
a plot-structure. The York cycle begins with *The Creation,
and the Fall of Lucifer*. It is worth noting that this play uses
the sophisticated technique of symbolism, iterating images
of filth and fading. The second play shows God alone, who
by the might of his voice effects the work of the first five
days of creation. The next three plays—*The Creation of Adam
and Eve, The Garden of Eden,* and *The Fall of Man*—take under
four hundred lines, nonetheless have complexity enough and

need for a plot-structure. The three plays are, indeed, three acts of a logically unified play.

1. Newly created, Adam and Eve, recognizing the wonder of the world and their own pre-eminence in it, speak their love, obedience, and worship to God.

2. Given lordship of the earth and Paradise as a dwelling place, they are instructed by God in how to live there and how to rule and sustain the world, which are to be their endeavor.

3. Will they be able to live in Paradise and sustain the world?

Climax: They disobey God, succumbing to the temptation of being his peers.

The consequence is, God tells them, their expulsion from Paradise and the necessity to live lives in which their whole labor will be to sustain themselves. (It is interesting that in the cycle's first play while other angels regarded their Lord, offering love and worship, Lucifer could see only his own perfections and power and succumbed to the temptation he used against man, "I shall be like unto him that is highest on height"; it is interesting, too, that in *The Fall of Man* Satan is given a motive for his rebellion, that he saw Godhead clearly and perceived God would take the nature of an order of created beings other than the angelic and so Lucifer was angry, thinking himself disdained, and he also became envious of man.) The sixth play is the sequel, which shows an Angel driving Adam and Eve from Eden. Adam, he says, will have to till the earth, sweating and laboring; Eve will bear children with pain. Adam and Eve quarrel, each blaming the other for the loss of their gladness and plenty between prime of day, when they awakened innocent in Paradise, and noontime, when their willful act changed bliss to misery and shame.

13/ PLAY PREMISES AND
AUDIENCE RESPONSE
Calderón's *The Surgeon of His Honour*
Chikamatsu's *The Love Suicides at Amijima*

Not all people who are nominally Christian believe in the God who begins the York cycle; indeed, not all practicing Christians do. Very few people believe in the existence of the Greek gods (they are not altogether dead in Greece). But such matters as the presence of God and angels and devils, or of Poseidon and Athena, even when they are believed not to exist in the actual world, are not conventions. They are, rather, premises of the world of the play, and premises may differ from age to age or country to country just as conventions do. One thinks readily of other supernatural premises: the witches in *Macbeth,* the ghosts in Zeami's plays. Of the witches and ghosts it may be said that we suspend our disbelief; yet it seems truer to our experience that we accept those existences as real. Or, to leave the supernatural, we may consider value premises, such as *honor* in Calderón or *obligation* in Chikamatsu. Premises are easier to accept as realities in the world of a play—whether as literal existences (say, angels or gods) or as powerful motives (say, the values in Calderón and Chikamatsu), whether they are familiar or unfamiliar, and whether they seem fictive or actual—than are unfamiliar conventions. There is no difficulty, of course, in accepting familiar conventions, such as the convention that the actors do not know that the audience is out there. It is easy enough to see how the literal existence of the archangel Gabriel or the sea god Poseidon is a premise of a play rather than a convention, and nothing further need be said about that. But to make clearer the reference to value premises that act as powerful motives, it may be well to show *honor* and *obligation* at work in plays. The emotional values of honor in Calderón's *The Surgeon of His Honour* and of obligation in Chikamatsu's *The Love Suicides at Amijima* do not exist in our actual experience, and we may doubt that they ever existed in any actual experience. Although these emotional values are not ours, they are capable of being accepted as immediate and real to us, not simply as something that may have existed in other cultures.

To a modern audience the premise of honor in Calderón must seem extreme; yet it can be accepted because it is so skillfully fitted to the rest of the play logically and psychologically. Here is what happens in *The Surgeon of His Honour* (1635).[1] I give the Spanish play and the Japanese one in detailed summary because, as the reader will find, the *texture* of the plays is just as important as the structure in creating and making credible the value premises.

Act I. There is a sound of galloping and Prince Don Henry falls as if from a horse and then cries, "Christ save me!" The meanings of the fall and of the words are suspended in the play. His brother King Pedro is vexed at this hindrance to his course and rides on to Seville. Henry's companion, Arias, exclaims, "This shows his fierce and cruel disposition—/ To leave a brother in the arms of death." From a nearby villa Doña Mencía has seen the fall; her description of the cavalier riding and his mishap shows her deeply attracted to him even before she knows who he is. (Before her marriage the prince courted her and she returned his love; but when he had to go away on duty and her father, she thought, was going to put her in a convent, she married Don Gutierre.) When Henry is carried to her house, only her respect for her honor restrains her from giving way to grief; and she realizes that "virtue only can be proved by trial." The prince, learning of her marriage, in a passion ignores his injury and calls for his horse. To Gutierre he invents a story analogous to his, the prince's, own to explain his unrest and jealousy; Doña Mencía suggests that the woman in the story (who is Doña Mencía) could perhaps excuse herself. Gutierre presents the prince with a fine mare to ride. Gutierre's servant Coquín jokes, the jollity endearing him to the prince. After the prince's departure, Gutierre expresses his love and asks his wife leave to go to pay homage to the king and attend the prince. Mencía accuses him of wanting to visit Leonor, a former love (the psychology is subtle), and ambiguously gives him leave to go.

In the Alcazar the king responds swiftly and generously to petitioners. Leonor implores the king to make Gutierre pay for her sustenance and upkeep in a convent, as her honor cannot be restored now that he is married. The king promises justice but must hear Gutierre's side. He has her hide behind a screen at Gutierre's approach. His jesting servant Coquín comes in first; the king, unlike the prince, takes no pleasure in the *gracioso*. The king forces a cruel pact on the jester. If Coquín can make him laugh—it is said the king never laughs—the king will give him gold each time; if he fails for a month, all his teeth will be drawn. Coquín thinks the king will have to laugh at the month's end when he sees how ruefully the jester studies the old age in his toothless mouth. Gutierre makes a restrained defense of himself, not wishing to say a word against Leonor's honor, but in face of the king's anger says that he saw a man leaping from Leonor's balcony. Leonor comes out to deny the accusation, and the king is pleased with the apparent success of his device, thinking Gutierre was practicing a deception. It turns out that there was a man, Don Arias, visiting another lady in the house (who later died); he says he fled not to prejudice Leonor's position, and is ready to fight in defense of her name. The king is angry when the two men grasp their hilts and orders them imprisoned. Gutierre is more vexed that he will not be able to see his wife than by the king's rigor.

Act II. The prince steals into Mencía's garden, pleading that she has told him to give her a hearing. She is dismayed that he is there (although confessing her fault in the matter). Gutierre comes, full of love. His jailer has given him liberty for the night. She makes the prince hide and by a trick effects his escape, but Gutierre finds a dagger. (In a brief scene Coquín says he will have nothing to do with honor; he prefers life.) Gutierre hides his suspicion and shame, and alone addresses his honor as though it had a personal existence.

In the Alcazar the king speaks of walking the city at night to observe things as they are and of having routed a gang of "gallants." Coquín cannot make him laugh, and complains that he

is unnatural. The prince has begged of the king the forfeit lives
of Gutierre and Arias, who are released from prison. Gutierre
recognizes the prince's sword as matching the dagger he has found,
and makes an ambiguous warning that the prince is alert to. In
a long monologue (nearly a hundred lines), Gutierre, enraged and
sorrowing, tries to excuse his wife's actions as possibly innocent
and to think the matching of the sword and dagger accidental.
Torn, he resolves to take remedies against the sickness endangering
his honor. He will dissemble his anguish, returning to his house
to make further diagnosis.

(A scene between Arias and Leonor, although it bears on the
theme of honor, comes to nothing in the action of the play.)

Now it is Gutierre's turn to steal into his garden, thinking
his suspicions vile; but he must clear away his doubts. He disguises
his voice and awakens his sleeping wife. At first he is full of joy
at her responses, believing her faithful, until she addresses his
figure in the night as "Your Highness" and angrily says that the
prince thinks he can hide again and have her play the same trick
for his escape. Gutierre, shaken, misunderstands what she says,
and in a fiery rage turns his mind to vengeance. He leaves and
returns in his own person, dissimulating delight while with double
meanings hinting at his purposes. She thinks he must be jealous.
No, he says, but if he felt the slightest twinge of jealousy (whatever
it may be like), even the least suspicion of a slave, he would tear
her heart out with his hands and wolf it raw and drink the blood.
He catches himself, and apologizes to Mencía, his dearest love,
for his derangement and excess. But she knows that she has heard
the rattle of her death.

Act III. Gutierre craves a private audience with the king. In
speaking he weeps for the only two things that do not cause a
man scandal for his tears, love and honor. He supplicates for justice
against Henry, not that he knows for certain the prince has infected
his honor but that the least cause for suspicion, even if only
imagined, calls one who lives for honor to act. If there actually
were treachery, only blood could wash away the offense—

No, do not start, your Majesty! I mean
The blood of my own flesh: not yours, not yours!
That Henry's royal blood is safe with me
Rest well assured.

And he gives the king the prince's dagger as witness to the prince's
safety. The prince comes, and the king adopts the device he used

with Leonor, letting Gutierre hide behind the screen. When the king warns his brother not to pursue Mencía, Henry claims to be the affronted one, having loved the girl before she married. The king, vexed that Gutierre is hearing this—for it is more than Gutierre knows and creates a "frightful quandry"—accuses the prince of inventing an excuse and shows the dagger as proof of guilt. The prince, receiving the dagger from the king, accidentally cuts his brother's hand. The king believes it purposeful, and the prince, not to be suspected of aiming at his brother's life, resolves to go to a distant place, and in his confusion drops the dagger before he leaves. The king sees a vision of himself dead, and prays that what has happened be not the cause of the land being deluged with blood.

Gutierre has heard too much. The prince's dagger will be the instrument of his wife's death. As the affront is secret, the vengeance must also be secret so that he does not proclaim his own dishonor.

But would that pitying heaven would first take
My life, before I come to do the deed,
So that I do not have to see or feel
The tragic end of such a luckless love!

In his house Mencía has come to realize that it was her husband, not the prince, she spoke to in the garden; and when Coquín comes with the news that the prince is going into exile, she interprets it to mean that her name will be bandied in the streets as the cause. She takes the advice, as the lesser of two evils, to write the prince asking him not to go. Gutierre breaks in on her writing, seizes the letter only just begun which says, "Your Highness, do not go away—" It is decisive. Because he loves her, he gives her two hours to save her soul.

Gutierre brings a leech blindfolded to his house and forces him at the point of the dagger to bleed his veiled wife to death; he will then allege the bandages became undone by accident. He intends, too, to kill the leech but is intercepted by the king who is following his custom of walking the streets; Gutierre escapes without being recognized. The king hears the monstrous story from the leech, who marked the house for recognition with bloody handprints. Coquín finds the king in the streets and tells of Gutierre's having been deceived by false appearances—may the king liberate Mencía from death. The king repays Coquín's loyalty by making him free of the pact, saying, "For laughter/ This is no season." And the jester cries, "No! When was it ever?"

The king uses a pretext to enter Gutierre's house. On the door he sees the bloody handprints and knows what Gutierre has done, but reflects,

I do not well know how to act, so cunningly
And cautiously he settled his affront.

(As he has the proof of Gutierre's guilt, he must mean that the secret vengeance conceals his brother's stain on the royal honor as well as Gutierre's fancied dishonor and is swayed by his self-interest. He is a man generous and just, cruel and unjust.)

Gutierre emerges from his house, crying out the tragic accident; nor need we think his grief altogether feigned. The king decides on prudence, controlling his feelings stirred up by the "cruel and most terrible revenge." He insists, ironically, on consolation for so great a grief: Gutierre will marry Leonor. Gutierre does not want to, but the king commands the marriage, refusing to listen privately to excuses—Gutierre, he says, credited base suspicions, and he reveals, too, only to Gutierre, that he knows what has been done. The bloodstained hand on the door, Gutierre replies, is a sign of the business of his honor, which "can only be washed in blood." He warns Leonor that the hand he is giving her is stained with blood, and in the concluding speech to the audience says,

Pardon its many errors, my good friends.

The action of the play is a significant whole. Here is the main plot-structure.

1. The beginning of change: Gutierre, who loves his wife and who lives for honor, discovers in the dagger reason to suspect cause for an affront to his honor by the king's brother.

2. The middle: Putting his wife to the test, he is led by false appearances to certainty of the affront.

3. To be settled by the end: Will he be able to redeem his honor?

Climax: He so cunningly has her killed, concealing the affront, that the king for the sake of royal honor does not execute justice.

There is another plot-structure for Mencía, whose psychology is interesting. Although innocent in deed if not in thought and feeling, her own deceits bring on her death.

1. Married to a man of honor, she suggests to the prince, her former lover, that she can justify herself.

2. In the consequent interview, surprised by her husband she uses a deception so that the prince can escape.

3. Will she be able to keep her husband from suspecting her?

Climax: In the garden scene she addresses her husband as "Your Highness" (later she nails down her own coffin with the letter she begins to write to the prince).

It has been said that the "generic characteristic of the Spanish drama is, of course, the fact that it is essentially a drama of action and not of characterization" and that the "significant whole" of the action "discloses a theme that has a significant bearing on experience." We could almost conclude, then, that the honor theme of the play was a kind of moral lesson. Moreover, the honor theme was typical of the *comedia* (the generic term for the plays of the Spanish golden age; it does not mean comedy). The "whole ideological system of the *comedia*" was built on honor and faith. We are now concerned with honor, which "upholds the individual as a social being," his honor being a matter both of his own dignity and his reputation. If honor is lost, the act of restoring it is a duty, even a ritual, involving the sacrifice of a victim to society. The form of the Spanish *comedia* may have been "created, primarily by Lope de Vega, to symbolize the communal feeling of the Spanish people." But there is, nonetheless, this question to ask. Did the honor plays reflect the actual values of the society? C. A. Jones, who has most closely studied this matter, is "not at all sure of the accuracy of the claim that Lope . . . reflected in his theatre the social system of contemporary Spain." It was Lope who established the theme of honor in the Spanish *comedia,* but his nondramatic works show reservations about the code, and when a gallant eloped with his daughter he did not try to take the vengeance the code called for. The code "although not entirely divorced from reality or morals, is closely concerned with neither of these things . . . it is bound up with the popular entertainment of the time." Manuals for confessors thought life more important than honor (which is the realistic point of view of the *gracioso* Coquín in our play), although they grant that reputation is better than all other earthly possessions. As a practical motive in the plays, "Honour was a strong social force, which in the close society portrayed in the plays, could not help exercising a good deal of pressure on persons and make them act in an interesting, exciting and sometimes moving way."[2]

We may conclude, then, that honor if not an actual motive in daily life, except in sporadic cases, was a critical enough matter in the mentality of the place and time for the audiences immediately to accept honor as a motive on which situations turned and by which characters acted. They would easily have understood the secrecy with which Gutierre acted, for otherwise his reputation, an aspect of his honor, would have been smirched. Just as in logic conclusions follow from premises, so in a play actions follow from premises, in this play from the premises of honor.

A question still remains. If honor is not the vital matter in our mentality that it was for the audiences of Lope and Calderón, how is it that we can respond to the play? I have already said that the premise of honor is an harmonious part of the logical design of the play. But before attempting the problem further, let us consider the premise of obligation in *The Love Suicides at Amijima* (1721),[3] which in the eyes of many is Chikamatsu's masterpiece.

Act I. Scene One: A Street in Sonezaki New Quarter, Osaka; Time: November 4, 1720. The Narrator begins with apparently meaningless syllables in a lively rhythm. His first words are, "The love of a prostitute is deep beyond measure; it's a bottomless sea of affection that cannot be emptied or dried." The licensed quarters were prominent in city life, and the relations of townsmen with prostitutes were socially acceptable. The great courtesan was a cultivated woman, somewhat like the *hetaira* of ancient Greece or like the courtesan of Venice who, the Elizabethan traveler Thomas Coryat wrote, enchants with her voice and lute and is an "elegant discourser." But she is crafty, and if you try not to pay her after "conversing [in Elizabethan England "conversation" also had the meaning of intercourse], she will have her ruffian cut your throat." In Venice in the late Renaissance even ordinary prostitutes enjoyed good regard, but in Japan the common prostitute at, say, a bathhouse, enjoyed no more regard than the common prostitutes at bathhouses in medieval Europe and were commonly thought to be without feeling for their customers. Koharu, the heroine of this play, has been "graduated from the smock of a bath attendant in the South to the garments of love in the New Quarter"—not likely because of a "bottomless sea of affection." Nonetheless, we are to accept the opening words as a major premise of the play. Her bounty, like Juliet's, "is as boundless as the sea," her "love as deep." Her only craftiness is meant to serve honorable ends as we shall see.

The Narrator gives a lively picture of men roaming the streets of the houses in the New Quarter and of a servant of one of the houses pouncing on a valuable customer and dragging him along. (This little incident is an example of something happening which is not a dramatic action in that it has no consequence; it is textural, and is in the play for the mood of the Quarter, so different from the tone of the lovers' story.) "Among the flowers on display," the Narrator chants while the puppets mime, "is Koharu of the Kinokuni House." Then comes a death motif, iterated skillfully in the play. "Is her name 'Second Spring' [literally "little spring," i.e., Indian summer] a sign that she is fated to leave behind a fleeting name in November?" Another prostitute encountering Koharu twits her that her master examines all of her customers to make certain it is not Jihei because of whom scarcely any business comes to her; the prostitute has also heard that Koharu is to be ransomed by Tahei to be his wife. Tonight Koharu has a samurai for a customer, and is worried that she might meet the dreadful Tahei. A street minstrel is not far off, singing a song about a love suicide, "mixing his nonsense with the burden of a hymn" to Amida Buddha, whose Western Paradise reckons importantly in the play. Tahei is in the crowd surrounding the minstrel.

Scene Two: The Kawachi House, a Sonezaki Teahouse. Koharu slips away into the Kawachi House, where the proprietress welcomes her loudly and Tahei, who is outside and overhears, breaks in. He mocks Jihei's paper business as about to collapse; his, Tahei's, money will win out, and he will have her tonight. He sings a burlesque prayer to Amida Buddha, again mocking Jihei who is "like scrap paper/ You can't even blow your nose on." As he is prancing and roaring, he sees a man at the gate whose face is covered with a wicker hat, and thinking it is "Toilet Paper" (Jihei) drags in the customer, who is the samurai. The samurai "patiently endures the

fool" and Tahei swaggers off. Koharu, depressed by Tahei, annoys
the samurai; he has not come to a teahouse to play the part of
a nursemaid. The proprietress explains that it is Koharu's love
for Jihei that interferes with her entertaining properly. Koharu,
weeping, asks the samurai if those who die in the Ten Nights (a
special religious period during which Acts II and III take place)
become Buddhas. He brusquely tells her to ask the priest. Then
she asks whether suicide by cutting the throat or by hanging is
the more painful. He has never tried either. The Narrator chants
that Jihei and Koharu have sworn that if they can meet again,
they will end their lives together; and he is now distractedly trudging
to the Quarter. Jihei hears gossip that Koharu has a samurai customer, and decides he must act tonight. Looking through the latticework window, he weeps to see her pale face and at his need
to be silent because the samurai customer is there. The samurai
says that it is clear she intends suicide, an act which is foolish.
She is the one who will be shamed, and she will go to hell, not
become a Buddha. Yes, she says, she has agreed to die because
it would disgrace Jihei's honor if someone else ransomed her, but
now she regrets it all. She begs for the samurai's help. Jihei's manly
heart is frantic at the exposure of the "rotten she-fox." In anger
and chagrin he weeps. Through her tears Koharu asks, Will the
samurai become her regular customer so that he can interfere
whenever Jihei comes? "Exactly what you'd expect from a whore,"
Jihei flares angrily; and in his jealousy wants to beat and trample
her. Unable to control himself, he thrusts his dirk through the
latticework at her shadow, but it falls short and the samurai instantly
seizes his hands and with his sword knot ties them to the window
upright. Koharu, recognizing the dirk, suggests that the samurai
let the crazy man go, but he will not and takes her inside. Tahei
returns, beats and kicks Jihei, and cries out that he's a captured
burglar. The samurai rushes out, throws Tahei into the dust, kicks
him, and pushes him under Jihei's feet to be stamped on. Tahei
pulls himself up, swears revenge, is laughed at by the spectators,
and makes his escape. When the crowd disperses, the samurai
removes his hood and Jihei recognizes his brother, Magoemon;
and ashamed, sinks to the ground weeping. (That he failed to
recognize his brother's voice earlier is a convention of disguise,
present in Shakespeare also; that he weeps so copiously is a premise
of men's conduct.) Koharu runs out of the house and Jihei seizes
her, exclaiming, "She-fox! I'd sooner trample on you than on
Tahei!" His brother stops him, saying, "That's the kind of foolish-

ness responsible for all your trouble. A prostitute's business is to deceive men. Have you just now waked up to that?" (That this attitude also exists pronouncedly in the play, and that a prostitute can be desired as a wife by Tahei, are factors making Koharu's relationship to Jihei and the notion that the "love of a prostitute is deep beyond measure" premises that can be accepted. There are other important factors to come that make the premise of the prostitute's love credible.) Magoemon is so furious with himself for cutting a ridiculous figure, putting on swords for the first time in his life "like a bit player in a costume piece" and announcing himself as an officer, that he can scarcely hide his tears behind grimaces. Jihei, still in tears of shame and mortification, gives his brother proof of breaking with the vixen by flinging at Koharu the twenty-nine written oaths they have exchanged at the beginning of each month. (Such a circumstance as the ceremonious exchange of oaths seems questionable to a Western mind, but since it is treated as a custom of the time and place we can accept it, and our being able to accept one seemingly unlikely matter eases the way to accepting others.) Jihei also tells his brother to collect his pledges from Koharu, which she surrenders tearfully. Among them is a letter from Osan, Jihei's wife, that Magoemon does not return but he swears that he will show it to nobody, not even his wife. Before the two brothers go, Jihei in his anger kicks Koharu on the forehead and breaks into tears, and the unhappy Koharu laments. Jihei does not know her true feelings, the Narrator chants concluding the act, which are hidden in the words of Osan's letter.

Act II. Scene: The House and Shop of Kamiya Jihei; Time: Ten Days Later. The act opens with a domestic scene that could take place in any country, anytime: Osan worrying about her missing younger child, who when last seen by the older boy was bawling her head off for her milk; the irresponsible fool of a servant who says, "You know, I must've lost her somewhere. . . . Should I go back for her"; and the child finally turning up on the back of another servant, even as Osan is screaming at the nitwit, who found the child in tears on the corner. (Such familiar matter also helps make the strange acceptable, as both are of one piece in the play.) Then Osan, learning that Magoemon and her mother are coming, wakens Jihei—a businessman sleeping in the afternoon!—who pretends to be busy at the abacus. Osan's mother, who is also Jihei's aunt, at the Ten Nights service (the period when anybody who dies becomes a Buddha) has heard gossip that a patron is going to ransom Koharu. Her husband is sure it is Jihei and intends to take his daughter back before Jihei starts selling her clothes. Magoemon is angry at being played for a fool. Jihei denies the rumor, declaring that it is Tahei who will redeem her, and Osan confirms her husband's version. Magoemon asks for a written oath to show Osan's father, and Jihei signs one, making Osan happy to have a religious pledge of affection. Her mother is grateful to the Buddha of the Ten Nights. When his brother and aunt leave, Jihei slumps down and weeps enough tears to float in. Osan is outraged. For two years her bed has been an empty nest, and tonight she thought she would hear sweet words again, and he is heartless to her, ignoble. But Jihei protests his tears are of anger not of grief. He has no attachment for that vampire Koharu, who said she would kill herself rather than be delivered to Tahei under any circumstances; now Tahei will boast, will say that Jihei's business has failed, and he will be dishonored. Osan pales, and says unexpectedly, "Koharu will surely kill herself." Jihei is sure that on the contrary the faithless creature is taking medicines to prolong life. Osan, not to commit a crime, says that there is no deceit in Koharu, that in a letter she begged Koharu to break with him in order to save his life; and Koharu replied that although he was more precious to her than life, she would end relations "because she could not shirk her duty" to Osan. (This is the social doctrine of *obligation* that controls conduct, in opposition to natural sentiments, as strongly as honor does in Spanish drama.) Such a "noble hearted woman," Osan goes on, would not marry Tahei, she will surely commit suicide; Jihei must save her. "I'd be failing in the obligations I owe her as another woman if I allowed her to die." What can Jihei do? Even if he crushed his body to powder, he says, he would have no money to administer the saving dose. Osan has more than half the money needed, which she has scraped together by pawning her clothes to pay for bills for paper about to fall due, and will pawn the rest of her clothes and the children's, even though they will go cold this winter, for the balance of the money. Her husband's reputation and Koharu's life are what concern her most. The ransoming of Koharu, Jihei foresees, is a dead end. What will become of Osan? He will have no money to keep Koharu elsewhere, and so he will have to bring her here; one or the other he must do. He cannot accept such generosity from his wife, and bowing before her asks for forgiveness of his crimes. Osan nonetheless makes him put on his finery to go to Koharu. But before he leaves her father breaks in. Gozaemon, seeing his son-in-law in a silken cloak and with a fine dirk in his sash, is full of irony; and he demands

a divorce for Osan. Neither Osan's pleas nor Jihei's promise of
repentance can make him yield, and when he discovers her ward-
robe empty of her dowry clothes, which are bundled up to be
sold, he again stringently demands a bill of divorce. Jihei lays his
hand on his dirk, saying that he will divorce her by suicide instead,
but she clings to him. Gozaemon drags her away while the children
weep, and "the twin-trunked bamboo of conjugal love is sundered
forever."

Act III. Scene One: Sonezaki New Quarter, in Front of the
Yamato House; Time: That Night. At two in the morning a palanquin comes to the Yamato House to take back Koharu of the
Kinokuni House, for Tahei's money for the ransom has been
accepted, news that "before morning will turn Jihei and Koharu
to dust." The master of Yamato says that she is asleep and will
spend the night; the palanquin leaves. There is frost in the cold
river-wind. Jihei comes through the open door, tells the proprietor
not to awaken Koharu until after sunrise for her return, and settles
his account generously, saying he is off to Kyoto on business. About
to go, he remembers that his dirk is in the house. The dirk given
him, they make their farewells, and Jihei hides near the door.
Magoemon comes through the dark. The whole family is in an
agony of suspense over Jihei, afraid that the dishonorable loss of
his wife may make him do something rash. Learning that he has
missed his younger brother, he weeps, but is relieved to know
that Koharu did not leave with Jihei. Jihei's son, there with
Magoemon to dissuade Jihei from a rash act, is cold. Magoemon
goes off in search of his brother. Jihei thinks himself unworthy
of such kindness, and prays for his children. Koharu comes,
impatient to escape, and they steal away, their hearts pounding.

Scene Two: The Farewell Journey of Many Bridges. It is the
night of the full moon, this last night of the Ten Nights, yet Jihei
cannot see his way, perhaps because of the darkness in his heart.
The lovers will melt away even sooner than the night's frost, symbol
of human frailty. They are making their michiyuki, a longer convention in puppet plays than in the Noh, and cross twelve bridges
on their way to death. Through their tears Koharu says they have
nothing to grieve for; after death they will be husband and wife
forever, reborn on one lotus.

Scene Three: Amijima. Koharu, fearful of being despised by
Osan as a one-night prostitute without decency, asks Jihei to kill
her in one place and himself in another so that their dead bodies
will not reveal a lovers' suicide. Jihei protests: Osan's father took

her away, and he has divorced her. None can be critical of their dying together. But in tears she insists and Jihei gives in. Then he uses the dirk to cut off his hair, making himself a monk. As he is now unattached to wife, children, and possessions, Koharu no longer has any obligation to Osan. Happy, she cuts off her flowing tresses and throws them away. Nevertheless they will honor their duty to Osan and die in separate places, pretending the nearby higher ground is a mountain for the place of her death, while he will hang himself with her sash by the river. His only unhappiness now is thought of his children; she has no regrets. They each take the blame for what is about to be. There will be no tears on her face when she is found later. They make their final invocations, *Namu Amida Butsu,* and he thrusts in the saving blade (the blade removes natural obstacles even as the invocation removes spiritual obstacles). The thrust misses her windpipe, the Narrator chants, she twists in agony, and Jihei summons strength to draw her close and stab her again, turning the blade, and she dies. As the prayers in the nearby temple reach their close, asking grace for the dead, he jumps from the sluice gate, the sash around his neck. He writhes until the passage of his breath is stopped. In the morning fishermen find the body in their net, an image for Buddha's catching living creatures for salvation.

The premises of this play, while *obligation* was probably more of an actual motive in Japanese daily life than *honor* was in Spanish daily life, seem just as far from our modern mentality as do the Spanish premises. Yet we can accept the world of either play as real, even if strange. It may be that our awareness that we too live by imperatives, although different imperatives, makes us able to accept the Spanish or Japanese imperatives. But human history suggests otherwise; we have generally been intolerant of imperatives, whether social or religious, different from ours. It is dubious, too, that we can participate emotionally and intellectually in the mind of a Gutierre, whose honor prompts him to act on the least cause of suspicion or even on an offense only imagined and whose action would be so far from being thought deranged as to be approved by his society; and who could wash his honor clean, not with the blood of the offending prince, for royal blood is safe with Gutierre, but with the blood of his wife whom he loves. Nor can we any more become Osan, whom the social doctrine of obligation controls at the expense of her natural and (to us) right sentiments; it is the obligation she owes Koharu as another woman and no other reason that prompts her to take an action that must sacrifice her marriage and the welfare of her children. We cannot really say, "Although her conduct might not be ours, it is honorable conduct and we respect it." At least we will not say that if we take her conduct out of the play, away from the logical relations of which it is a part, and into our world. For we could not in our actual world think that the stated motive for her conduct could justify the consequences.

Defining the quality of universality in literature in the sense that we can imaginatively participate—whether emotionally, intellectually, or morally—in what happens, most of us will likely conclude that the actions of Gutierre and Osan are not universal, although they were intended to invite the emotional and moral participation of their own audiences. We may feel much closer to the values of the classical Greek world than to Spanish or Japanese values, but in fact the separateness of other times and places is as much true of Greece as of Spain and Japan. In Greece family and religion and morality were lived differently from ours, social and political and economic structures were different, the very mentality of the Greeks was (and still is) different from ours. According to M. I. Finley, when in *Oedipus the King* the chorus " 'will go no more to Apollo's inviolate shrine . . . Religion is dying' . . . because what a god has prophesied seemed not to be fulfilled; worse, seemed to have been successfully thwarted by human artifice"; when the chorus "say this, [Finley now quotes John Jones] 'we should allow them to mean what they say.' " But it is extremely hard, no, impossible, for us to participate in their meaning; it is deceptive to say that we can participate because we have a religion although a different one, or because we also have had a belief that we have lost, or because we can suspend disbelief for the sake of the myth. "*Oedipus* ends on the note: 'Call no man happy until he is dead,' " and Finley again quotes Jones, "we 'know nothing in the least' like the 'bottomless, relativistic insecurity' of the Sophoclean faith. . . . For this and similar reasons . . . Greek drama 'remains desperately foreign,' 'very alien.' 'Probably not much of the ancient tragic experience is recoverable by us.' The best we can do is to foster 'what awareness we can of its near-accessibility.' "[4] It would no doubt be worth having "awareness" of the "ancient tragic experience"—but for historical and intellectual reasons, not for literary and esthetic ones. The separateness of times and places legislates that our experience of the play must be different. The play, however, remains as an objective existence with *a* determinable and absolute meaning apart from what anybody may or may not think—indeed, whether anybody thinks about it or not. If the nature of an experience is the product of what is experienced and the experiencer, it follows that although there is an absolute meaning in the play, our experience must be different from that of the Greeks for we are different. It does not follow, however, that every interpretation is equally valid; as there is an absolute meaning interacting with the experiencer, interpretation is not a wholly subjective matter.

To say that there is an absolute meaning is not to say that only one interpretation is possible in any one time and place, for no interpretation can correspond perfectly to the play. Moreover, "an absolute meaning" in no sense equals the whole meaning. While the self-contained system that is the world of a play is nothing like the universe, let us compare small things to great as we listen to Whitehead on Plato: "His Dialogues are permeated with a sense of the variousness of the Universe, not to be fathomed by our intellects, and in his Seventh Epistle he expressly disclaims the possibility of an adequate philosophic system. The moral of his writings is that all points of view, reasonably coherent and in some sense with an application, have something to contribute to our understanding of the Universe . . . " So may the critic think of interpretations of a play.

The self-existent world of a play gives a perspective of knowledge. "The perspective of knowledge," says Feibleman in *Aesthetics,* "is both permissive and restrictive; it is permissive in that it enables the individual to obtain a view of existence; but it is restrictive in that it insures that the view of existence

shall be a partial view and therefore to some extent distorted."
If Gutierre's and Osan's views of existence seem to us distorted, we must remember that our view is, in both senses
of the word, partial. In any case, their views, being "reasonably
coherent and in some sense with an application, have something to contribute to our understanding of the Universe."

If we cannot become Gutierre or Osan, we can experience
sympathy with them, whether approving or unapproving.
It is, of course, possible to participate in the life of the characters as though theirs were an actual world: we participate,
observes Jung in *Analytical Psychology,* on "a psychological
level where there is no conscious discrimination between subject and object." Obviously, I do not refer to those cases
on record of men and women in the audience calling out
warnings or rushing onto the stage to attack a character;
nor do I imply that only the unsophisticated participate on
a psychological level. Whenever a character in a play speaks
in character to the audience, the cosmos of the play and
actuality intersect. The cosmos of *Waiting for Godot* intersects
with actuality thus: *"Vladimir. . . . Off you go! Quick! (He
pushes Estragon towards auditorium. Estragon recoils in horror.)
You won't? (He contemplates auditorium.)* Well I can understand
that." Zeami used the technique in *Sanemori,* when the Man
of the Place says to the audience, "If any of you happen
to hear him [the priest in the play] talking to himself, please
let me know," and when he later exhorts the people, i.e.,
the audience, not to fail to attend the prayers of the priest.
Whether the modern or Japanese audience psychologically
participated in the play is questionable. More likely the reaction was dual: amusement *at* the device together with a
momentary underlay of acceptance of the intersection making the two worlds one at that point. We have seen such
intersection both with words and actions in medieval plays,
where the audience did participate on a psychological level.
As Allardyce Nicoll puts it in *English Drama: A Modern Viewpoint,* not only did the actors become the real Herod and
the true Jesus. "Still further, when Christ was led to Calvary,
not only was this journey a matter of deep concern for the
participants, the spectators became mysteriously transformed

into the very crowd who had been present at the historical scene centuries before." Nor may we think them simple people. They knew very well that a play is not actuality but that it is a *game*—they used that word for a "play," just as they used "players" for actors. They knew as well as Johan Huizinga that all "Play is distinct from 'ordinary' life" and that *"Poiesis* . . . is a play-function." Nonetheless, they could psychologically participate in the sacred happening.

In modern theory this is all wrong. Kenneth Muir: "Shakespeare's characters are not real people: They are characters in a play . . . determined by the plot." L. C. Knights: " 'Character' . . . is merely an abstraction from the total response in the mind of the reader or spectator, brought into being by written or spoken words." G. Wilson Knight: "The persons, ultimately, are not human at all, but purely symbols of a poetic vision." Those with such a point of view are more likely to approve a Japanese audience than an English medieval audience. For the Japanese, says Earle Ernst, the "art object contains within itself to a large degree the quality known as esthetic distance, and the average Japanese accepts the line of contact and division between art and reality without question or discussion. The Kabuki audience is at all times completely, consciously aware that it is seeing a play." Nicoll believes, "in general, the imaginary and the real are held distinct in the theatre," but Gassner has observed that rather a "duality of experience" exists "for both the performer and the audience: action in the theatre is both make-believe and actual for them."[5]

Let us assume that we remain conscious of ourselves and of the fictiveness of the play while we are somehow involved with the world of the play. How is it that we may respond with tears to the end of *King Lear?* Dr. Johnson has it in his *Preface to Shakespeare,* "Imitations produce pain or pleasure, not because they are mistaken for realities, but because they bring realities to mind." Or, we may say, because they bring the possibility of realities to mind. To turn from the neo-classicist to the romanticist, Hazlitt on the question of reality says, "Hamlet is a name; his speeches and sayings but the idle coinage of the poet's brain. What then, are they not real? They are as real as our own thoughts. Their reality is in the reader's mind. It is *we* who are Hamlet." The sentence that counts is, I think, "They are as real as our own thoughts"; that *we* are Hamlet or Lear is, at least for many, simply not true. It is easier for us to believe, as a modern critic, Elder Olson, observes, that "our feelings at a play are such feelings as we have, not for ourselves, but for others."

Whether we participate psychologically or imaginatively (as we can do even while remaining conscious of ourselves) in a play, or simply watch the play, it is worth considering theories on what the conditions are for a response to beings, like Lear, who seem worlds away from us, or to values, like Gutierre's, which seem incredible. Jung would say that the separateness of people, times, and places that I have talked of does not exist. "Our mind has its history, just as our body has its history. . . . Our unconscious mind, like our body, is a storehouse of relics and memories of the past." These are mythological contents belonging to "mankind in general, and therefore they are of a *collective* nature." In the collective unconscious "we are no longer separate individuals, we are all one. . . . Because the basic structure of the mind is the same in everybody, we cannot make distinctions when we experience on that level. There we do not know if something has happened to you or to me."[6] If we experience a play with our unconscious, no being is worlds away, no value is incredible; there is no separateness, we are all one in our mental nature.

Claude Lévi-Strauss believes that the same structural laws are to be found in all human minds, that is to say all minds function alike, whether primitive or civilized, whether neurotic or normal. "These structures as an aggregate form what we call the unconscious." In Lévi-Strauss' view the unconscious is not the "repository of a unique history which makes each of us an irreplaceable being. It is reducible to a function . . . which no doubt is specifically human, and which is carried out according to the same laws among all men, and actually corresponds to the aggregate of these laws." The unconscious "is always empty . . . As the organ of a specific function, the unconscious merely imposes structural laws upon inarticulated elements which originate elsewhere—impulses, emotions, representations, and memories." These are each person's "vocabulary of his personal history," and "this vocabulary becomes significant, for us and for others, only to the extent that the unconscious structures it according to its laws and thus transforms it into language." Because these "structures are not only the same for everyone" but are also "few in number, . . . the world of symbolism is infinitely varied in content, but always limited in its laws. [By "symbolism" Lévi-Strauss apparently means any kind of representation.] There are many languages, but very few structural laws which are valid for all languages. A compilation of known tales and myths would fill an imposing number of volumes. But they can be reduced to a small number of simple types if we abstract, from among the diversity of characters, a few elementary functions."[7] If the mechanism of the human mind is everywhere alike and limits and determines our mental processes and behavior, human nature is everywhere alike. Evidence for the mind working everywhere alike, its structural laws determining thought and action, is that all languages have the same basic structure; and further, many other human activities show the same basic structure the world over, as reflected in myths, kinship practices, and cooking. So Lévi-Strauss believes. It is as though cultures, no matter how separate in time and place, were all manifestations of a limited number of paradigms which are the common store of all human minds. The differences in values, then, are seeming rather than real. And since we all experience a play with a similar mental nature, again we may conclude, as we did with Jung, that no person or value represented is foreign to us.

Interesting as Jung's analytical psychology and Lévi-Strauss' structuralism are, their reductive tendencies may be inapplicable to literary experience. It is the variousness of literary experience, of all artistic experience, that counts. Each work is its own meaning. The differences from work to work are no less important than their likenesses in our apprehension of meaning, that is in our apprehension of the formal structure

(which includes content). Moreover, not only are we conscious
of differences—whether emotional, intellectual, or esthetic—
between works and from our own values, but *consciousness on
our part and particularity of meaning on the part of the work* are
among the necessary conditions for a literary experience.
Camus goes so far as to say, "Everything begins with consciousness and nothing is worth anything except though it." In
Joyce's view it is only "esthetically permissible" to apprehend
an esthetic object as "that thing which it is and no other
thing."

The investigations of the epistemologist Jean Piaget are
also interesting. Piaget postulates that our own logic gives
us much of our understanding of external reality; our perception and judgment of external reality do not come to us
from that reality. Jung writing on the matter of the contents
of consciousness says, "Sensation tells me that something *is:*
it does not tell me *what* it is. . . . Thinking in its simplest
form tells you *what* a thing is. . . . It adds a concept because
thinking is perception and judgment." He goes on, "Feeling
informs you through its feeling-tones of the *values* of things
. . . what a thing is worth to you."[8] (It is tempting to make
an analogy between these three stages of apprehension and
the three phases of artistic apprehension that Joyce speaks
of, the apprehension of unity, harmony, and radiance. The
analogy between the first two stages, at least, seems close.
Joyce says that the "synthesis of immediate perception is followed by the analysis of apprehension.")

Piaget found that the human mind follows a certain order
in its development. At first, when children are under two
years old, they can reason without language. For example,
"to grab a stick in order to draw up a remote object is an
act of intelligence . . . Here, an instrument, a means to an
end, is coordinated with a pre-established goal. In order to
discover this means, the subject must first understand the
relationship between the stick and the objective." In that stage
of sensorimotor intelligence, before language is learned, the
mind can also reason by using mental pictures, that is, without
the objects reasoned about being present in the subject's per-
ceptual field. After language is learned, for about five years,

from about two to about seven, words are realities, the name
is the thing. Let the child designate a rug as a pet kitten
and he will become upset if anyone steps on his kitten-rug.
During that period reasoning does not advance far; if the
child is shown pairs of sticks in a series of two pairs in which
A is smaller than B, and then B is smaller than C, he cannot
deduce that A is smaller than C unless the differences are
large enough to remain in his memory as picture images.
He is in a pre-logical stage and remains so until about the
age of seven. At that age he can construct the series, make
the deduction and can reverse the operation. Logic has begun
to operate.

Such a logical operation is, of course, the logic inherent
in the coordination of actions, not the logic in words. Piaget
insists, however, "There is no basic difference between verbal
logic and the logic inherent in the coordination of actions,
but the logic of actions is more profound and more primitive."
Indeed, "the source of logical operations is action itself, which,
of course, takes place only in connection with objects."[9] From
about seven to about eleven the mind goes through the stage
of these concrete operations, which mark the beginning of
logic. An operation "is a type of action: it can be carried
out either directly, in the manipulation of objects, or internally, when it is categories or (in the case of formal logic)
propositions which are manipulated." The concrete operations "are based on the logic of classes and the logic of
relations; they are means for structuring immediately present
reality,"[10] that is, they are applied to things that can be manipulated; the manipulation can be a real action or an imagined
one. To put it another way, "the [concrete]logical act consists
essentially of *operating,* hence of acting on things and toward
people. An operation is, in effect, an internalized action . . ."[9]
*(At every turn in Piaget's theory we see that the relation between
logic and action is natural to the human mind, and this natural
relation suggests the source of the strength of the logical design
of action in drama.)* During the stage of concrete operations
the child can do in his head what he formerly had to do
in actions. For example, the younger children could match
six sticks, when instructed to take the same number from

a pile, but could not take six sticks by counting. The older children, between seven and eleven, could count the six sticks and then count six from the pile. During these years they are good at arranging colors in a series, and can reason concretely about colors. If shown, first, that Edith has darker hair than Lily, and then that Edith's hair is lighter than Susan's, they can easily enough deduce which of the three has the darkest hair. But although good at arranging colors, they cannot at nine or ten answer the classic question, when Edith and Lily and Susan are now spoken of in a series of two pairs, "Edith has darker hair than Lily. Edith's is lighter than Susan's. Which of the three has the darkest hair?" For the mind at that age these names are "fictive personages . . . presented in the abstract as pure hypotheses."

It is formal thought that permits the mind "to draw conclusions from pure hypotheses and not merely from actual observations." These "formal operations" contrast to concrete operations in engendering a "logic of propositions" rather than a logic of relations and classes.[9] The stage of formal operations comes between about twelve and fifteen. Now the mind can think about thought, reason from assumptions that are contrary to fact, and understand metaphor. Pertinent to the way the mind works in responding to a play is that "at the formal level the subject subordinates *reality* to *possibility*," that is, "in order to avoid inconsistencies as new facts emerge, from the start he seeks to encompass what appear to be the actual relations in a set of relations which he regards as possible . . . the subject tends to insert links, which in the first instance he assumes as real, in the totality of those which he recognizes as possible."[10] That is not a far cry from the child who can believe in his fictions. There "may be several realities for the child, and these realities may be equally real in turn."[11] There is a modern ontology that holds there are two universes equally real and valuable, the possible and the actual.[12] In this view the fictive as possible is real. When we respond to the artifice of a play as real, returning as it were to the immediacy of a childhood response, equating possibility with reality, we may be responding truly.

The stage of concrete operations is of particular interest

in connection to drama. The ability to reason concretely comes at about the same age and with about equal force everywhere in the world, whether in primitive or civilized society, whether in slums or in middle-class homes. (It is in the region of formal operations, of abstract reasoning, that the ways part.) Now, when we watch a play our minds are using these profound concrete operations, reasoning on the basis of premises that we see before us; when we read a play, we do the same thing by means of mental pictures (children under two can so reason). Further, we overlay our concrete operations by encompassing what appears before us (or before our mind's eye) in a set of relations we regard as possible and assume as real. The only demand we need to make is that there be logical relations between the parts. For example, a child walking through the streets believes the moon is following him. It would be logical for him to believe, then, that the moon is watching him, even that the moon is alive. The logical relations may be expressed in the form of syllogisms. (The child, of course, has no traffic with syllogisms, but that need not stop us from using them so long as we remember that syllogisms are only one way of expressing logical relations.)

The moon follows me.
Things that follow me are watching me.
The moon is watching me.

The moon is watching me.
Things that watch me are alive.
The moon is alive.

It remains, I think, natural and easy for adults to reason concretely and easy to accept that which has logical coherence. We can probably accept any premises in a play, although we may not personally value them, if the structure (and texture) of which they are a part are coherent, that is, if the parts fit together well. It is even possible for a play to have such premises that a conclusion of incoherence or absurdity would be necessary for the logical structure. So it is that we can respond to persons in a play who seem worlds away from us and to values that would not be credible to us if they were isolated and removed from the play. We gather in a meaning from a knowledge of logical relations, and to gather a meaning into our minds is a considerable pleasure. Through the sympathy of our feelings (sympathy in the sense that a tuning fork vibrates to another) we give a value to the meaning we apprehend. Our apprehension is esthetic apprehension of a formal structure; our means of apprehension are sensational, emotional, intellectual, and imaginative, means that may work together or separately.

If these speculations are one valid way of explaining response to drama, that is to say, if all things do contain logical relations among their parts and to everything else that exists, and if we respond to such logical relations as we perceive, then this study of logical relations in drama is theoretically justified. But whether it be thought theoretically justified or not, will not, I trust, disturb its practical value for the understanding of drama.

14/ MODERN DRAMA

We have seen the logically unified plot-structure the world over. Except for theaters such as the Kabuki or the Peking opera in which the performer is more important than the play, and except in the Sanskrit whose *rasa* is at cross-purposes with such a structure, the logically unified plot-structure is the prevailing mode of constructing a play, and in Western experience such plays are the most satisfying. But if we have seen the syllogistic plot-structure the world over, we have not yet seen it in a body of drama that fairly lays claim to greatness—the modern. By modern I do not mean simply of our times, but modes of drama that have not been used before, such as the expressionistic or absurd. It is a contemporary critical notion that if a play is made well, it may be dismissed from serious criticism as worth no more than something mechanical. Critics holding such a notion do not stop to think that Shakespeare used syllogistic plot-structures in both his mainplots and subplots, which he unified by making an action in one plot the cause of an action in the other. Or, if these critics do think of Shakespeare, they maintain, "Yes, Shakespeare was great, but if he were writing today he would not use that dead formal principle. Look at the great plays of our time. They do not have plots." By great plays they mean those in the new modes. Well, then, let us look at the formal structures of plays in new modes,

plays whose greatness is acknowledged and which have been
greatly influential.

These new modes as Maurice Valency writes in *The Flower
and the Castle* typically bring "together in the theatre things
which in real life are not normally related." It was with Strindberg's *A Dream Play* and *Ghost Sonata,* Valency continues,
that this "new chapter opened in the history of drama," whose
modes also rejected "the principle of logical sequence."
Before we examine *A Dream Play* for its formal structure,
we may reflect that an audience accepts the violation of its
sense of actuality in expressionistic or absurd plays in the
same way that it can accept the premises in traditional plays.
Even dreams have their logical relations.

A Dream Play, written in 1902, was not August Strindberg's
first extraordinary experiment in expressionism but it has
been the most influential on modern drama. He wrote in
a prologue to the play, four years later, that the "writer has
tried to imitate the disjointed but apparently logical form
of a dream. Anything may happen: everything is possible
and probable. Time and space do not exist. . . . The characters
are split, doubled, and multiplied; they evaporate and are
condensed, are diffused and concentrated. But a single consciousness holds sway over them all—that of the dreamer."
(The expressionistic may also take form in memory, as in
Tennessee Williams' *The Glass Menagerie;* or an expressionistic
world may be presented directly, without recourse to dream
or memory, as in Eugene O'Neill's *The Hairy Ape.* In our
own time Williams' *Camino Real* is a dream play.) O'Neill,
in his expression of gratitude for having received the Nobel
prize in 1936, paid tribute to Strindberg by saying, "Strindberg was the greatest genius of all modern dramatists," that
he remains, indeed, "more modern than any of us."

Since *A Dream Play* seems to imitate the disunited form
of dreams and its sequences are therefore difficult to
remember, and since we are interested to discover whether
or not there are logical relations in the sequential happenings,
we ought to examine what happens scene by scene. (I have
used the translation of Arvid Paulson.)

Scene 1, The Prologue: In the Clouds. The Daughter of Indra decides to go down to earth to see whether its people have cause always to complain and lament; her father has nothing good to say for them.

Scene 2: Outside the Growing Castle. She will enter the castle to set free, at any cost, who waits there for her; it is her duty.

Scene 3: Inside the Castle: The Officer's Room. The Officer does not know whether he wants to be free; whatever he chooses will mean suffering.

Scene 4: Inside the Castle: The Mother's Room. The mother is dying; she and her husband exchange forgiveness for their having failed and tormented each other. She tells the Officer he has no right to complain of a childhood injustice having warped his life; he allowed his brother to be punished for a wrong he himself did. She tries to do something good for their maid and thereby offends her husband. Then comes the first statement of the theme: "Humanity is to be pitied!" says the Daughter of Indra. "Life is hard," she says to the Officer, "—but love conquers all! Come—and see!"

Scene 5: The Alleyway Outside the Opera House. Wearing the shawl of the Portress (which holds human agonies), the Daughter takes the Portress' place by the gate to learn what she can about life. The Officer, radiating happiness, has been waiting seven years for his love, the singer Victoria. The season changes from summer to autumn. The Officer has turned gray, shabby, and wilted; Victoria never comes. He wants to have a door in the alleyway opened; nobody knows what is behind it. The season changes to summer. People standing around anticipate the opening of the door, but a policeman forbids its being opened in the name of the law.

Scene 6: The Attorney's Office. To find out what the law says, the Officer and the Daughter go to the Attorney, who suffers all the agonies of his clients. Murder cases are bad enough, he says, but the very worst is having to separate a married couple (he and the Daughter will marry and the marriage will not last). The theme is repeated, as it is many times in the play, by the Daughter: "Man is to be pitied!" The Attorney is to have conferred on him the degree of a doctor of laws.

Scene 7: The Interior of a Church (The Chancel; The Organ). Because he has championed the poor and spoken a good word for the wicked, the Attorney is considered unworthy of the degree. The Daughter gives him a more appropriate wreath, a wreath of thorns.

Scene 8: Fingal's Cave. The wailing of mortals reaches no farther than this cave. There is only one thing in life to rejoice over, says the Attorney, "love—a wife and a home," which is the sweetest and bitterest experience, the most sublime and the most hollow. She wants to submit herself to the test of marriage, despite all the pitfalls—"All that matters is that we love each other!" If they tire of each other, the child when it comes will bring a constant joy. He is persuaded to a union of their destinies.

Scene 9: The Attorney's Living Quarters Behind His Office. The child turns out to be a cause of their undoing; and their antipathies drive them apart. Turning the doorknob to his office, he twists the Daughter's heart and is stopped only by the entrance of the Officer, who tells her, "There is always a way out, so long as you have someone to love you." He asks her to go with him to Fairhaven, where there are sun and youth and flowers and exuberant life. The Attorney knows that when he closes the door behind him he will open the way for the Daughter.

Scene 10: Foulstrand. The Officer and the Daughter land here rather than in Fairhaven. The rich live here in misery. A poet occasionally comes for the mud to toughen himself. A prodigal girl is being feted while her sister, who has always done her duty, suffers cruelly. The Daughter finds it is difficult to cope with the idea of justice. Two lovers (one of them the Officer's Victoria) are made miserable although guiltless owing to the Officer's jealousy; their love does not conquer. The Daughter knows now that love is not a way out of human misery.

Scene 11: Fairhaven. Plainlooking Edith, although her playing of Bach fascinates the guests in the casino who appear in the doorway to listen, breaks off playing, agonized by seeing a naval officer put his arm around the waist of a girl and take her down to the jetty.

The Officer is a pupil along with children in a schoolroom, and despite his degree of doctor of philosophy cannot do simple arithmetic. The quarantine master rescues him, taking him to the casino to dance before the plague breaks out.

Outside the casino a couple just married decide to die in their bliss and forestall the unhappiness certain to come.

The Attorney enters and tells the Daughter that she has not met with the worst, which is to learn the same lesson over and over again, and summons her to her duties, i.e., to "everything that is vile, loathsome, and painful . . ." She would rather die than return to the humiliation and dirt in the Attorney's house. But

before she returns to heaven she wants to learn the secret behind
the door in the alleyway outside the opera house. First she will
go to the lonely wilderness to find her own self again.

Scene 12: A Beach on the Mediterranean. "This is Paradise!"
says the Daughter, and she hears a coalheaver say, "This is hell!"
and at the end of the scene she hides her face and says "This
is not Paradise."—She has retraced her steps from heaven to hell.

Scene 13: Fingal's Cave. Here the Master of Heaven listens
to the voice of humanity lamenting dusty lives. The Daughter and
the Poet watch a shipwreck; when Christ appears walking on the
waves to save the crew, they scream in horror at the sight of their
Savior and leap to their death in the sea.

Scene 14: The Alleyway Outside the Opera House. The four
faculties—theological, philosophical, medical, and legal—summoned to give their thoughts about the door, attack each other.
The door opens; nothing is behind it. Only the Daughter understands the meaning of that, and she does not explain the riddle.
The "righteous-minded" threaten her. She tells the Poet to go to
the wilderness with her, where she will answer the riddle to him
alone. The Attorney appears, saying her duty is to her crying child.
She suffers a cleaving in her soul, but chooses her higher duty.
All those present are her children.

Scene 15: Outside the Growing Castle. The Daughter explains
to the Poet the meaning of the riddle: Brahma, the divine force,
was tempted by Maya, the Mother of the Universe, to propagate
himself: thus the fall of heaven into sin; mankind and existence
are a dream, an illusion. But Brahma's offspring try to make themselves free of earth-matter; suffering becomes the liberator.
However, suffering is in conflict with enjoyment and love. Thus
love is a mixture of the greatest in suffering and the greatest in
enjoyment. The struggle between the two elements produces
energy.

The Daughter has suffered all human sufferings a hundred-
fold. Then follows a sacrificial scene. The Daughter throws her
shoes—the earth, clay—into the fire; the Portress, her shawl; the
Officer, the roses he held for Victoria; the Glazier, the diamond
that opened the door; the Attorney, his documents; Victoria, her
beauty—her sorrow; but Don Juan in his wheelchair only cries
to She and the Lover, "Make haste, make haste! Life is short!"
and leaves with the couple.

The moment before the Daughter enters the castle she feels
the utter pain of human *being*. As the castle burns—only fire can free

her from her mortal guise—a chrysanthemum bud on the roof of the castle opens into a giant flower.

Other than the theme "Man is to be pitied," thematic elements in the play that are common to most of the expressionists are the Daughter of Indra's longing to reconcile the finite and the infinite (which was an earlier preoccupation of Romanticism) and her search for a better life. It is perfectly apparent that the play does not have a tight unity, but it is not true that, as Valency states, "seldom has a plot had less relation to a play." This many-scened play, as is typical of many-scened expressionistic plays, is a vehicle for theme, and as many of the incidents are here for the sake of theme (and so are logically related texturally) the structure, as the summary shows, is loose. But even in the looseness so caused there are cause and effect in the chain of events (as there are in Sanskrit drama). More important, however, to the structure of the play is its plot, which gives the play a syllogistic although submerged unity.

1. The beginning of change: The Daughter of Indra, come from heaven to earth to see whether humanity has cause for always lamenting, and having learned that humanity is to be pitied, says to the suffering Officer, "Life is hard, but love conquers all! Come—and see!" (scene 4)

2. The middle of change: When the test of marriage she submitted herself to with the Christlike Attorney fails, she leaves with the Officer, believing his echo of her, "There is always a way out, so long as you have someone to love you." (scene 9)

3. To be settled by the end: Will she find a way out of the misery on the earth?

Climax: She realizes that love is not a way out when she sees two lovers made miserable although they are guiltless.

The climax determines the end, her return to heaven, but she returns with a new wisdom (the secret behind the locked door) and returns only after sacrificial rites for the sake of humanity. Clearly, the plot-structure has very much relation to the play.

Some think O'Neill the greatest successor of Strindberg

in expressionism. *The Hairy Ape* (1922), like *A Dream Play,* is many-scened, and typical of such plays (whether expressionistic or not) we watch a character's progress through a series of circumstances at many times and in many places. But *The Hairy Ape* is not at all episodic; it has a simple, strong, coherent plot-structure. In the way of expressionism the play stylizes, distorts and exaggerates scenery, stage properties, lighting, physical movements and appearance, sounds, and the use of voices—it all makes for an unnaturalistic atmosphere in which the play is submerged. The atmosphere is also typically created by symbolism, which has the function of expressing the infinite in the finite. Typically too, the many scenes and distortions serve the theme. Here is the plot-structure.

1. Yank is insulted by Mildred, a creature of a different world from his.
2. He swears revenge.
3. Will he succeed?
Climax: Searching for Mildred, he throws a punch in anger at a Gentleman and thereby lands in jail.

He will lose out to the world which is different from him. A later scene in which he tells a local of the Industrial Workers of the World that he wants to blow up her father's steel works puts him into his coffin, as it were, for they think him a clumsy government agent and throw him out, leaving him with no resource.

The thematic beginning of change happens when Yank is in jail. Learning that Mildred's father is President of the Steel Trust, he realizes that he, Yank, does not belong to steel. Earlier he had said, "Steel, dat stands for de whole ting!"—steel makes the world move—"I'm steel—steel—steel!" The thematic climax is his being thrown out by the IWW, which makes him realize that he belongs nowhere, that he is a busted Ingersoll. Death is all that's left.

Untypically of expressionistic plays, *The Hairy Ape* is close to the traditional concept of tragedy. As tragic protagonist, Yank is superior to those about him: he is physically and emotionally more powerful, and, more important, his absolute honesty with himself gives him ethical superiority. He attempts to the limit of his capacity but lacks the intellect (his flaw) to execute his desire. He experiences a recognition, that his shipmate Paddy's world of warm sun, cloudless skies, and wind for sailing ships was worth having but that it cannot be for him. And finally, he meets catastrophe without cringing.

Nor does *The Hairy Ape* support the scholarly view that the belief "that art is essentially and inevitably subjective [which is not even true of all Romantic poetry] . . . is indeed the foundation upon which all manifestations of Expressionism are built."[1] We do not have a revelation of the writer, which is what subjectivity generally means.

About the time that Strindberg created expressionism, Anton Chekhov invented a mode of drama commonly unrecognized for what it is structurally and therefore regarded as a plotless mode. During his first period of drama, Chekhov wrote mainly short farces adapted from his stories; in his second period, in the last decade of his life (he died at 44 in 1904), he composed his great plays. Eric Bentley thinks *The Three Sisters* (1901) Chekhov's supreme achievement. Certainly it is in this play that Chekhov perfectly achieved his new mode, a structure in which none of the most interesting characters is the character central to the plot. It is the better known *The Cherry Orchard* (1904), however, which has given Chekhov the reputation as the founder of a kind of play in which "nothing happens." Remarking on the play's being "often accused of having no plot whatever," Francis Fergusson says "it is true that the story gives little indication of the play's content or meaning." Its beginning, middle and end, if I understand him well, exist in time but not as a logical structure. On the contrary, a syllogistic plot-structure holds this play together and is revelatory of its content and of meaning. Moreover, unlike *The Three Sisters,* it is the character who is the most interesting who is central to the plot-structure.

1. Mme. Ranevsky, having left Paris and the scoundrel she loved to come back to Russia which she loves and to her estate whose meaning to her is her early innocence, learns that the only way to save the estate is to change what it means to her and learns too that there are telegrams for her from Paris.

2. When pressed to make the estate profitable, which would make it possible for her to stay in Russia, she says it would be vulgar and also laments her life in Paris to which she is being implored to return.

3. Will she stay in Russia or go to Paris?

Climax: She learns that the estate has been sold at auction (after we learn that she still loves the man in Paris, although she knows he is a millstone around her neck, and that she cannot live without that stone).

The play ends with her returning to Paris, where her life will at least have meaning and reality in the present. The play uses an unusual technique: the deuteragonist in the syllogism, her lover in Paris, never appears; but his telegrams are an existence in the play like a character. (Similarly, in Edward Albee's *The Zoo Story* a bench and then a knife have the force of characters.)

Much of the meaning and content of *The Cherry Orchard*, of course, are not revealed by the plot-structure; I maintain only that the plot-structure is revelatory of narrative content and meaning and that perceiving the unity the plot-structure creates is necessary to our primary artistic apprehension. Other elements of meaning in the formal structure, corresponding to the second phase of artistic apprehension of a work, are textural.

Instead of studying Chekhov's *The Three Sisters* for the new mode that he invented, we shall turn to a descendant, Sean O'Casey's *The Plough and the Stars* (1926). Distinguished drama historians praising this play speak of it as a naturalistic, mass drama having little structural design. Of O'Casey George Freedley writes, "His sense of plot has always been slight." Allardyce Nicoll believes that *The Plough and the Stars* is a play "almost without a plot . . . a series of vivid scenes." John Gassner says, "O'Casey here wrote a triumphant example of the 'mass drama' as first developed by the pioneering

naturalists."[2] The exception always proves—that is, tests—the
rule, and if *The Plough and the Stars* truly has little structural
design, the acknowledged greatness of this play would make
unassailable the position of those critics who maintain that
greatness can, no, *should* be achieved in rebellion against the
"tyranny of the plot." But although the design of the play
does not readily reveal itself, it is an intricate and firm design
with at least three interdependent plot-structures.

As the curtain goes up, Fluther Good "is repairing the
lock of the [Clitheroes'] door"—the lock that is to bring on
Bessie's explosion when she enters the play. "The room
directly in front of the audience is furnished in a way that
suggests an attempt towards a finer expression of domestic
life"—Nora's doing, we soon learn. Mrs. Gogan, gossipy and
envious, speaks to Fluther of Nora and Jack Clitheroe. We
glimpse what is happening to their marriage, and, despite
Mrs. Gogan, our sympathies are with Nora and against
Clitheroe. This opening exchange, including the announce-
ment of the "Great Demonsthration" and the account of
Clitheroe posturing in his Sam Browne belt, makes Nora
and Clitheroe our first focus as the play at once prepares
for what the act is building to: the commanding scene between
Nora and her husband at the end of the act.

Tracking the plot-structures, we may pass by the comic
scenes, noting only that the Covey's provocation of Uncle
Peter serves Nora's entrance: in her reaction to the two men
we see her as mistress of the household, desiring gentility.
She calls an end to their quarrel: "Jack 'll be in any minute,
an' I'm not goin' to have th' quiet of his evenin' tossed about
in an everlastin' uproar." Then O'Casey with quiet structural
skill brings the lock into the play. Nora turns to Fluther,
who invites her attention to his handiwork. "As Nora is opening and shutting the door, Mrs. Bessie Burgess appears in
it. . . . She looks scornfully and viciously at Nora." Angered
by the lock, as though it were an affront to her honesty,
and by Nora's trying to shut the door in her face, she grips
Nora by the shoulders and, shaking her, violently exclaims,
"You little overdhressed throllope, you, for one pin, I'd paste

th' white face o' you!" As Fluther breaks Bessie away from
the frightened Nora, Clitheroe enters. In his face is the "desire
for authority, without the power to attain it." He pushes
Bessie out. Then—this is the consequence of Bessie's
action—he comforts Nora, kissing her, although, as we have
heard earlier, Nora "dhresses herself to keep him with her,
but it's no use."

Soon after tea Nora and Clitheroe are alone. We perceive
that the world has broken in on their love; they no longer
have a common center of gravity. She is being pulled toward
her notion of a better place in life, he toward a captaincy
in the Irish Citizens Army. They quarrel at first over the
meeting that night and the I.C.A., but, Nora coaxing, they
make up. For a moment they are as close as in the days
of their honeymoon. Then a knock sounds on the door.
Clitheroe discovers that Nora has burned the letter with the
news of his appointment as a commandant, and is fierce
to her. She tries to keep him at home and fails, crying, "Your
vanity 'll be the ruin of you an' me yet." Putting on his Sam
Browne belt, he struts out to the meeting. The "pitifully
worn" Mollser comes to sit with Nora and wonders if she
will "ever be sthrong enough to be keepin' a home together
for a man." We hear a brass band and singing soldiers march-
ing through the street outside. Bessie Burgess appears "as
the chorus ends, and the music is faint in the distance again";
she delivers her commentary and prophecy of disaster.

The first act has ended, we do not yet know who the character central to the plot is, but we already have a sense of
firm structural design and we have aligned ourselves with
Nora.

Nora does not enter the second act at all. The second
act is played out against the background of the meeting
toward which much of the first act built. The voice of the
man whose shadow we see in the window of the publichouse
is a crescendo of madness, to which the prostitute Rosie's
seaminess is a counterpoint. The reactions of Rosie, Peter,
Fluther, and the Covey to the Voice of the Man; the collisions
between the Covey and Rosie, and between Fluther and the
Covey; Rosie's seduction of Fluther—these are all essentially

thematic and tonal elements. However important they are to the play's dimension and its comic and satiric power, however successfully O'Casey controls their textural harmony in the whole formal design of the play, they are not shaped into a plot-structure. The various actions of these characters have no logical unity and do not move the play forward.

Early in the third act Nora returns, supported by Fluther. She is passionately unhappy and worn out after searching for her husband in the barricades. When Clitheroe appears on the street, she again fails to hold him. The consequence of this failure is her emotional and physical collapse, the stillbirth of her child, and, in the fourth and last act, her deeply moving madness. Nora absorbs our interest and sympathy more than any other character in the play, but she is not central to the plot; she does not advance the action of the play, she is not a doer of acts that cohere into a complete plot-structure. Clitheroe, on the other hand, does have a plot-structure, although not the main one. The logical unity of his action is worked out in relationship to Nora:

1. Clitheroe, discovering that Nora has burned the letter containing his appointment as a commandant, leaves her to go to the rally.

2. Inflamed by the oratory, he subordinates Nora to the Irish cause, declaring that "Ireland is greater than a wife."

3. Will he stay committed to the cause or return to Nora?

Climax: Ashamed that Nora searched for him in the barricades, stung by Brennan's and Bessie's taunts, he is afraid of being thought a coward and renegade.

Consequently he deserts Nora in her desperate need. The end of his action falls near the close of the third act. In the last act his death is reported. Because he has no part in the final action of the play, which takes place in the significant fourth act, he cannot be central to the plot.

Who, then, is central? There is no question that Nora and Clitheroe are our main focus of interest—but the advance of the play's action and its culmination belong mainly to Bessie. She, indeed, has two plot-structures, the main one in relationship to Nora, another in relationship to Mrs. Gogan. The first of these is the main plot-structure of the play:

   1. Bitterly at odds with her neighbors, Bessie attacks and insults Nora.

   2. When, however, Nora collapses following the desertion by her husband, Bessie carries her into the house. (Earlier in the act when Nora was brought back from the barricades by Fluther, Bessie taunted her mercilessly, so that even Fluther lost control and called Bessie an "ignorant oul' throllope.")

   3. Will her change toward Nora be lasting?

   Climax: When Nora screams, in spite of the danger Bessie goes for the doctor. It is an act which confirms her in kindness and an inclination to care for others, a quality suggested earlier when she gave a mug of milk to Mollser and when she helped the sick child into the house.

The question raised by the middle is settled in Act IV: we see Bessie caring for Nora. She is no longer at odds with her neighbors. The Covey reflects, "I don't know what we'd have done only for oul' Bessie: up with her [Nora] for th' past three nights, hand runnin'," and Fluther adds approvingly, "I always knew there was never anything really derogattory wrong with poor Bessie." Bessie's bitter resentment breaks out again only when, in the irony of the play's end, she is fatally shot while pulling the irresponsibly mad Nora from the danger of the window.

We may note in O'Casey's structural design, as fundamental to the play's sense of wholeness, that Bessie's plot-structure has Clitheroe's involved in it. Not only is Nora common to both plot-structures; Bessie's taunting of Clitheroe is an important cause of his climax, his yielding to a sense of shame. His climax then determines the end of his action, the desertion of Nora. The desertion, in turn, occasions the middle action of Bessie, the carrying of the collapsed Nora into the house. It is such interdependence of plot-structures in a play that makes each integral to the whole.

Bessie's plot-structure in relationship to Mrs. Gogan springs from the same source as her plot-structure in relationship to Nora and grows parallel to it:

   1. Bitterly at odds with her neighbors, Bessie picks a fight with Mrs. Gogan.

2. She suspends hostilities, however, to use a pram with Mrs.
Gogan during the looting.
3. Will she remain reconciled to Mrs. Gogan?
Climax: She becomes a veritable bosom companion in thievery.

We see the end of the action of this plot-structure briefly
in Act IV: Bessie is courteous to Mrs. Gogan, who in turn
offers regard to Bessie for having been kind to Mollser. The
plot-structure of Bessie and Mrs. Gogan involves and satiri-
cally illuminates themes of the play; like Clitheroe's plot-
structure, it is revelatory of the tone. Have we not seen
everywhere that the people in the play do not know how
to live together? The first occasion to bring any of them together emerges from the opportunity that the Easter Rebellion gives them to plunder. There are redeeming elements,
of course, to which the sufferings of the Rebellion give sharp
outline: Nora's flaring love, Bessie's strain of goodness,
Fluther's (limited) manliness. But the satirical tone prevails;
the vision the play presents is intensely critical.

The contemporary welcome accorded the so-called "plotless" play may well issue from a misunderstanding of the
modern structural mode. It may be, as Moody Prior reflects,
that to "say that action is the primary formal principle in
a serious play is not the same as saying that the plot is the
supremely interesting thing about it, or the feature which
fascinated the dramatist most," but being the primary formal
principle the plot-structure must be perceived if there is to
be accurate and full artistic apprehension.

There are critics who also fail to see syllogistic plot-
structures in the theater of the absurd. They maintain, as
George Wellwarth writes, that the "formlessness and illogical-
ity of plot line remains and has become one of the avant-
garde's identifying characteristics." As in such expressionistic
plays as Strindberg's and as in plays written in the mode
that Chekhov invented, the plot-structure of absurd plays
is submerged—but it is there and is formally essential. Without it the plays would collapse like a body without a skeleton.
Friedrich Duerrenmatt believes, "Every great age of the
theatre was possible because of the discovery of a unique

form of theatre, of a particular style, which determined the way plays were written." *Common to the new modes of theater in the twentieth century is the submerged plot-structure, which is not the main focus of interest.*

Such a structure is not an absolutely new invention. In Zeami's Noh drama *Kiyotsune* (c. 1400) the *shite,* or main performer, is the Ghost of Kiyotsune, but it is his wife who is central to the plot-structure:

1. The Wife of Kiyotsune, learning of her husband's suicide, does not take his keepsake.

2. Reproached by his Ghost, she reproaches him in turn, weeping in grief.

3. Will she be able to reconcile herself to him?

Climax: She is moved by his tale.

(The complete play is printed at the end of this book.)

The "mass drama" lends itself to the submerged plot-structure; but in such plays, because the dramatists were less concerned with the architecture of form, the plot-structure may not be proportioned so that it holds the design of the whole play together. Of Maxim Gorki's *The Lower Depths* (1902) Chekhov told Gorki that he had left the most interesting characters out of the last act. These characters are those in the pattern of the play's submerged plot-structure: the young thief Pepel, who is the central character, the pilgrim Luka who acts as a catalyst in the play and persuades Pepel and Natasha that they ought to escape to a better life, Natasha's sister Vassilisa whose cruelty to Natasha provokes Pepel and who goads Pepel to kill her husband. The killing is the play's climax. Pepel must consequently go to jail; and Natasha, deranged by torture, misconstrues what happened and turns against Pepel. So ends the third act. It may be said that life always goes on, but the fourth act shows it going on after the play is in effect over. Perhaps more important to Gorki than naturalistically letting life go on, the last act serves as a vehicle for his ideas.

Rather than examining in detail an "example of the 'mass drama' as first developed by the pioneering naturalists," let us consider Lope de Vega's *Fuenteovejuna*[3] (written probably

between 1612 and 1614), which is said to have a "mass protagonist" in the citizens of the village of Fuenteovejuna, or
Sheepwell. A summary of some detail will give a sense of
the life of the citizens and their conflict with the Commander,
which performance highlights.

Act I. The play opens with Fernando Gomez, Chief Commander of the Order of Calatrava, proud and irritated, waiting
for the young Master of the Order, for whose Masterhood Fernando
risked much. He persuades the young man to take the part of
Portugal against Aragon and Castile, and to storm Ciudad Real
on the frontier of Castile.

Laurencia, in the next scene, declares to Pascuela that she
will have nothing to do with the Commander. She is called on
to arbitrate a dispute on love, Mengo maintaining that there is
only self-love, that the elements are at discord in the world and
in the human body, against the view that all is harmony, which
is pure love. Does Laurencia love?—yes, her honor.

Flores, preceding his master the Commander, gives a brilliant
description of his master and the storming of the city. Musicians
celebrate the return of the Commander, who accepts the gifts of
the village Fuenteovejuna where he has his headquarters. He would
add to those gifts Pascuela and Laurencia, who break away from
Flores and run.

The next scene opens with Queen Isabel advising King Fer-
dinand to proceed swiftly against Portugal. But he will take time
to gather his forces and allies fully, and he sends forces to retake
Ciudad Real which is an entrance for Portugal.

In Fuenteovejuna Laurencia encourages Frondoso, whom she
has been putting off. They hear the Commander, who is hunting,
and she makes Frondoso hide. The Commander turns to her as
quarry, and puts down his crossbow. To prevent the rape Frondoso
takes up the crossbow. The Commander is not fearful. Frondoso
does not shoot, for, he says, "A peasant cannot kill his overlord."
(But in the end he implies that he was the one who killed the
Commander.)

Act II. The peasants have heard how the Commander treated
Laurencia, and would gladly see him hanged as a whoremaster
and tyrant. The Commander comes to tell Esteban (a joint mayor
of the town) that he wants his daughter Laurencia. Esteban warns
him of both divine and human justice. "You will not persuade
us to live without honor or respect."

The Commander speaks with his servants of the women available for his pleasure, whom he little values. The conversation is cut short by a soldier coming to announce the siege of Ciudad Real. Admirable as a soldier, the Commander goes at once with only the fifty men at his command.

Laurencia confesses to Mengo that Frondoso's bravery has made her love him. Jacinta comes, pursued. Pascuela and Laurencia can do nothing to protect her, and go. Mengo, despite his believing only in self-love, stays with his sling and stones, and challenges Flores and the soldiers; but he can do nothing when the Commander appears. The Commander has him flogged and Jacinta given to the soldiers as army baggage.

Frondoso risks his life by coming out of hiding to ask Laurencia to marry him. She says "yes," and her father joyfully gives his consent after teasing her.

The Commander and the Master of Calatrava are escaping from Ciudad Real. The Commander tells the young Master that his hopes are at an end, and that the blood the enemy has lost has made the day a tragedy for victor and the defeated alike.

The wedding is being happily celebrated, when the Commander breaks in and arrests Frondoso. Esteban warns him that the king will put down tyrannic disorder. The Commander then orders Laurencia taken under guard. "The wedding has turned to mourning."

Act III. The townsmen meet in council, and are divided over the question of attempting revenge. Laurencia comes in, having escaped from violation by the soldiers, cut and bruised by their brutality. She taunts the townsmen and inflames them to action. Then she rallies the women.

The Commander is about to have Frondoso hanged from a tower of his house, when he hears the townsmen breaking down the doors. He has Frondoso untied so that he can go out, unharmed, to pacify the attackers. The Commander is warned to escape, but overconfident he stays. The peasants rush in and will listen to no talk of redress for their wrongs. Offstage we hear Esteban cry, "Die, treacherous Commander!" The women take part in the carnage, Pascuela exulting, "I will die killing."

The King and Queen hear of the assassination from the escaped Flores. The king sends a judge and a captain to confirm the truth of the matter and to chastise the guilty.

The peasants are celebrating the death of the tyrant and honoring the king and queen. Esteban is aware that an inquiry must

come and advises that all say only "Fuenteovejuna" did it. The
town agrees, and watches a rehearsal with the comic and sturdy
Mengo.

The Master of Calatrava would raze the village, but the king
now rules there whom he must recognize as sovereign.

Laurencia is terrified at what may happen to her husband
and wants him to escape, but he cannot leave the others in agony
to save his own skin. Not children, nor women, nor the old break
under torture. Mengo on the rack mocks his torturers. The judge,
weary, puts an end to it. Then, after Mengo is feted, there is a
little scene between Frondoso and Laurencia in which he implies
he killed the Commander. (Esteban's advice to the town rules him
out as the one who killed the Commander; he is too honorable
to save himself at their expense.)

In the royal palace Rodrigo, the Master of Calatrava, pays
homage to the king. The matter of Fuenteovejuna no longer con-
cerns Rodrigo, says the king. The judge tells the king that since
there is no proof of guilt, he must pardon or execute the entire
population. Esteban, Frondoso, and Mengo plead their case.
Although the crime is great, the king pardons and takes the village,
which has set up the royal arms on the town hall, under his direct
authority until a commander "worthy of its charge shall emerge."

And so this tale of Fuenteovejuna ends in happiness.

We do indeed have in the play a sense of the life of the
town, but the townspeople are not a mass protagonist. For
the play has a (submerged) plot-structure, and the character
central to that structure is always the protagonist.

*1. Laurencia, saved from the Commander by Frondoso, agrees
to marry him.*

*2. At the wedding, come upon by the Commander who orders
Frondoso arrested, Laurencia is put under the guard of the Commander's men.*

3. Will she come to an unhappy end?
Climax: Escaping, she inflames the townsmen to rebellion.

Just as *Fuenteovejuna* shows that the "mass drama" is not
a modern invention, Lope's play also shows, like Zeami's *Kiyot-*
sune, that the submerged plot-structure does not belong
absolutely to modern drama. That is not very strange. It

would be stranger still if no changes had been rung on drama's primary formal principle, a plot-structure with logically related actions, before our time. But nearly always, in Western drama before our time, the character central to the plot-structure was also the main focus of interest, as in such classic examples as *Oedipus the King, Macbeth,* and *Hedda Gabler.*

15/CONTEMPORARY DRAMA

Submerged Structure in
Beckett's *Waiting for Godot*

If the submerged plot-structure was sporadic before our time, in Zeami and Lope separated by half a world and two centuries, in the new modes of drama it is consistently and everywhere artfully used. Yet we hear that "In the Theatre of the Absurd," it is Martin Esslin speaking, "the action does not proceed in the manner of a logical syllogism." We may expect, then, his observation that Samuel Beckett's *Waiting for Godot* "does not tell a story." Indeed, it is generally thought, even insisted on, that in this play "nothing happens." It is true that the play is highly theatrical—its comic elements especially profit from a first-rate performance—but it is also true that the language of the play is its sufficient medium, and therefore the play is a fair, although severe, test of the main theme of this book. According to Esslin, "Beckett's plays lack plot even more completely than other works of the Theater of the Absurd."[1] *Waiting for Godot* (1952) is the cornerstone of the theater of the absurd (Antonin Artaud's *The Theatre and Its Double* gave the blueprints for the absurd theater); and, to shift the image, *Godot* is the most seminal play in the modern theater of the last quarter century.

The philosophical idea of the absurd got its currency from Albert Camus, who in *The Myth of Sisyphus* wrote, "In a world that cannot be explained the divorce between man and his life, the actor and his setting, is properly the feeling of absurdity. . . . The Absurd is not in man . . . nor in the world, but in their presence together" as "man stands face to face with the irrational." The absurd man "demands of himself . . . to live solely with what he knows, to accommodate himself to what is, and to bring in nothing that is not certain. He is told that nothing is. But this at least is a certainty. . . . It was previously a question of finding out whether or not life had to have a meaning to be lived. It now becomes clear, on the contrary, that it will be lived all the better if it has no meaning." Living an absurd fate, a man must do "everything to keep before him that absurd brought to light by consciousness"; otherwise, he will "elude the problem. The theme of permanent revolution is thus carried into individual experience. . . . Just as danger provided man the unique opportunity of seizing awareness, so metaphysical revolt extends awareness to the whole of experience. . . . It is not aspiration, for it is devoid of hope. That revolt is the certainty of a crushing fate, without the resignation that ought to accompany it." Also, "an absurd attitude, if it is to remain so, must remain aware of its gratuitousness. So it is with the work of art. If the commandments of the absurd are not respected, if the work does not illustrate divorce ["between man and his life, the actor and his setting," i.e. the man acting in the world] and revolt, if it sacrifices to illusions and arouses hope, it ceases to be gratuitous."[2] The issue of hope is in the very plot-structure of *Godot*.

We may well listen to a playwright on the impulse and purpose of the absurd theater, Edward Albee. "As I get it The Theatre of the Absurd is an absorption-in-art of certain existential and post-existential philosophical concepts having to do, in the main, with man's attempts to make sense for himself out of his senseless position in a world which makes no sense—which makes no sense because the moral, religious, political and social structures man has erected to 'illusion' himself have collapsed." He goes on to quote Martin Esslin and to express an Amen to this passage: "Ultimately, a phenomenon like The Theatre of the Absurd does not reflect despair or a return to dark irrational forces but expresses modern man's endeavor to come to terms with the world in which he lives. It attempts to make him face up to the human condition as it really is, to free him from illusions that are bound to cause constant maladjustment and disappointment. . . . For the dignity of man lies in his ability to face reality in all its senselessness; to accept it freely, without fear, without illusions—and to laugh at it." The issue of illusion is woven into the texture of *Godot*.

If the metaphysical theme of absurdity underlies absurd drama, it does not follow that absurdity and the consequent anguish define such drama. The absurd sense of the meaningless of life in the world, or of purposelessness—as Ionesco puts it succinctly, "Absurd is that which is devoid of purpose"—is present in plays by Sartre and Camus, by Giradoux and Anouilh, but these dramatists, says Esslin in his standard book, give "their sense of the irrationality of the human condition in the form of highly lucid and logically constructed reasoning, while The Theatre of the Absurd" openly abandons "rational and discursive thought . . . in trying to achieve a unity between its basic assumptions and the form in which these are expressed." It is probably truer to say, with William Oliver, that absurd "plays appear to be utterly illogical until we realize that the logic of the author's thought is not directly expressed but rather symbolically stated in language."

It is dramatic technique that distinguishes absurd plays from other plays using the premise of metaphysical absurdity. For example, in those plays that use the absurd premise, but are not absurd, the syllogistic plot-structure has a central character who is dominant in the play. Absurd plays, on the other hand, may have submerged syllogistic plot-structures and the play may have no dominant character, which we shall see to be the case in *Godot*. The absurd plays make technical capital of the "logic of the absurd" which is in comedy; according to Théophile Gautier, that logic defines comedy. Such plays also use expressionistic dreamlike technique as comedy for, in Henri Bergson's words, "Comic absurdity is of the same nature as that of dreams." The meaning of absurd that these two notions have in common can easily be bent to the philosophical meaning. The comic in absurd plays may be of a texture so closely interwoven with the tragic as to be indistinguishable. Absurdists use the obscure and the inexplicable symbolically, often for the obscure and the inexplicable existing in the causes of terror and pain that ravage human lives. They use the unrealistic, even the fantastic, making them harmonious with the realistic by the logical relations that exist between the unrealistic and the realistic as deductions from absurd premises. Such premises may, for example, fit together pieces of experience without regard to their influence in time or their relation in space, as is done in dreams. Their language may be stylized, unexpectedly simple for the thoughtful content. In their stylized language meaning may come through rhythmic movement of words, rhythmic repetitions of words, and images also used rhythmically; the rhythm giving a sense of control over the hopelessness and meaninglessness. They also use trivia in a patterned way that makes trivia formally and thematically significant; often the pattern is comic; and there is tension between pattern and trivia as there is between rhythm and meaninglessness. These techniques are not exhaustive chapter headings for an absurd poetics and are not always all present in an absurd play, but they are sufficient to characterize a play as absurd (the premise of metaphysical absurdity always being present). All are present in *Waiting for Godot.*

The play[3] opens with Estragon and Vladimir on a country road in the evening, nothing in the landscape but a bare and unaccommodated tree, like a poor, forked man turned upside down, if I may so interpret the tree, which nonetheless will sprout four or five leaves even as an unaccommodated man sprouts hope. Estragon three times tries to take off his boot and gives up, saying, "Nothing to be done"; Vladimir reflects, "I'm beginning to come round to that opinion. All my life I've tried to put it from me, saying, Vladimir, be reasonable, you haven't tried everything yet. And I resumed the struggle. (*He broods, musing on the struggle.*)" Vladimir thereby not only gives the concrete a universal meaning, he raises the question of whether he will sustain hope, which makes struggling possible, and that question is central to the play. Estragon, who is too irritated to get up for an embrace by Vladimir, has spent the night in a ditch and been beaten, whether by the "same lot as usual" he doesn't know. He feebly calls for help with his boot. The passage that follows uses the rhythm of repetition and trivia in a pattern that is comic:

Vladimir. It hurts?
Estragon. (angrily) Hurts! He wants to know if it hurts!
Vladimir. (angrily) No one ever suffers but you. I don't count. I'd like to hear what you'd say if you had what I have.
Estragon. It hurts?
Vladimir. (angrily) Hurts! He wants to know if it hurts.
Estragon. (pointing) You might button it all the same.
Vladimir. (stooping) True. *(He buttons his fly.)* Never neglect the little things of life.

When Estragon uses the phrase "the last moment" in its casual sense, Vladimir muses on death and deferred hope. When he sometimes feels death coming, he goes all queer, feeling relieved and appalled at the same time. *"(He takes off his hat, peers inside it, feels about inside it, shakes it, puts it on again.) . . .* AP-PALLED. *(He takes off his hat again, peers inside it.)* Funny. *(He knocks on the crown as though to dislodge a foreign body, puts it on again.)* Nothing to be done. *(Estragon with a supreme effort succeeds in pulling off his boot. He peers inside it, turns it upside down, shakes it, looks on the ground to see if anything has fallen out, finds nothing, feels inside it again, staring sightlessly before him.)* "Well?" And Estragon replies, "Nothing." When Estragon will not try to put his boot on again, Vladimir says, "There's man all over for you, blaming on his boots the faults of his feet. *(He takes off his hat again, peers inside it, feels about inside it, knocks on the crown, blows into it, puts it on again.)*" By now we know that the meanings of the boots and hat are closely related. There follows a passage on the two thieves, repentance (For what, says Estragon, "Our being born?"), and salvation, ending with Estragon's exclamation "People are bloody ignorant apes" and Vladimir's picking up a boot (while Estragon limps off and gazes into the distance), peering into it, and manifesting disgust.

The business of the boots and of the hat will be repeated

in the way of symbolism as elements of textural meaning. Estragon goes through business with his boots, his feet hurting, each time a boy comes with a message from Godot, both before and after Vladimir's interview with the messenger. The boots reckon in other ways. A different pair turns up in place of them the second day (at first Estragon says they fit and don't hurt, but then says they're too big). Twice Vladimir picks up a boot, peers into or sniffs it, and manifests disgust. When Pozzo is talking and *"Estragon is fiddling with his boot again, Vladimir with his hat,"* and *"Lucky is half asleep,"* Pozzo cracks his whip for attention. *"Lucky jumps. Vladimir's hat, Estragon's boot, Lucky's hat fall to the ground."* Pozzo then speaks of the passage of the day and the bursting of night upon us, ending "That's how it is on this bitch of an earth." Vladimir reflects, "We're used to it," and *"He picks up his hat, peers inside it, shakes it, puts it on."* A few moments later to cheer up Estragon and Vladimir who have been civil to him and who are having a dull time, Pozzo has Lucky dance (it is a tortured dance). He is about to tell them about the one time Lucky refused when he is distracted and forgets. He exclaims, "Help me!"

> *Estragon.* Wait!
> *Vladimir.* Wait!
> *Pozzo.* Wait!
> *All three take off their hats simultaneously, press their hands to their foreheads, concentrate.*

But the wrong thing is remembered, they realize, and they give up trying to remember and *"They put on their hats."* Then the two tramps want Pozzo to make Lucky think, and Pozzo says, "He can't think without his hat." Vladimir puts Lucky's hat on. Lucky's consequent tirade makes Pozzo suffer, and Estragon and Vladimir protest violently. They all three heap themselves on Lucky, but they can only make him stop his tirade by Vladimir's seizing Lucky's hat. Then *"Vladimir examines the hat, peers inside it."* In the second act, after a try at conversation to help pass the time—first there is a poetic passage on dead voices, and then other tries—Estragon following a silence says with comic pathos, "That wasn't such a bad little canter," but they need to find something else. Each *"takes off his hat, concentrates,"* but when they put on their hats nothing emerges. Later on Vladimir picks up Lucky's hat, left on the ground, and puts it on in place of his own which he hands to Estragon. Then follows a comic routine with the three hats going from one hand to the other. (A similar comic routine is in the Marx Brothers' *Duck Soup*.) Vladimir finally throws his own hat down. *"He takes off Lucky's hat, peers into it, shakes it, knocks it on the crown, puts it on again"* —by now a familiar piece of business. That the business has symbolic meaning connected to thinking is clear, but that meaning is neither easy nor lucid if we try to understand it by translation into words. But however obscure and ambiguous it seems to our reflective thought, the various business with the hat, and with the boot, can be accepted easily by our direct experience, by our perception of the concrete, as having meaning and (absurd) logical relations.

Unlike these textural elements (the textural patterns are infrequently obscure or ambiguous; and when they are, it is with a purpose), the plot-structure is not obscure, for although submerged it can be clearly seen, and is not ambiguous in the rhetorical sense although the end may be liable to two interpretations (that is, the interpretations being contradictory, they cannot exist together as various meanings do in the rhetorical device of ambiguity).

After the passage on the two thieves, Estragon says, "Let's go."

> *Vladimir.* We can't.
> *Estragon.* Why not?
> *Vladimir.* We're waiting for Godot.

This is the first reference to Godot. In Vladimir's mind there is no doubt of the rightness of waiting or of the rightness of the time and place for their waiting. Estragon, who does not want to wait, asks questions that insinuate they've come to the wrong place and then that they are waiting at the wrong time. The exchange culminates in Vladimir's "What'll we do?" It is an expression of doubt. They stop talking. Vladimir walks back and forth agitatedly, stopping only to look into the distance (for Godot) while Estragon falls asleep on a mound. Vladimir—because he is lonely—awakens Estragon. They are at odds—Vladimir won't listen to Estragon's nightmare—but they finally dissolve the anger with an embrace. Needing something to do while they wait, Estragon suggests hanging themselves, and becomes highly excited over the prospect when Vladimir reflects that it would give them an erection; but the notion fizzles out. It's safer to wait. They speak of Godot. When Estragon wants to know if they're tied, Vladimir replies, "To Godot? Tied to Godot? What an idea! No question of it. *(Pause.)* For the moment." The last phrase implies the possibility of breaking the tie. Estragon, chewing on a carrot, comments, "Funny, the more you eat the worse it gets." But for Vladimir it's the opposite (who again informs the concrete with the universal), "I get used to the muck as I go along."

> *Estragon.* No use struggling.
> *Vladimir.* One is what one is.
> *Estragon.* No use wriggling.
> *Vladimir.* The essential doesn't change.
> *Estragon.* Nothing to be done.

The passage echoes, with some change, the opening of the play. Then there is a terrible cry, miming of their fright, and Pozzo and Lucky enter, Lucky tied by a rope around his neck to Pozzo. Vladimir wants to help Lucky, but Estragon holds him back. Estragon asks whether it is Godot. They do not know Pozzo, they explain to him, because they are not from these parts. Nonetheless, he says, they are human, they are of the same species as he (laughing), "Made in God's image!" They are waiting on his land, says Pozzo, but the road is free to all, which is a disgrace. Pozzo has his picnic, using the stool and basket that Lucky carries along with a suitcase (filled with sand, we later learn). Scandalizing Vladimir, Estragon asks for the chicken bones left from Pozzo's picnic, and gets them when Lucky for the first time refuses a bone. Vladimir thinks it a scandal that Pozzo treats a human being as he does, and wants to go, but Pozzo holds him there by reminding him of his appointment "with this

. . . Godet . . . Godot . . . Godin." When Estragon asks a question, and Vladimir presses for an answer, Pozzo measures the change in the two. "A moment ago you were calling me Sir, in fear and trembling. Now you're asking me questions." Vladimir's reactions to Pozzo—his wanting to go, his pressing for an answer—are structurally significant as they prepare for the change in his mind in relation to Godot. Pozzo speaks of his enslaved Lucky, who is trying by all means he can to mollify Pozzo so that his master won't get rid of him. Sixty years ago Pozzo took Lucky as a jester, who taught Pozzo all he knows about beauty, grace, and truth of the first water. Now Lucky has white hair.

    Vladimir. And now you turn him away? Such an old and faithful servant.
    Estragon. Swine!

They are no longer afraid. This change in relations means, dramatically, that something has happened. What has happened is not a part of the plot-structure, but is connected to the plot-structure. Toward the end of the play, when night has come after the second day and Godot can no longer be expected that day, Estragon not wanting to return tomorrow asks, "If we dropped him?" and Vladimir replies, "He'd punish us." But that thought is not a determinant, for with the change in relation to Pozzo they are learning not to be afraid and what they are learning will become stronger in their minds the next day. When the tramps berate him, Pozzo becomes more and more agitated, but not over what they say; he collapses over the way Lucky goes on. And the passage ends comically with the tramps' reversal, Vladimir exclaiming to Lucky, "How dare you! It's abominable! Such a good master! Crucify him like that! After so many years!" The "Crucify" may be another linking of Pozzo and Godot.

    When the scene with Pozzo and Lucky ends, the master and his "pig" gone, Vladimir reflects after a long silence, "That passed the time." Estragon wants to go, but Vladimir says they can't because they're waiting for Godot. A moment later his mind is in a condition of doubt, wondering whether the very changed Pozzo and Lucky are not the same two they've known before (Estragon insists that he does not know them); Vladimir says three times, "Unless they're not the same . . ." Right after his third expression of a doubtful mind, the Boy, the messenger from Godot, calls out "Mister" from a distance to Vladimir, who says to the voice, "Approach, my child." Vladimir is gentle, Estragon rough because he is unhappy. Estragon limps away to take off his boots, and Vladimir alone conducts the interview, as he does on the second day also. The message is, "Mr. Godot told me to tell you that he won't come this evening but surely tomorrow." The boy, like Vladimir, doesn't know if he is unhappy or not. When the boy asks what he is to tell Mr. Godot, Vladimir replies, "Tell him . . . *(he hesitates)* . . . tell him you saw us. *(Pause.)* You did see us, didn't you?" Vladimir, apparently, wants the boy to confirm a doubtful existence. The boy leaves and night falls.

Estragon puts his boots down at the edge of the stage; he will go barefoot, like Christ.

> *Vladimir.* Christ! What has Christ got to do with it? You're not going to compare yourself with Christ?
> *Estragon.* All my life I've compared myself to him.
> *Vladimir.* But where he lived it was warm, it was dry!
> *Estragon.* Yes. And they crucified quick.

The implication is, of course, And we crucify slowly. Vladimir tries to raise his friend's spirits with hope. "To-morrow everything will be better"—because the child said Godot was sure to come. As they go for cover Estragon looks at the tree. "Pity we haven't got a bit of rope." (Rope for a hanging will be in the climax of the plot-structure.) Estragon wonders whether they wouldn't have been better off alone these past fifty years.

> *Vladimir.* (Without anger) It's not certain.
> *Estragon.* No, nothing is certain.

But it's not worth while parting now. They are silent. Then:

> *Estragon.* Well, shall we go?
> *Vladimir.* Yes, let's go.
> *They do not move.*

The curtain descends. The emphasis on nothing being certain, which includes Godot's coming tomorrow, raises the question of whether they will go on waiting.

Act II takes place "Next day. Same time. Same place." The tree now has four or five leaves. When Estragon comes, Vladimir wants to embrace him, as at the beginning of the first act. Estragon doesn't want to be touched at first—he has had another night of senseless beating, which again is made vague to us—but they do embrace. They will wait for Godot.

> Estragon. And if he doesn't come.
> Vladimir. (after a moment of bewilderment) We'll see when the time comes.

They have difficulty finding matter to talk about. Thinking is not the worst. The worst is to *have* thought; their past thoughts are a pile of corpses and skeletons. Their attempts to converse peter out. Vladimir suddenly sees the leaves on the tree.

> Estragon. Leaves.
> Vladimir. In a single night.
> Estragon. It must be the Spring.
> Vladimir. But in a single night!

"In a single night" makes it seem a miracle; and if it is Spring, hope can take root and grow, like life. But Estragon says they weren't there yesterday, that Vladimir had another of his nightmares. Vladimir tries to get Estragon to remember yesterday, and at one pass calls him "pig!" as Pozzo did Lucky. The word marks a change in their relationship, underlined by Vladimir's making Estragon expose the leg that Lucky kicked and saying triumphantly, "There's the wound! Beginning to fester!" Estragon wants to go, but Vladimir still says they can't because they're waiting for Godot. To pass the time, Estragon agrees to try on the boots that have been left in place of his own. When Estragon later sleeps, Vladimir touchingly lays his coat across Estragon's shoulders, making himself cold, and comforts Estragon when he comes wildly out of a nightmare. Again they say:

> *Estragon.* Let's go.
> *Vladimir.* We can't.
> *Estragon.* Why not?
> *Vladimir.* We're waiting for Godot.

Vladimir finding Lucky's hat is sure they are in the right place and their troubles are over. Then follows a comic routine with the hats. Next Vladimir suggests they play at Pozzo and Lucky—yesterday's encounter gives them something to do today, but they can make little of it. They need to pass the time somehow to go on living. When told to "Think, pig!" Vladimir cannot, and when told to "Dance, hog!" Estragon writhes and exits precipitately. He returns in fear, crying, "They're coming!" Vladimir triumphantly exclaims, "It's Godot! We're saved!" But Estragon rushes away, only to come back in terror. There is no place to hide. The causes of his terror do not come. They quarrel and make up. Lucky and Pozzo come. Estragon twice wants to know if it is Godot and then says it is. Vladimir's reaction is, "We were beginning to weaken. Now we're sure to see the evening out." (Thus something has happened; the appearance of Pozzo and Lucky is a dramatic action, having a consequence.) Pozzo, who is blind and groaning on the ground, begs for pity and help. He will pay. "How much?" says Estragon, at last responding. "One hundred francs." "It's not enough." In the first act Estragon begged for five francs. "Two hundred!" Vladimir goes to help—because it's a diversion that should not be let go to waste. Vladimir falls down trying to pull Pozzo to his feet, and himself cannot get up. Estragon tries to help Vladimir after Vladimir promises he will go away with Estragon, only to fall down in like case. When Pozzo is at it again, calling "Pity! Pity!", Vladimir strikes him, and he crawls away. The tramps manage to get up, but Vladimir will not go away; they must wait for Godot. They learn, after picking Pozzo up, that he is blind and Lucky is dumb. Pozzo does not remember having met anybody yesterday. After Lucky, also fallen to the ground, stirs and gets up when furiously kicked by Estragon, Pozzo orders him "On. Whip. Rope." They go, and Estragon

asks Vladimir if it was Godot. Vladimir says "Not at all!"
three times, each time less sure. Estragon's feet hurt, and
after struggling with his boots he dozes. Vladimir reflects,
"At me too someone is looking, of me too someone is saying,
He is sleeping, he knows nothing, let him sleep on. *(Pause.)*
I can't go on!" Then another boy comes from Godot. "I can't
go on" connects with what follows.

> *Vladimir.* You have a message from Mr. Godot.
> *Boy.* Yes Sir.
> *Vladimir.* He won't come this evening.
> *Boy.* No Sir.
> *Vladimir.* But he'll come tomorrow.
> *Boy.* Yes Sir.
> *Vladimir.* Without fail.
> *Boy.* Yes Sir.
> *Silence.*

The exchange tells us that Vladimir knows that Godot will
not come this evening, knows what will be said now but not
done tomorrow, and knows (the tone of "Without fail") that
hope will not be fulfilled. He gives the boy the same message
for Godot, that the boy saw Vladimir. When Estragon awakes,
he says "I'm going." And Vladimir for the first time says,
"So am I." But then says, "We have to come back tomorrow."
They stand before the tree, the only thing that's not dead.
They think to hang themselves and they test for strength
the cord holding up Estragon's trousers.

> *They each take an end of the cord and pull. It breaks. They
> almost fall.*

We may feel the pathos even as we laugh. They have to
come back tomorrow, when they will bring a good piece of
rope.

> *Vladimir.* We'll hang ourselves to-morrow. *(Pause.)* Unless
> Godot comes.
> *Estragon.* And if he comes?
> *Vladimir.* We'll be saved.

But we have seen that Vladimir knows Godot won't come,
that the case is hopeless. The play ends,

> *Vladimir.* Well? Shall we go?
> *Estragon.* Yes, let's go.
> *They do not move.*

It is pretty clear, I think, even without the formulation of the plot-structure, that the general notion of critics that "nothing happens" in the play is false. Here is the formulation:

> *The beginning of change: Vladimir, with strong conviction waiting for Godot, begins to doubt.*
> *The middle: He is told that Godot will come the next day.*
> *To be settled by the end: Will he go on waiting?*
> *Climax: He tests the rope with Estragon and it breaks.*

There is no alternative but to wait; the waiting, however, will be without hope. The change that takes place in Vladimir is from hopefulness to loss of hope.

In an interview in the restaurant La Closerie des Lilas on Montparnasse in 1967, as Alden Whitman reported in *The New York Times* on the occasion of Beckett's winning the Nobel prize, Beckett said that his play "is not supposed to have a dominant character." (He was objecting to Bert Lahr's having played Estragon as the dominant character.) It is no contradiction that Vladimir, although central to the submerged plot-structure, is not dominant in the play. But Beckett also said, and this remark does contradict my interpretation of the end of the play, "*Godot* is not despair, but hope. *Godot* is life—aimless, but always with an element of hope." It is possible, of course, so to interpret the end of the play. It is equally possible to interpret the play as ending with a loss of hope (Vladimir having begun to lose hope, as we have seen, at the very outset of the play). In any case, even if it is believed that hope revives in Vladimir at the end, he nonetheless knows that the case is hopeless (some think this paradox is central to Beckett's thought). His knowing the case is hopeless is the change that takes place in the play, and the plot-structure stands.

CODA

Without external evidence it cannot be asserted that Beckett
rationally formulated a logically unified plot-structure, however evident it is that a careful mind wrote the play. But
we can assert on the strength of the empirical evidence that
the unity of logical relations is inherent in the formal structure
of drama, when the essential medium of the drama is language. With the exception of the Sanskrit, drama acknowledged to be great and unflawed is formed, whether consciously or intuitively, according to that law of its nature.
There are, of course, great plays that are flawed, structurally
or otherwise; such a one is Aeschylus' *The Persians*. Structurally flawed as that work is, it is far greater than very many
an unflawed work in the history of drama, but it is no match
for the perfection of the power and beauty of his structurally
flawless *The Seven Against Thebes*. From Aeschylus to Beckett
we have seen that plays are like vertebrate creatures. Their
bones give them a shape—the better the shape for its purpose,
the better the play works—and the shape gives meaning.
It is meaning that counts finally.

NOTES

1/ THE PLAY: ABOUT WHOM? ABOUT WHAT? A MODERN TEST CASE

1. Jean Anouilh, *Becket*, tr. Lucienne Hill (New York, 1960).
2. Bernard Grebanier, *Playwriting* (New York, 1961); William T. Price, *The Analysis of Play Construction and Dramatic Principle* (New York, 1908). In Price and Grebanier the plot-structure is termed the Proposition, which does not include the climax. It expresses the logic in the three steps of the main action only, paralleling the form of a syllogism. By Grebanier the three steps are termed the condition of the action, the cause of the action, and the resulting action; in Price "condition" is "conditions" and the "resulting action" is the "result of the action."

2/ THE PLAY: ABOUT WHOM? ABOUT WHAT?
A CLASSICAL TEST CASE

1. Thornton Wilder, "Some Thoughts on Playwriting," *The Intent of the Artist*, ed. Augusto Centeno (Princeton, 1941), p. 85.
2. The translation is that of David Grene in *The Complete Greek Tragedies*, ed. David Grene and Richmond Lattimore (Chicago, 1957). Occasionally I have used a variation from *The Tragedies of Sophocles*, tr. Sir Richard C. Jebb (1904; reprinted New York, 1940).
3. The best commentary on the meaning that centers in Philoctetes and on the meaning in the symbols of the play is Lillian Feder's "The Symbol of the Desert Island in Sophocles' *Philoctetes*," *Drama Survey* (Spring-Summer 1963), pp. 33-41.

3/ THE NATURE OF ACTION IN A PLAY

1. Bertolt Brecht, *The Caucasian Chalk Circle*, tr. Eric Bentley (New York, 1966).
2. *Jean Racine. Five Plays*, tr. Kenneth Muir (New York, 1960).

4/ STRUCTURE AND TEXTURE

1. Antonin Artaud, *The Theater and Its Double*, tr. Mary Caroline Richards (New York, 1958), pp. 84, 94, 37, 39, 44, 51, 79.
2. James Joyce, *A Portrait of the Artist as a Young Man*, ed. Richard Ellman (New York, 1964), p. 212.

3. G. Wilson Knight, *The Wheel of Fire* (London, 1930), pp. 180, 182; L.C. Knights, *"How Many Children Had Lady Macbeth?" Explorations* (1933; London, 1946), pp. 4, 16-17; Una Ellis-Fermor, *The Jacobean Drama: An Interpretation*, 4th ed. (London, 1958), p. 38; Marvin Rosenberg, "A Metaphor for Dramatic Form," *The Journal of Aesthetics and Art Criticism*, XVII (December 1958), 174-180; Richard D. Altick, "Symphonic Imagery in *Richard II*" *PMLA*, LXII (March 1947), 339, 340.

5/ JAPANESE DRAMA

1. *The Noh Drama: Ten Plays from the Japanese*, tr. The Special Noh Committee, Japanese Classics Translation Committee (Rutland, Vt., and Tokyo, 1961), p. ix.

2. *The Nō Plays of Japan*, tr. Arthur Waley (New York, 1957), pp. 43, 35, 36. Waley quotes a passage from Zeami which I have slightly re-arranged without quotation marks.

3. The Noh plays in this section are chiefly from *The Noh Drama*; *Kumasaka* is in Waley.

4. *Six Kabuki Plays*, tr. Donald Richie and Myoko Watanabe (Tokyo, 1963), contains the 1960 libretti except for *Kanjincho*; the 1969 libretti are in the special program for the performances, *Kabuki* (New York, 1969); Namiki Gohei III, *Kanjincho*, tr. James R. Brandon and Tamako Niwa, *Evergreen Review*, IV (September-October 1960), 28-57.

5. *Major Plays of Chikamatsu*, tr. Donald Keene (New York, 1961), p. 32.

6/ CHINESE DRAMA

1. *Anthology of Chinese Literature*, ed. Cyril Birch, associate editor, Donald Keene (New York, 1965). One is the comedy *Li K'uei Carries Thorns* by K'ang Chin-chih (fl. 1279), tr. J.I. Crump; the other is the tragic *Autumn in the Palace of Han* by Ma Chih-yüan (fl. 1251), tr. Donald Keene.

2. Hung Sheng, *The Palace of Eternal Youth*, tr. Yang Hsien-yi and Gladys Yang (Peking, 1955).

7/ SANSKRIT DRAMA

1. A. Berriedale Keith, *The Sanskrit Drama in its Origin, Development, Theory & Practice* (London, 1924), pp. 277, 283, 294.

2. The *Natyasastra*, ascribed to Bharati-muni, tr. Manomohan Ghosh (Calcutta, 1950).

3. Tr. Arthur W. Ryder, 1912; reprinted in *Shakuntala and*

Other Writings by Kalidasa (New York, 1959); and by A. Hjalmar Edgren, 1894, reprinted in *Six Sanskrit Plays*, ed. Henry W. Wells (Bombay, 1964).

4. Bhavabhuti, *Rama's Later History*, tr. C.N. Joshi, reprinted in *Six Sanskrit Plays*.

5. *The Little Clay Cart*, tr. Revilo Pendleton Oliver, reprinted in *Six Sanskrit Plays*.

8/ A TRUE PLOTLESS PLAY

1. James Weldon Johnson's *Trumpets of the Lord*, adapted by Vinnette Carroll from *God's Trombones*. Directed by Theodore Mann. Musical adaptations, arrangements, and direction by Howard Roberts.

2. For copies of the play for performances write to Will B. Sandler, 292 Madison Avenue, New York, N.Y., or telephone (212) MU 6-0644.

9/ SO-CALLED "PLOTLESS" PLAYS

1. Gilbert Murray, *Euripides and His Age* (London, 1965), p. 116; and his *The Classical Tradition in Poetry* (1927; New York, 1957), pp. 26, 32.

2. Allardyce Nicoll, *The Theatre and Dramatic Theory* (New York, 1962), p. 16; Jane Ellen Harrison, *Themis: A Study of the Social Origins of Greek Religion*, 2nd ed. (London, 1912), p. 43; Susanne K. Langer, *Feeling and Form* (New York, 1953), p. 364; J.L. Styan, *The Elements of Drama* (Cambridge, 1960), p. 7, and his *The Dramatic Experience: A Guide to the Reading of Plays* (Cambridge, 1965), p. 14; Nicoll, pp. 45, 47; Alan Reynolds Thompson, *The Anatomy of Drama*, 2nd ed. (Berkeley, 1946), p. 2; Molière quoted by Eric Bentley, *The Play* (Englewood Cliffs, 1951), p. 9. Nicoll's quotation from *Knights* is from "How Many Children Had Lady Macbeth?" *Explorations* (London, 1946), p. 4; G. Wilson Knight, *The Wheel of Fire* (1930; New York, 1957), p. 13.

3. Edith Hamilton, tr., *Three Greek Plays* (New York, 1937), p. 25; Richmond Lattimore, tr., *The Trojan Women*, introduction in *Euripides III* of *The Complete Greek Tragedies*, ed. David Grene and Richmond Lattimore (Chicago, 1958); G.M.A. Grube, *The Drama of Euripides* (London, 1941), p. 80; D.J. Conacher, *Euripidean Drama: Myth, Theme, and Structure* (Toronto, 1967), p. 139.

4. The translation is Edith Hamilton's in *Three Greek Plays*.

5. Aeschylus, *Oresteia*, tr. Richmond Lattimore (Chicago, 1953).

10/ The Trilogy as a Dramatic Form

1. Aeschylus, *Oresteia*, tr. Richmond Lattimore (Chicago, 1953).
2. *Selected Plays of Kuan Han-ching*, tr. Yang Hsien-yi and Gladys Yang (Shanghai, 1958).

11/ Shakespearean Structures

1. It is the First Folio that gives this emphasis to Hotspur.
2. Dover Wilson, ed., *The First Part of the History of Henry IV* (Cambridge, 1946, 1958), p. 185, note for V.iii.35-38; for contemporary quotations concerning such practices see A.R. Humphreys, ed., *The First Part of King Henry IV* (London and Cambridge, Mass., 1960), p. 153.
3. Kenneth Muir, ed. *Macbeth* (New York, 1964), footnote for II.i.26-28.

12/ The Medieval Achievement

1. Claude Lévi-Strauss, *Tristes Tropiques*, tr. John Russell (New York, 1961), pp. 262, 302, 274-275, 214, and his *Structural Anthropology*, tr. Claire Jacobson and Brooke Grundfest Schoepf (New York, 1967), p. 98; Paul Radin, *The World of Primitive Man* (New York, 1960), pp. 28, 12; *Structural Anthropology*, p. 227.
2. Thornton Wilder, "Some Thoughts on Playwriting," *The Intent of the Artist*, ed. Augusto Centeno (Princeton, 1941), pp. 94-95.
3. Good paperback anthologies of medieval plays in modern English are *Everyman and Medieval Miracle Plays*, ed. A.C. Cawley (New York, 1959) and *Medieval and Tudor Drama*, ed. John Gassner (New York, 1963). There are also complete cycles in modern English: *The Wakefield Mystery Plays*, ed. Martial Rose (London, 1961) and *The York Cycle of Mystery Plays*, ed. J S. Purvis (London, 1962).

13/ Play Premises and Audience Response

1. Calderón de la Barca, *The Surgeon of His Honour*, tr. Roy Campbell (Madison, 1960).
2. A.A. Parker, "The Approach to the Spanish Drama of the Golden Age," *Tulane Drama Review*, IV (Autumn 1959), pp. 42, 43; originally published in *Diamante* VI (London, 1957); Arnold G. Reichenberger, "The Uniqueness of the *Comedia*," *Hispanic Review*, XXVII (1959), 308, 304-305; C.A. Jones, "*Honor* in Spanish

Golden-Age Drama: Its Relation to Real Life and Morals," *Bulletin of Hispanic Studies*, XXXV (1958), 199-210 passim.

3. *Major Plays of Chikamatsu*, tr. Donald Keene (New York, 1961).

4. M.I. Finley, *Aspects of Antiquity* (New York, 1968), pp. 1, 3, quoting from John Jones, *On Aristotle and Greek Tragedy* (New York, 1962).

5. Kenneth Muir, "The Jealousy of Iago," *English Miscellany II* (Rome, 1951), p. 67; L.C. Knights, *Explorations* (London, 1946), p. 4; G. Wilson Knight, *The Wheel of Fire* (London, 1930), p. 16; Earle Ernst, *The Kabuki Theatre* (New York, 1956), p. 80; Allardyce Nicoll, *The Theatre and Dramatic Theory* (New York, 1962), p. 23; John Gassner, *Directions in Modern Theatre and Drama* (New York, 1965), p. 210.

6. C.G. Jung, *Analytical Psychology: its Theory and Practice* (London, 1968), pp. 45, 40-41, 46.

7. Claude Lévi-Strauss, *Structural Anthropology* (New York, 1967), pp. 198-199.

8. Jung, pp. 11-12.

9. Jean Piaget, *Six Psychological Studies*, tr. Anita Tenzer and ed. David Elkind (New York, 1967), pp. 11, 79, 127, 121, 62-63.

10. Barbel Inhelder and Jean Piaget, *The Growth of Logical Thinking from Childhood to Adolescence*, tr. Anne Parsons and Stanley Milgram (New York, 1958), p. 246.

11. Jean Piaget, *Judgment and Reasoning in the Child*, tr. Marjorie Warden (London, 1928), p. 246.

12. James K. Feibleman, *Aesthetics* (1949; New York, 1968), p. 27.

14/ MODERN DRAMA

1. Richard Samuel and R. Hinton Thomas, *Expressionism in German Life, Literature, and the Theatre (1910-1924)* (Cambridge, 1939), p. 72.

2. George Freedley, "England and Ireland," *A History of Modern Drama*, ed. Barrett Clark and George Freedley (New York and London, 1947), p. 227; Allardyce Nicoll, *World Drama: From Aeschylus to Anouilh* (New York, 1950), p. 807; John Gassner, *A Treasury of the Theatre* (New York, 1960), p. 634.

3. Lope de Vega, *Fuenteovejuna*, tr. Jill Booty, in *Lope de Vega (5 Plays)*, (New York, 1961).

15/ CONTEMPORARY DRAMA

1. Martin Esslin, "The Theatre of the Absurd," *Tulane Drama*

Review, IV (May 1960), 14; *The Theatre of the Absurd* (Garden City, 1961), p. 13.

2. Albert Camus, *The Myth of Sisyphus and Other Essays*, tr. Justin O'Brien (New York, 1955), pp. 5, 23, 21, 39-40, 75.

3. Samuel Beckett, *Waiting for Godot* (New York, 1954).

BIBLIOGRAPHY

Adams, Joseph Quincy, ed. *Chief Pre-Shakespearean Dramas*. Boston, 1924.

Albee, Edward. "Which Theatre Is the Absurd One?" *The New York Times*, February 25, 1962.

Altick, Richard D. "Symphonic Imagery in *Richard II*," *PMLA*, LXX (March 1947), 339-365.

Anthology of Chinese Literature from Early Times to the Fourteenth Century. Ed. Cyril Birch, associate ed. Donald Keene. New York, 1965.

Araki, James T. *The Ballad-Drama of Medieval Japan*. Berkeley, 1964.

Aristotle. See Fyfe.

Arrowsmith, William. "The Criticism of Greek Tragedy," *Tulane Drama Review*, III (March 1959).

Artaud, Antonin. *The Theater and Its Double*. Tr. Mary Caroline Richards. New York, 1958.

Auerbach, Erich. *Mimesis: The Representation of Reality in Western Literature*. Tr. Willard R. Trask. Princeton, 1953.

Beare, William. *The Roman Stage*. 3rd ed. New York, 1965.

Beckerman, Bernard. *Dynamics of Drama: Theory and Method of Analysis*. New York, 1970.

Bergson, Henri. *Laughter*. In *Comedy*. Ed. Wylie Sypher. New York, 1956.

Bentley, Eric. *The Playwright as Thinker: A Study of Drama in Modern Times*. 1946; Cleveland, 1955.

————. *What Is Theatre?* Boston, 1956.

Bieber, Margarete. *The History of the Greek and Roman Theatre*. Princeton, 1939.

Bodkin, Maud. *Archetypal Patterns of Poetry: Psychological Studies of Imagination*. London, 1934, 1963.

Bowers, Faubion. *Theatre in the East: A Survey of Asian Dance and Drama*. New York, 1956.

Bowra, C.M. *Sophoclean Tragedy*. Oxford, 1944.

Brecht, Bertolt. *The Caucasian Chalk Circle*. Tr. Eric Bentley. New York, 1966.

Browne, E. Martin. *Religious Drama 2*. New York, 1958.

Camus, Albert. *The Myth of Sisyphus and Other Essays*. Tr. Justin O'Brien. New York, 1955.

Carroll, Vinnette. *Trumpets of the Lord.* Adapted from James Weldon Johnson's *God's Trombones.* c 1964 by Theodore B. Mann and Will B. Sandler.

Chambers, E.K. *The Medieval Stage.* 2 vols. Oxford, 1903.

Ch'ên Shou-yi. *Chinese Literature. An Historical Introduction.* New York, 1961.

The Chester Plays. Ed. H. Deimling and G.W. Matthews. Early English Text Society, Extra Series, 62 and 115. 1892, 1916; reprinted Oxford, 1959.

Clark, Barrett H. *European Theories of the Drama. With a Supplement on the American Drama.* Revised by Henry Popkin. New York, 1965.

Clark, Barrett H. and George Freedley. *A History of Modern Drama.* New York and London, 1947.

The Complete Greek Tragedies. Ed. David Grene and Richmond Lattimore. Chicago, 1959.

Conacher, D.J. *Euripidean Drama: Myth, Theme and Structure.* Toronto, 1967.

Craig, Hardin. *English Religious Drama of the Middle Ages.* London, 1955.

Dowson, John. *A Classical Dictionary of Hindu Mythology and Religion, Geography, History, and Literature.* 1879; 11th ed., London, 1968.

Duerrenmatt, Friedrich. "Problems of the Theater," tr. Gerhard Nellhaus, *Tulane Drama Review,* III (October 1958), 3-26; also in Clark, *European Theories of the Drama.*

Ellis-Fermor, Una. *The Jacobean Drama: An Interpretation,* 4th ed. London, 1958.

Else, Gerald F. *Aristotle's Poetics: The Argument.* Cambridge, Mass., 1957.

Empson, William. *Some Versions of Pastoral.* London, 1935.

Ernst, Earle. *The Kabuki Theatre.* New York, 1956.

Esslin, Martin. *The Theatre of the Absurd.* Garden City, 1961.

———. "The Theatre of the Absurd," *Tulane Drama Review,* IV (May 1960), 3-15.

Feder, Lillian. "The Symbol of the Desert Island in Sophocles' *Philoctetes,*" *Drama Survey* (Spring-Summer 1963), 33-41.

Feibleman, James K. *Aesthetics: a Study of the Fine Arts in Theory and Practice.* 1949; reprinted New York, 1968.

———. *The Theory of Human Culture.* 1946; reprinted New York, 1968.

Fergusson, Francis. *The Idea of a Theatre.* Princeton, 1949.

Finley, M.I. *Aspects of Antiquity. Discoveries and Controversies.* New York, 1968.

Frank, G. *The Medieval French Drama.* Oxford, 1954.

Frye, Northrop. *The Anatomy of Criticism. Four Essays.* 1957; New York, 1967.

Friedländer, Ludwig. *Roman Life and Manners under the Empire.* Vol. II. London and New York, n.d.

Fyfe, W. Hamilton, tr. *Aristotle, The Poetics,* rev. ed. London and Cambridge, Mass., 1932.

Gassner, John. *Directions in Modern Theatre and Drama, an expanded edition of Form and Ideas in Modern Theatre.* New York, 1965.

————. *A Treasury of the Theatre: from Henrik Ibsen to Eugene Ionesco.* New York, 1960.

Gelb, Arthur and Barbara. *O'Neill.* New York, 1961.

Ghéon, Henri. *The Art of the Theatre.* New York, 1961.

Grebanier, Bernard. *Playwriting.* New York, 1961.

Grotowski, Jerzy. *Towards a Poor Theatre.* New York, 1968.

Grube, G.M.A. *The Drama of Euripides.* London, 1941.

Harrison, Jane Ellen. *Themis: A Study of the Social Origins of Greek Religion.* 2nd ed. Cambridge, 1927.

Hazlitt, William. *Characters of Shakespeare's Plays.* London, 1817; reprinted 1966.

Henriques, Fernando. *Prostitution in Europe and the Americas.* London, 1963.

Holland, Norman N. *The Dynamics of Literary Response.* New York, 1968.

Huizinga, Johan. *Homo Ludens. A Study of the Play-Element in Culture.* 1944; Boston, 1955.

Hung Lou Mêng, or the Dream of the Red Chamber. By Tsao Hsueh-chin and Kao Ngoh. Tr. Florence and Isabel McHugh. New York, 1958.

Hung Sheng. *The Palace of Eternal Youth.* Tr. Yang Hsien-yi and Gladys Yang. Peking, 1955.

Ingalls, Daniel H.H., tr. *Sanskrit Poetry.* Cambridge, Mass., 1968.

Inhelder, Barbel and Jean Piaget. *The Growth of Logical Thinking from Childhood to Adolescence.* Tr. Anne Parsons and Stanley Milgram. New York, 1958.

Jaeger, Werner. *Paideia: the Ideals of Greek Culture.* 3 vols. Tr. Gilbert Highet. Volume I. New York, 1939.

Japanese Folk-Plays: The Ink-Smeared Lady and Other Kyogen. Tr. Shio Sakanishi. Rutland, Vt., 1960.

Jean Racine: Complete Plays. Tr. Samuel Solomon. 2 vols. New York, 1967.

Jean Racine: Five Plays. Tr. Kenneth Muir. New York, 1960.

Johnson on Shakespeare. 2 vols. Ed. Arthur Sherbo. New Haven, 1968. Vol. I.

Jebb, Sir Richard, tr. *The Tragedies of Sophocles.* 1904; New York, 1940.

Jones, C.A. "*Honor* in Spanish Golden-Age Drama: Its Relation to Real Life and to Morals," *Bulletin of Hispanic Studies,* XXXV (1958), 199-210.

Jones, John. *On Aristotle and Greek Tragedy.* New York, 1962.

Joseph, B.L. *Elizabethan Acting,* 2nd ed. Oxford, 1964.

Joyce, James. *A Portrait of the Artist as a Young Man.* Ed. Richard Ellmann. New York, 1964.

Jung, C.G. *Analytical Psychology: its Theory and Practice.* London, 1968.

———. *Introduction to a Science of Mythology.* Tr. R.F.C. Hull. London, 1951.

———. "On the Relation of Analytical Psychology to Poetic Art," *Contributions to Analytical Psychology.* Tr. H.G. and Cary F. Baynes. London, 1928.

———. *Symbols of Transformation.* Tr. R.F.C. Hull. New York, 1956.

Kaufmann, Walter. *Tragedy & Philosophy.* Garden City, 1968.

Keene, Donald. *Japanese Literature. An Introduction for Western Readers.* London, 1953.

———. *Major Plays of Chikamatsu.* New York, 1961.

Keith, A. Berriedale. *The Sanskrit Drama in its Origin, Development, Theory & Practice.* Oxford, 1924.

Kitto, H.D.F. *Form and Meaning in Drama. A Study of Six Greek Plays and of Hamlet,* 2nd ed. London, 1964.

Knight, G. Wilson. *The Wheel of Fire. Interpretation of Shakespeare's Tragedy.* 1930; 5th rev. ed., Cleveland, 1957.

Knights, L.C. *Explorations.* London, 1946.

Kolve, V.A. *The Play Called Corpus Christi.* Stanford, 1961.

Kuan Han-ching. See *Selected Plays.*

La Meri. *The Gesture Language of the Hindu Dance.* 1941; New York, 1964.

Langer, Susanne K. *Feeling and Form: A Theory of Art* developed from *Philosophy in a New Key.* New York, 1953.

Lawler, Lillian B. *The Dance in Ancient Greece.* Middletown, Conn., 1965.

Lesky, Albin. *Greek Tragedy.* Tr. H.A. Frankfort. London and New York, 1965.

Lévi-Strauss, Claude. *Structural Anthropology.* Tr. Claire Jacobson and Brooke Grundfest Schoepf. New York, 1967.

———. *Tristes Tropiques.* Tr. John Russell. New York, 1961.

Ludus Coventriae. Ed. K.S. Block. Early English Text Society, Extra Series, 120. 1922.

Mahabharata. Selected verses tr. by C.V. Narasimhan. New York, 1965.

Medieval French Plays. Tr. Richard Axton and John Stevens. London and New York, 1971.

Moulton, Richard G. *The Ancient Classical Drama.* Oxford, 1890.

Mueller, Karl O. *History of the Literature of Ancient Greece,* new ed. Tr. George Cornwall Lewe. London, 1847.

Muir, Kenneth. "The Jealousy of Iago," *English Miscellany II.* Rome, 1951.

———. See *Jean Racine: Five Plays.*

Murray, Gilbert. *The Classical Tradition in Poetry.* 1927; New York, 1957.

———. *Euripides and His Age.* With a new Introduction by H.D.F. Kitto. London, 1965.

Namiki Gohei III. *Kanjincho.* Tr. James R. Brandon and Tamako Niva. *Evergreen Review,* IV (September-October 1960), 28-57.

The Natyasastra. A Treatise on Hindu Dramaturgy and Histrionics. Ascribed to Bharata-muni. Tr. Manomohan Ghosh. Calcutta, vol. I, 1950, vol. II, 1961.

Nicoll, Allardyce. *English Drama: A Modern Viewpoint.* New York, 1968.

———. *Masks Mimes and Miracles: Studies in the Popular Theatre.* 1931; New York, 1963.

———. *The Theatre and Dramatic Theory.* New York, 1962.

———. *World Drama: From Aeschylus to Anouilh.* New York, 1950.

The Noh Drama: Ten Plays from the Japanese. Tr. the Special Noh Committee, Japanese Classics Translation Committee. Rutland, Vermont, and Tokyo, 1955.

The Nō Plays of Japan. Tr. Arthur Waley. 1921; New York, 1957.

Norwood, Gilbert. *Greek Tragedy,* 4th ed. London, 1948.

Oliver, William I. "Between Absurdity and the Playwright," *Educational Theatre Journal,* XV (1963), 224-235.

Olson, Elder. *Tragedy and the Theory of Drama.* Detroit, 1961.

Pantin, C.F.A. *The Relations Between the Sciences.* Cambridge, 1968.

Parker, A.A. "The Approach to the Spanish Drama of the Golden Age," *Tulane Drama Review,* IV (Autumn 1959), 42-59; originally published in *Diamante* VI, London, 1957.

Piaget, Jean. *Judgment and Reasoning in the Child.* Tr. Marjorie Warden. London, 1928.

———. *Six Psychological Studies.* Tr. Anita Tenzer and ed. David Elkind. New York, 1967.

———. See also Inhelder.

Pickard-Cambridge, Sir Arthur. *The Dramatic Festivals of Athens,* 2nd ed. Rev. John Gould and D.M. Lewis. Oxford, 1968.

Plato with an English Translation. Vol. V. *Symposium.* Tr. W.R.M. Lamb. Cambridge, [Mass.] and London, 1925. Vols. IX and X. *Laws.* Tr. R.G. Bury. London and New York, 1926.

Powys, John Cowper. *Rabelais.* London, 1948.

Price, William T. *The Analysis of Play Construction and Dramatic Principle.* New York, 1908.

Prior, Moody E. *The Language of Tragedy.* New York, 1947.

Radin, Paul. *The World of Primitive Man.* 1953; New York, 1960.

Racine, Jean. See Muir and Solomon.

Ransom, John Crowe. *The New Criticism.* Norfolk, Conn., 1941.

Reichenberger, Arnold G. "The Uniqueness of the *Comedia,*" *Hispanic Review,* XXVII (1959), 303-316.

Richards, Ivor Armstrong. *Practical Criticism, a Study of Literary Judgment.* London, 1929.

Rosenberg, Marvin. "A Metaphor for Dramatic Form," *The Journal of Aesthetics & Art Criticism,* XVII (December 1958), 174-180.

Rossiter, A.P. *Angel with Horns and Other Shakespeare Lectures.* Ed. Graham Storey. London, 1961.

Rojas, de, Fernando. *La Celestina.* Tr. J.M. Cohen under the title *The Spanish Bawd.* Baltimore, 1964.

Samuel, Richard and R. Hinton Thomas. *Expressionism in German Life, Literature and the Theatre (1910-1924).* Cambridge, 1939.

Scott, A.C. *The Classical Theatre of China.* New York, 1957.

Seami's Sixteen Treatises. Tr. Michitaro Shidehara and Wilfred Whitehouse. In *Monumenta Nipponica,* IV (July 1941), 204-239 and V (December 1942), 180-214 (Of the projected translations only *Kwadensho* was published.)

Selected Plays of Kuan Han-ching. Tr. Yang Hsien-yi and Gladys Yang. Shanghai, 1958.

Shakuntala and Other Writings by Kalidasa. Tr. Arthur W. Ryder. New York, 1959.

Six Sanskrit Plays. Ed. H.W. Wells. Bombay, 1964.

Snell, Bruno. *The Discovery of the Mind: The Greek Origins of European Thought.* 1953; New York, 1960.

Stanislavski, Constantin. *My Life in Art.* Tr. J.J. Robbins. New York, 1924.

Strindberg, August. *A Dream Play.* Tr. Arvid Paulson. In Gassner, *A Treasury of the Theatre.*

Styan, J.L. *The Dramatic Experience: A Guide to the Reading of Plays.* Cambridge, 1965.

————. *The Elements of Drama.* Cambridge, 1960.

Sypher, Wylie. "The Meanings of Comedy." In *Comedy.* Ed. Wylie Sypher. New York, 1956.

Thompson, Alan Reynolds. *The Anatomy of Drama*, 2nd ed. Berkeley, 1946.

————. *The Dry Mock: A Study of Irony in Drama.* Berkeley, 1948.

Three Japanese Plays from the Traditional Theatre. Ed. Earle Ernst. New York, 1956.

The Towneley Plays. Ed. G. England and A.W. Pollard. Early English Text Society, Extra Series, 71, 1897, 1952.

Traditional Chinese Plays. Tr. A.C. Scott. New York, 1957.

Turnell, Martin. *The Classical Moment: Studies of Corneille, Molière, and Racine.* New York, n.d.

Two One-Act Plays of Bhasa. Tr. G.K. Bhat. Kolhapur, n.d.

Valency, Maurice. *The Flower and the Castle. An Introduction to Modern Drama.* New York, 1963.

Van Laan, Thomas F. *The Idiom of Drama.* Ithaca, 1970.

Varma, K.M. "La Base du Théâtre Classique Indien," in *Les Théâtres D'Asie.* Ed. Jean Jacquot. Paris, 1961.

Vinaver, Eugène. *Racine and Poetic Tragedy.* Tr. P. Mansell Jones. Manchester, 1955.

The Wakefield Mystery Plays. Tr. Martial Rose. London, 1961. See also *The Towneley Plays.*

Webster, T.B.L. *Greek Theatre Production.* London, 1956.

Wells, Henry W. *The Classical Drama of the Orient.* New York, 1965.

————. *The Classical Drama of India.* London, 1963.

Wells, Stanley. *Literature and Drama: with special reference to Shakespeare and his contemporaries.* London, 1970.

Wellwarth, George E. *The Theater of Protest and Parodox.* New York, 1964.

Whitehead, Alfred North. *Adventures of Ideas.* New York, 1933.

Whitman, Cedric H. *Sophocles: A Study of Heroic Humanism.* Cambridge, Mass., 1951.

Wilder, Thornton. "Some Thoughts on Playwriting." In *The Intent of the Artist.* Ed. Augusto Centeno. Princeton, 1941.

————. *Three Plays: Our Town, The Skin of Our Teeth, the Matchmaker* New York, 1957.

Wilson, Dover, ed. *The First Part of The History of Henry IV.* Cambridge, 1946, 1958.

The York Cycle of Mystery Plays. Tr. J.S. Purvis. London, 1957.

York Plays. Ed. Lucy Toulmin Smith. Oxford, 1933.

Young, Karl. *The Drama of the Medieval Church.* 2 vols. Oxford, 1933.

Zeami. *Kadensho.* Tr. Chuichi Sakurai and others. Tokyo, 1968. See also *The Noh Drama, The Nō Plays of Japan,* and *Seami's Sixteen Treatises.*

Zoete, de, Beryl and Walter Spies. *Dance and Drama in Bali.* New York, 1939.

SUPPLEMENT/The Text of Zeami's *Kiyotsune*

THE NOH STAGE

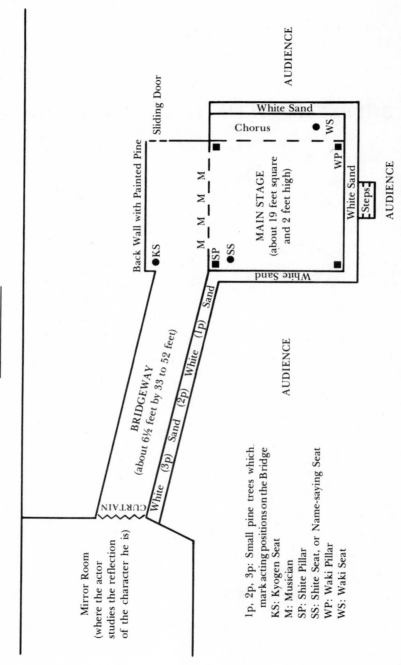

Mirror Room
(where the actor
studies the reflection
of the character he is)

CURTAIN

BRIDGEWAY
(about 6½ feet by 33 to 52 feet)

White (3p) Sand (2p) White (1p) Sand

Back Wall with Painted Pine

Sliding Door

White Sand

Chorus

WS

KS

M M M M

SP
SS

WP

MAIN STAGE
(about 19 feet square
and 2 feet high)

White Sand

White Sand

Steps

AUDIENCE

AUDIENCE

AUDIENCE

1p, 2p, 3p: Small pine trees which
mark acting positions on the Bridge
KS: Kyogen Seat
M: Musician
SP: Shite Pillar
SS: Shite Seat, or Name-saying Seat
WP: Waki Pillar
WS: Waki Seat

Kiyotsune*

(As we cannot, of course, include an anthology of Eastern drama, we have chosen to present a Noh play—the most difficult kind of Eastern play to approach without a specimen of a text.)

Introduction

The play is built round a very touching incident recorded in the *Heike Monogatari*. After a series of disastrous reverses at the hands of the Genji late in 1183, the Heike army was forced back to the northeastern corner of Kyushu in the neighbourhood of the famous Hachiman Shrine[1] at Usa. Desiring to know the fate which lay in store for the clan, the leaders requested the god to grant them an oracle. When the god replied that they must give up all hope, Kiyotsune, the third son of Taira-no-Shigmori,[2] who was lieutenant-general of the Left Wing of the Imperial Body-guard, immediately decided to throw himself on the mercy of Buddha and thus ensure his future bliss. Eager to enter the Western Paradise, invoking the name of Amida he leapt one night from his boat into the sea and drowned himself. Subsequently a lock of his hair was discovered in the boat apparently cut off by him and left as a keepsake for his wife in

---

*From *The Noh Drama: Ten Plays from the Japanese*, selected and translated by the Special Noh Committee, Japanese Classics Translation Committee (Rutland, Vt., and Tokyo: Charles E. Tuttle Company, 1955). By permission of the publisher.
[1]Ancient Shinto shrine in Buzen Province, Kyushu, dedicated to the Emperor Ojin. In the ninth century, in accordance with an oracle, another shrine was built near Kyoto known as Otoko-yama Hachiman, which came to be especially revered by the Genji as the shrine of their patron deity just as that on Miyajima in the Inland Sea was by the Heike clan.
[2]Unlike his father Kiyomeri who was a typical dictator, Shigemori was righteous, merciful and refined, and tried to restrain his father's policy of violence. After his son's death at a comparatively early age, Kiyomori gave full rein to his inordinate lust for power which ultimately led to the downfall of the family.

Miyako, which his faithful retainer, Awazu-no-Saburo, took upon himself
to deliver.

The feelings of mingled sorrow and resentment aroused in Kiyotsune's
wife by the news of her husband's suicide, lead up to a moving scene
between her and the ghost of Kiyotsune which appears to her in a dream.
The play ends with a remarkable dance performed by Kiyotsune's ghost
in which he evokes the strife-torn world of the *Asuras* described by the
chorus. (The Asuras inhabit a world of transmigration. Full of jealousy
and hate, they are continuously engaged in fighting one another as a
punishment for their deeds of violence in their previous life, until they
have worked out their *karma* or until through invocation of Amida they
have achieved enlightenment and are reborn in the Western Paradise.)
In answer to his tenfold invocation of Amida[3] at the time of his death
Kiyotsune, purified at last from all thoughts of hate, enters the Western
Paradise by virtue of the saving vow of Amida.

The main theme of the present drama might perhaps best be described
as the strife of love and death in a dream. These two motives not only
dominate, but provide the main dramatic interest, which is further en-
hanced by the tragic historical events which destroyed the wedded happiness of Kiyotsune's wife who was separated from her husband, first by the
war and then by his wilful and seemingly unnecessary suicide. The play
also develops not less clearly but with greater subtlety than other Noh
plays the underlying Buddhistic theme that it is only through faith in the
Great Vow of Amida that man can escape rebirth and achieve ultimate
blessedness.

As regards its production, the following points are worth noting because
of their dramatic significance. At the beginning of the dream the *waki*
(Awazu-no-Saburo), instead of leaving the stage by the Bridgeway, as is
customary, retires though the Sliding Door. When the *shite* (Kiyotsune)
appears in his wife's dream towards the end of the scene, he enters softly
while the chorus is singing, thus indicating the passage from reality to
dream. The *tsure* (Kiyotsune's wife) remains on the stage throughout the
performance, while the *waki*, contrary to the general practice in most Noh
plays, only appears in the earlier part. In the later scenes only two persons
are on the stage, the *tsure* (who never moves from the *Waki* Seat) and the
shite. Since the latter is really a dream figure existing only in the wife's
imagination and not a real ghost, the whole play may be regarded, in
effect, as a one-person play. Finally, the absence of the *kyogen* is due to
the fact that, apart from its being a one-act play, a comic interlude would
introduce a discordant note and destroy the emotional tension created by
the dream-scene.

[*the* tsure *in
Noh drama is
an attendant of
the* shite]

---

[3] According to the tenets of the Amidist sects prevalent in those days, tenfold repeti-
tion just before death of the formula "Namu Amida Butsu" (I put all my faith in
Amida Buddha) had the power to ensure the immediate rebirth into the Western
Paradise.

Author: Zeami Motokiyo (1363-1443)

Source: *Gempei Seisuiki* (History of the Rise and Fall of the Genji and the Heike), Vol. XXXIII: "Episode of Kiyotsune's Suicide"; *Heike Monogatari* (Tale of the Heike), Vol. VIII: "The Heike's Evacuation from the Dazaifu."

Persons

WIFE OF KIYOTSUNE	*Tsure*
AWAZU-NO-SABURO	*Waki*
GHOST OF KIYOTSUNE	*Shite*

Place

Hiding-place of Kiyotsune's wife in Miyako

Season

Late autumn

Wife of Kiyotsune *appears on the Bridgeway and advancing across it, enters the stage and sits on the* Waki *Seat. She wears a* tsure *mask, wig, painted gold-patterned under-kimono and brocade outer-kimono.*

1

While the entrance music shidai *is being played,* Awazu-no-Saburo *appears, crosses the Bridgeway and stops by the* Shite *Pillar. He wears a striped kimono,* kake-suo *robe, white broad divided skirt, short sword, mushroom hat and amulet-bag hanging from his neck.*

Awazu. Crossing the surges of the eightfold sea,
shidai [en- Crossing the surges of the eightfold sea,
trance music] I must return to where the Court
Stands within its nine gates.[4]

Chorus. Crossing the surges of the eightfold sea,
jidori [repeti- I must return to where the Court
tion of shidai] Stands within its nine gates.

Awazu. I am a retainer of the late Kiyotsune, Lieutenant-General of the Left Wing of the Imperial Body-guard. Awazu-no-Saburo is my name. My late master was defeated in the battles in Tsukushi,[5] and since his retreat to Miyako was cut off, he probably preferred to take his own life rather than perish at the hands of the common soldiery no better than wayside weeds. So, late one moonlit night, he plunged from his boat into the sea off the coast of Yanagi.[6] Later, when searching the boat, I found a lock of hair he had left behind him as a keepsake. Having undeservedly escaped with my life, I am now carrying this keepsake to his wife in Miyako.

---

[4] Conventional epithet for the Imperial City.
[5] Ancient name for Kyushu now rarely used.
[6] Town on the eastern coast of Buzen Province.

michi-yuki   In recent years
[*travel song*]   I have lived a country life,
                      I have lived a country life.
                      My heart is filled with sadness,
                      Since, when I return,   *Retiring to*
                      Miyako's glorious springtide no more will   *the Stage-*
                          greet me.   *attendants'*
                      Past is mournful autumn,   *Seat, removes*
                      And the wintry rain   *his mushroom*
                      Beats down upon my dress.   *hat and slip-*
                      Grieving at my unhappy fate,   *ping the*
                      My sleeves are drenched with tears,   *amulet-bag*
                      As in disguise my journey I pursue,   *inside the fold*
                      As in disguise my journey I pursue.   *of his kimono,*
            Travelling in haste, I have quickly reached Miyako.   *moves to the*
                                                                     Shite *Pillar.*

2

Awazu. A visitor is announcing his arrival. It is Awazu-no-Saburo just   *Turns*
come from Tsukushi. Please announce him.   *towards the*
    Wife. What? Is it you, Awazu-no-Saburo? You need not be announced.   Waki *Seat.*
Pray enter. What message do you bring me from my lord?
    Awazu. A message I am loath to deliver to my lady.   *Kneeling in*
    Wife. A message you are loath to deliver? Has my lord perchance   *the centre of*
renounced the world?   *the stage, and*
    Awazu. No, he has not renounced the world.   *placing both*
    Wife. I have heard he has come safely through the recent battles in *hands on the*
Tsukushi.   *floor, makes a*
    Awazu. Yes, my lady, he has come safely through the recent battles   *deep*
in Tsukushi. But since his way to Miyako was cut off, my lord thought   *obeisance.*
to put an end to his own life rather than lose it at the hands of nameless
soldiery no better than wayside weeds and while we were off the coast
of Yanagi in Buzen Province, late one moonlit night, he leapt overboard
and was drowned.
    Wife. What! You mean he cast himself into the sea?
                      Never can I forgive him such an end!
                      Had he in battle perished
                      Or died of illness,
                      I could resign myself to fate;
                      But that he himself should seek
                      A watery grave
                      Proves all his vows
                      Were lying words.
                      Oh! Woe is me,
                      Naught's left me in this world
                      Save my vain rancour against my lord!

Chorus.	How dream-like now appear
sage-uta	Our wedded joys!
age-uta [*low-*	Through all these troubled years[7]
pitched and	I've hid from prying eyes,
high-pitched	I've hid from prying eyes—
singing	My sobs voiceless as the rustle of *susuki*
respectively]	grass[8]

Swayed by autumn winds
In the hedge round my dwelling.
From whom need I to-day conceal my
    grief?
Like to the cuckoo[9]
Crying until the moon-beams
Grow pale in the dawn sky,
Freely and openly I'll weep,
Freely and openly I'll weep!

Awazu. Later I searched the boat and found this lock of my lord's hair left you as a keepsake. Pray gaze on it and soothe your grieving heart.

<table>
<tr><td>Wife.</td><td>Is this the raven lock of my
    late lord?
My eyes are blinded,
My spirit longs for its release
And ever stronger grows my yearning.
"Each time I look upon this lock
Grief tears at my heart;
I bid it hence return
Unto my sorrow's fountain-head."[10]</td><td>Places the
amulet-bag on
his fan and
offers it to
KIYOTSUNE'S
wife, who
takes it.</td></tr>
<tr><td>Chorus.
sage-uta
[low-pitched
singing]</td><td>As she repeats these lines,
The keepsake she returns
And seeks her couch.
Tears of longing fall,</td><td>KIYOTSUNE'S
wife places
the amulet-
bag on the
floor.

  Soon after
the CHORUS
begins,
AWAZU
retires through
the Sliding
Door.</td></tr>
</table>

[7]Allusion to the period following the abandonment of Miyako by the Heike in the autumn of 1183 and its occupation by the Genji troops. At that time Kiyotsune's wife was forced by her parents to remain in Miyako instead of following her lord into the west. The death of Kiyotsune took place three years later.

[8]*Miscanthus sinensis:* wild grass somewhat resembling pampas grass and found all over Japan. It reaches five or six feet in height, and in autumn puts forth tassel-like flowers.

[9]I.e. *hototogisu*, the Japanese species of the cuckoo genus which comes to Japan from the south in late spring and leaves in autumn. Unlike its Western relative, its cry consists of several notes instead of two and is often heard at night.

[10]The original contains a number of pivot-words which baffle any attempt at literal translation, such as "tsukushi" (to grieve or place-name), "kami" (hair or god) and "usa" (grief or the Shinto shrine of that name).

> The while she prays that he may come to
>   her
> If but in dream.
> Sleepless, in vain her pillow oft she shifts;
> Yet ever stronger grows her longing,
> Yet ever stronger grows her longing.

3

The GHOST OF KIYOTSUNE, *who has appeared during the last chorus, advances and stands by the First Pine. He wears a* chujo *mask, long black-hair wig, white head-band, tall black cap, embroidered kimono, gold-brocade robe with left shoulder uncovered, white broad divided skirt and sword.*

Kiyotsune.	'Tis said: "The sage is dream-free,"[11]
sashi	Yet for whom is life reality?
[recitatif]	"A mote within the eye
	May cause a man to feel
	The threefold world too small;
	But when his mind is free from care,
	His couch seems vaster than the world."[12]
	Past griefs are truly but illusion
	And present sadness but a dream;
	Which, like drifting cloud or running water,
	Do pass away, leaving no trace.
	O poor frail self that clings unto this world!
	"Since once I saw my lover in a dream,
	I've learned to trust in dreams."[13]
	O thou whom I once loved!
	Kiyotsune is here!
Wife.	O wondrous marvel!
	I see Kiyotsune by my pillow,
	And yet I know that he has drowned himself.
	How then can I behold him save
	in dream?
	Though but a dream,
	Yet I am thankful
	To see his form once more.
	But since, defying heaven's decree,
	You brought your life to an untimely end,

Advancing on to the stage, stands before his WIFE.

---

[11] Quotation from Ta-hui Sung-kao (1089-1163), a Chinese monk of the Zen sect. The same saying in a slightly altered form is traceable to Chuang-tse.

[12] Quoted from a Chinese poem by Muso Kokushi (1275-1351), a Japanese monk of the Zen sect.

[13] Poem by Ono-no-Komachi included in the *Kokinshu.*

	You've proved yourself untrue
	And bred resentment in my breast.
Kiyotsune.	Though you reproach me for my deed,
	You too are not unworthy of reproach.

Why did you spurn the keepsake I left to ease your pain?

Wife.	No! No! Why I did so
	Is set forth in a poem
	Which scarce conveys
	How deep the sight of it did stir me.
	"Each time I look upon this lock,
	Grief tears at my heart;
	I bid it hence return
Kiyotsune.	Unto my sorrow's fountain-head."

Unless you had grown weary of my love, you should have treasured the gift I took such care to leave you.

Wife.	You mistake my reason:
	You meant the keepsake as a comfort,
	But as I look upon that lock
	My mind becomes unruly like my hair.

Kiyotsune. Since you have spurned my gift and rendered vain my thoughtful care, I cannot forgive your cruelty.

Wife.	Nor I your wilful death.
Kiyotsune.	One taunts the other with reproaches,
Wife.	The other tauntingly replies.
Kiyotsune.	The keepsake is a source of woe.
Wife.	And a lock of hair
Chorus.	Becomes for us a source of strife,
age-uta	Becomes for us a source of strife.
[high-pitched	To-night the two lie side by side,
singing]	Each head pillowed on the other's arm,
	Wet by tears of anger;
	Estranged by anger, though in body joined,
	Sadly they lie as if they slept alone.
	"The keepsake brings new agony
	Recalls afresh to the bereaved
	The loss she had else forgot,"[14]
	And makes salt tears to flow,
	And makes salt tears to flow.

Both weep.

4

Kiyotsune. Listen while I tell you what befell me in the days gone by, and forget your grievance.

| *sashi* | Hearken to me! |
| *[recitatif]* | We chanced to learn |

Advances to the centre, and sits down on a stool.

---

[14]Anonymous poem included in the *Kokinshu.*

	The foe was marching through Kyushu
	Against our castle in Yamaga.[15]
	Dismayed, in haste we took to barges,
	Plying our oars the long night through,
	And reached Yanagi in Buzen Province.
Chorus.	Where, as its name bespeaks,

Chorus.   Where, as its name bespeaks,
An avenue of willows lines the sea-front;
Here rude buildings were put up
To house the Imperial Court.

Kiyotsune.   Then we were told
The Emperor would invoke Hachiman
At Usa Shrine;

Chorus.   Thither a store of gold and silver
And countless precious gifts,
And seven steeds sacred to the god,
Were brought as offerings to the Lord of
   War[16]

Wife.   Though you may think I still reproach you,
Was it not a rash and foolish deed
To cast away your life before the time,
While yet you knew not
The fate awaiting the Emperor and the
   Heike clan?

Kiyotsune.   Truly you would be right,
Had not the sacred oracle declared
Our cause past hope.
But pray, hear me to the end!

Chorus.   How while the Emperor and his court
Were keeping vigil at the shrine,
Offering up prayers and making vows,
Behind the curtain of brocade
That hangs before the holy place,
A voice divine proclaimed,—

Kiyotsune.   "No power hath the God of Usa
To change man's hateful fate on earth!
What serves it then to urge Him further?"

Chorus.   "Now the last hope
Grows faint as insects' dying song;
Forlorn indeed is autumn's eve!"[17]

---

[15]Situated in Chikuzen Province. The Heike when forced to abandon their base at the Dazaifu were given an asylum by the local lord in this castle.

[16]Emperor Ojin who, as Hachiman, God of War, is still regarded as the tutelar deity of warriors.

[17]Poem by Fujiware-no-Shunzei included in the *Senzaishu*

5

Kiyotsune.	Alas! Gods and Buddhas
Chorus.	Both forsake our cause.
	All confidence and spirit lost,
	Like a rumbling cart
	The Emperor we follow to his quarters.
	O woeful sight!
kuse [choral	Meanwhile we learn
chant]	The foe is marching into Nagato Province.
	Once more we embark,
	Wretched indeed our plight!
	Life is an ever-changing dream,
	And those who once in the Hogen era[18]
	Rioted like flowers in spring,
	Now, in the Juei autumn,[19]
	Alas, are scattered
	Like sere and yellow leaves
	Over the waves,
	Each leaf, a boat.
	Snowy-crested billows
	Urged by the autumn wind from Yanagi
	Are like a pursuing host.
	A glimpse of herons caught
	Amidst the distant pines
	Makes their spirit quail,
	Thinking they might be
	The snow-white pennants of the Genji host.
	Now as I ponder deeply
	Wherefore Hachiman's fateful words
	Run ever in my head,
	I, Kiyotsune, call to mind
	That in the head of an upright man
	God dwells.[20]
	Possessed by that single thought,
Kiyotsune.	I feel 'twould be but foolishness
	To save the dew-drop of my foredoomed life,
Chorus.	As though it could endure.

KIYOTSUNE
*leaves the
stool and
dances while
the following
lines are
chanted.*

---

[18]During this era (1156-1158) the Heike took over the political ascendancy previously enjoyed by the Fujiwara nobles.

[19]Autumn of 1183. See p. 249, note 7. The Heike took with them the young Emperor, nephew of Munemori, head of the clan.

[20]Supposed to have been the vow made by Hachiman, meaning that he would always guide and protect a just man.

Rather than trust to any boat
Floating like seaweed to and fro,
A prey to endless sorrow,
Like to a water-fowl
I'll dive into the sea,
And so end my life.
Keeping my own counsel
I stand and wait
Upon the bow-planks
While the autumn moon
Grows pale in the dawning sky.
Drawing forth my flute,
I blow a few clear silvery notes,
Then sing *imayo*[21] songs
And chant some ancient verses.
Musing upon the past and future,
Well do I see that soon or late
The glorious past forgot,
The present full of woe,
Perish I must
Like surf upon the shore.
Our life is but a travail
And I can quit this world without regret.
Others may deem my deed stark mad;
Well, let them judge me as they will!
The moon descends the western sky,
I'll follow her to the Western Paradise.
Namu Amida Butsu! Receive my spirit!
Thus praying, overboard I leap
And sink down to the oozy bottom of the   KIYOTSUNE
    sea.   *sinks weeping*
So pitifully ends my woeful life!   *by the*
                                             Shite *Pillar.*

6

Wife.   Hearing your tale, my mind is mazed;
               Sobs shake me
               And hot tears fall.
               O tragic ending to our wedded life!   *Weeps.*
Kiyotsune.   How true the saying,
               "Once fallen in the pit
               The selfsame grievous lot

---

[21]Song consisting of eight alternating lines of seven and five syllables, first invented
and very popular throughout the Heian period (794-1184).

Awaits all men."[22]

7

Kiyotsune.	Where'er I turn	
	In the *Asura* world,	*Rises and*
Chorus.	Where'er I turn	*dances while*
	In the *Asura* world,	*the following*
	The trees are foes,	*lines are*
	Arrows the falling rain,	*chanted.*
	Sharp swords strew the ground,	
	The hills are iron castles,	
	The clouds are battle-pennants,	
	Enemies thrust with their proud blades,	KIYOTSUNE
	Hate flashing in their eyes.	*draws his*
	Here all is strife:	*sword.*
	Anger and lust,	
	Greed and ignorance	
	Strive against the Holy Way;	
	Blind attachment and Buddha-nature	
	Grapple together.[23]	
	Now the foes advance in waves,	
	Now like the ebbing tide retreat.	
	The battles of Shikoku and Kyushu	
	Endlessly are fought again	
	Till, now at last, these torments cease.	KIYOTSUNE
	Relying utterly upon the Barque of Holy Law,	*throws down his sword.*
	The dying Kiyotsune uttered the tenfold prayer:	
	Kiyotsune, the "Pure"-hearted,	
	Kiyotsune, the "Pure"-hearted	
	Now enters the Western Paradise.	KIYOTSUNE
	Praised by Amida!	*stamps twice on the stage at the* Shite *Seat.*

---

[22] It is said that when Nichizo Shonin (886-985), a monk of the Hosso sect, visited Hell guided by Bodhisattva Zao, he saw the Emperor Daigo, famed for his benevolence, being tormented in the lake of molten iron. In answer to the monk's surprised enquiry why he was there, the Emperor repeated the lines quoted.

[23] These five lines are a tentative translation. The original passage is so corrupt that no satisfactory interpretation has yet been reached.

INDEX

absolute meaning, 13, 35, 185
absurd, the theater of
  dramatic techniques of, 216-217
  impulse and purpose of, 215
  philosophical idea of, 214
action, dramatic
  narrated, 51, 64, 99; see also text
    of *Kiyotsune*
  nature of, 27-28, 50-51
Aeschylus, 123, 131, 133, 138, 228
Agamemnon, 17, 128, 130, 131, 139-
  140
Albee, Edward, 203, 215-216
Altick, Richard, 60
Anouilh, Jean, 18-19, 25-26
Antigone, Sophocles', 17
Aristotle, 121, 123
Artaud, Antonin, 62, 63, 123, 214
Atkinson, Brooks, 17

Becket
  analysis of, 19-23, 27-33, 34-35
  reviews of, 13, 16-19, 23-25
  summary of, 14-15
Beckett, Samuel, 227, 228
Bentley, Eric, 51, 202
Bergson, Henri, 216
Bhasa, 92, 110
Bhavabuti, 92, 103-104, 109
The Birth of Christ, York, 167-168
Bowra, C.M., 138-139
Brecht, Bertolt, 51
Brenan, Gerald, 77
Britannicus, 17

Calderón de la Barca, 171
Camino Real, 196
Camus, Albert, 190
Carroll, Vinnette, 113
The Caucasian Chalk Circle, 51-52
central character, 17, 33, 35, 91

cheironomia, 122
Chekhov, Anton, 205
The Cherry Orchard, 202-203
Chikamatsu Monzaemon, 73-74,
  171
ching hsi theater, *see* Peking opera
ch'uan opera, 76
Claudel, Paul, 70
climax, 33-34, 35
comedia, 176
Conacher, D.J., 127
"contextual" form, 60
conventions, dramatic, 157-161
Craig, Hardin, 156
The Creation through *The Fall of
  Man*, York, 168-169
Crist, Judith, 24
The Crucifixion, Wakefield, 166
The Crucifixion, York, 165

dance drama, 122-123
dancing, 63, 64, 69, 90, 109, 120,
  121-123
dramatic action, *see* action
The Dream of the Red Chamber, 77
A Dream Play, 196-200

Eguchi, 65-66
Ellis-Fermor, Una, 59
entremeses, 62
Ernst, Earle, 187
Esslin, Martin, 214, 216
The Eumenides, 141
Euripides, 123, 138
expressionism, 196, 200-202

Feibleman, James K., 50, 185
Finley, M.I., 184
five-act structure, Elizabethan, 146
Freedley, George, 203
Fuenteovejuna, 209-213

256